DAY HIKING
Los Angeles

The high elevations and tall pines of Icehouse Canyon provide welcome relief from summer heat.

You will become well acquainted with Spanish bayonets on Mount Lawlor.

Previous page: Lewis Falls forms a delicate cascade.

Hiker and flagpole atop Mugu Peak

Lasky Mesa in spring

A perfect view of Santa Monica Bay from the Los Liones Trail

Humans aren't the only ones who enjoy California's wildflowers.

The author inside the Cave of Munits (Photo by Michael Liang)

Toyon berries aplenty in Santa Anita Canyon

Avoid tourist crowds at this unique view of the Hollywood sign from the Hollywood Reservoir (Hike 47).

Hikers are often surprised to find dense tree canopies in the San Gabriels, like along this trail in Santa Anita Canyon.

A hiker on the Mishe Mokwa Trail in winter.

DAY HIKING

Los Angeles

city parks • santa monica mountains • san gabriel mountains

Casey Schreiner

MOUNTAINEERS
BOOKS

This book is dedicated to the memory of my mother,
Bernadette Blankenburg Schreiner,
who was always sure to warn me about mountain lions.

Mountaineers Books is the publishing division of The Mountaineers,
an organization founded in 1906 and dedicated to the exploration,
preservation, and enjoyment of outdoor and wilderness areas.

MOUNTAINEERS
BOOKS

1001 SW Klickitat Way, Suite 201, Seattle, WA 98134
800.553.4453, www.mountaineersbooks.org

Copyright © 2016 by Casey Schreiner
All rights reserved. No part of this book may be reproduced or utilized in any form, or by any
electronic, mechanical, or other means, without the prior written permission of the publisher.

Printed in the United States of America
Distributed in the United Kingdom by Cordee, www.cordee.co.uk
First edition, 2016

Copy editor: Janet Kimball
Design and layout: Jennifer Shontz, www.redshoedesign.com
Cartographer: Pease Press Cartography
Cover photograph: *California poppies in Antelope Valley (Photo: Image Source)*
Frontispiece: *Some of the largest conifers in the San Gabriels, along the trail to Twin Peaks.*
All photographs by author unless otherwise noted.

Library of Congress Cataloging-in-Publication Data
Names: Schreiner, Casey, author.
Title: Day hiking Los Angeles : City parks, Santa Monica Mountains, San
   Gabriel Mountains / Casey Schreiner.
Description: First edition. | Seattle, WA : Mountaineers Books, [2016] |
   Includes index.
Identifiers: LCCN 2016017893 (print) | LCCN 2016025511 (ebook) | ISBN
   9781680510089 (paperback : alk. paper) | ISBN 9781680510096 (ebook)
Subjects: LCSH: Hiking—California—Los Angeles Region—Guidebooks. | Los
   Angeles Region (Calif.)—Guidebooks.
Classification: LCC GV199.42.C22 L658 2016 (print) | LCC GV199.42.C22 (ebook)
   | DDC 796.5109794/94—dc23
LC record available at https://lccn.loc.gov/2016017893

The background maps for this book were produced using the online
map viewer CalTopo. For more information, visit www.caltopo.com.

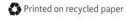 Printed on recycled paper

ISBN (paperback): 978-1-68051-008-9
ISBN (ebook): 978-1-68051-009-6

Table of Contents

City Parks

Verdugo Mountains/ San Rafael Hills

Antelope Valley

San Gabriel Foothills and Front Range

Central San Gabriel Mountains

Mount Baldy Area

Puente–Chino Hills

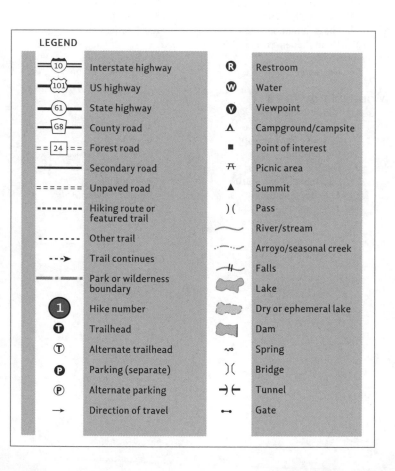

LEGEND

10	Interstate highway	**R**	Restroom
101	US highway	**W**	Water
61	State highway	**V**	Viewpoint
G8	County road	Λ	Campground/campsite
24	Forest road	■	Point of interest
	Secondary road	⊼	Picnic area
	Unpaved road	▲	Summit
	Hiking route or featured trail	)(	Pass
	Other trail		River/stream
--→	Trail continues		Arroyo/seasonal creek
	Park or wilderness boundary		Falls
1	Hike number		Lake
T	Trailhead		Dry or ephemeral lake
T	Alternate trailhead		Dam
P	Parking (separate)	~∞	Spring
P	Alternate parking	)(	Bridge
→	Direction of travel	→←⊢	Tunnel
		•⊢	Gate

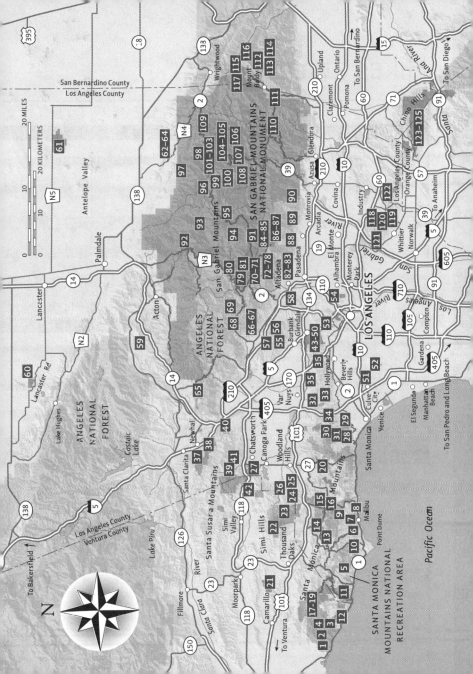

Hikes at a Glance

HIKE	DISTANCE (ROUNDTRIP)	DIFFICULTY	HIKEABLE YEAR-ROUND
PACIFIC COAST			
1. Mugu Peak	5.2 miles	3	•
2. La Jolla Canyon Loop	7.5 miles	3	•
3. The Grotto	3 miles	2	•
4. Sandstone Peak	6.1 miles	3	•
5. Charmlee Wilderness Park	2.8 miles	2	•
6. Escondido Falls	3.6 miles	2	•
7. Solstice Canyon	3.1 miles	2	•
8. Corral Canyon	2.5 miles	2	•
9. Castro Crest	7.6 miles	4	•
10. Zuma Ridge	5.3 miles	2	•
11. Nicholas Flat	6.9 miles	4	•
12. Serrano Canyon	8.6 miles	3	•
INLAND SANTA MONICA MOUNTAINS			
13. Rocky Oaks Park	1.4 miles	1	•
14. Paramount Ranch	2.8 miles	2	•
15. King Gillette Ranch	1.8 miles	1	•
16. Malibu Creek	8 miles	2	•
17. Old Boney Trail	11.4 miles	3	•
18. Upper Sycamore Canyon	4.1 miles	2	•
19. Tri-Peaks via Satwiwa	10.2 miles	5	•
20. Calabasas Peak	4.6 miles	2	•
SAN FERNANDO VALLEY/SIMI HILLS			
21. Wildwood Park	4.5 miles	2	•
22. China Flat and Simi Peak	5.5 miles	3	•
23. Cheeseboro and Palo Comado Canyons	10.4 miles	4	•
24. Las Virgenes Canyon	8.6 miles	3	•
25. Lasky Mesa Loop	5.1 miles	2	•
26. Cave of Munits	2.6 miles	2	•
27. Santa Susana Pass	5.3 miles	3	
EASTERN SANTA MONICA MOUNTAINS/HOLLYWOOD HILLS			
28. Parker Mesa via the Los Liones Trail	7.3 miles	3	•
29. Temescal Canyon	4.6 miles	3	•
30. Eagle Rock and Temescal Peak	7.4 miles	2	•

KID-FRIENDLY	DOG-FRIENDLY	WATERFALL	HISTORICAL	SHADE	RIVERS & STREAMS	VISTAS	ALPINE
						•	
						•	
•				•	•		
	•					•	
•	•		•			•	
•	•	•		•	•		
•	•		•	•	•		
	•					•	
						•	
	•					•	
						•	
						•	
•	•			•			
•	•		•				
•			•			•	
			•	•	•	•	
			•			•	
			•			•	
			•			•	
•	•					•	
•	•	•			•	•	
	•					•	
	•					•	
	•					•	
•	•		•			•	
•			•				
•			•			•	
						•	
				•	•	•	
						•	

HIKE	DISTANCE (ROUNDTRIP)	DIFFICULTY	HIKEABLE YEAR-ROUND
EASTERN SANTA MONICA MOUNTAINS/HOLLYWOOD HILLS *continued*			
31. Murphy Ranch	3.8 miles	2	•
32. Franklin Canyon Reservoir	1.4 miles	2	•
33. Hastain Loop	2.4 miles	2	•
34. San Vicente Mountain via Mandeville Canyon	5.1 miles	3	•
35. Wilacre Park	2.9 miles	2	•
36. Runyon Canyon	3 miles	3	•
SANTA SUSANA MOUNTAINS			
37. Mentryville	4.6 miles	3	•
38. Towsley Canyon	5.4 miles	3	•
39. Rocky Peak	5 miles	3	•
40. O'Melveny Park	4.5 miles	4	•
41. Michael D. Antonovich Regional Park at Joughin Ranch	3.9 miles	2	•
42. Corriganville Park	1.5 miles	1	•
GRIFFITH PARK			
43. Glendale Peak	3.1 miles	2	•
44. Mount Hollywood	4.6 miles	3	•
45. Beacon Hill	2.9 miles	2	•
46. Bee Rock and the Old L.A. Zoo	3.8 miles	3	•
47. Hollywood Reservoir	3.3 miles	1	•
48. Cahuenga Peak and the Wisdom Tree	3 miles	4	•
49. Mount Lee via Bronson Canyon	6.5 miles	3	•
50. Northside Loop	6.8 miles	4	•
CITY PARKS			
51. Baldwin Hills Scenic Overlook	1.3 miles	3	•
52. Kenneth Hahn Community Loop	2.6 miles	2	•
53. Elysian Park Loops	5.2 miles	3	•
54. Ernest E. Debs Regional Park	5.2 miles	3	•
VERDUGO MOUNTAINS/SAN RAFAEL HILLS			
55. Vital Link Trail and Verdugo Peak	5.8 miles	4	
56. Beaudry Loop	5.8 miles	3	
57. La Tuna Canyon Trail	4.2 miles	3	•
58. Descanso Trail	4.8 miles	3	•
ANTELOPE VALLEY			
59. Vasquez Rocks	3.4 miles	3	
60. Antelope Valley California Poppy Reserve	3.3 miles	1	

KID-FRIENDLY	DOG-FRIENDLY	WATERFALL	HISTORICAL	SHADE	RIVERS & STREAMS	VISTAS	ALPINE
•			•	•			
•	•		•	•			
	•					•	
	•		•			•	
	•						
	•					•	
•			•			•	
	•		•		•	•	
	•					•	
	•						
	•		•			•	
•	•		•	•			
	•					•	
	•		•			•	
	•					•	
	•		•			•	
•			•		•	•	
	•		•			•	
	•		•			•	
•	•		•			•	
	•					•	
•						•	
	•					•	
	•					•	
	•			•			
	•		•			•	
	•		•				
•						•	

HIKE	DISTANCE (ROUNDTRIP)	DIFFICULTY	HIKEABLE YEAR-ROUND
ANTELOPE VALLEY *continued*			
61. Saddleback Butte	4.8 miles	3	
62. Devils Punchbowl	1.3 miles	2	•
63. Devils Chair	7.3 miles	3	•
64. Burkhart Saddle	14.1 miles	5	
SAN GABRIEL FOOTHILLS AND FRONT RANGE			
65. Placerita Canyon	6.9 miles	4	•
66. Mount Lukens via Haines Canyon	8.4 miles	4	•
67. Mount Lukens via Stone Canyon	8.6 miles	4	•
68. Trail Canyon Falls	3.6 miles	3	•
69. Fox Mountain	11.3 miles	5	•
70. Switzer Falls	3.6 miles	2	•
71. Bear Canyon	6.8 miles	3	•
72. Dawn Mine Loop	5.9 miles	5	•
73. Millard Canyon Falls	1.2 miles	2	•
74. Echo Mountain	5.6 miles	3	•
75. Inspiration Point	9.9 miles	4	•
76. San Gabriel Peak and Mount Disappointment	4.3 miles	3	•
77. Mount Markham	6.3 miles	4	•
78. Mount Lowe	6.1 miles	3	•
79. Josephine Peak	8 miles	3	•
80. Strawberry Peak	10.8 miles	5	•
81. Mount Lawlor	4.2 miles	4	•
82. Eaton Canyon	3.8 miles	2	•
83. Henninger Flats	6 miles	3	•
84. Mount Wilson via Devore Campground	10.5 miles	4	•
85. Mount Wilson from Chantry Flat	12.8 miles	5	•
86. Santa Anita Canyon	8.7 miles	3	•
87. Hermit Falls	2.6 miles	2	•
88. Jones Peak	6.4 miles	4	•
89. Monrovia Canyon Falls	2.6 miles	2	•
90. Fish Canyon Falls	4.8 miles	3	•
CENTRAL SAN GABRIEL MOUNTAINS			
91. Shortcut Canyon	7 miles	4	•
92. Pacifico Mountain	11.7 miles	5	
93. Mount Hillyer	5.7 miles	3	•
94. Vetter Mountain	3.9 miles	2	•

KID-FRIENDLY	DOG-FRIENDLY	WATERFALL	HISTORICAL	SHADE	RIVERS & STREAMS	VISTAS	ALPINE
						•	
•	•						
	•					•	
	•					•	•
	•		•			•	
	•					•	
	•				•	•	
•	•	•			•		
	•					•	
•	•	•	•	•			
	•		•	•	•		
		•	•	•	•		
•	•	•		•	•		
	•		•			•	
	•		•			•	
	•		•			•	
						•	
	•		•			•	
	•					•	
						•	
						•	
•	•	•			•		
	•		•			•	
	•		•	•	•		
	•		•	•		•	
	•	•	•	•	•		
		•		•	•		
	•					•	
•	•	•		•			
	•		•	•	•		
	•		•	•	•		
	•					•	•
	•					•	
•	•		•			•	

HIKE	DISTANCE (ROUNDTRIP)	DIFFICULTY	HIKEABLE YEAR-ROUND
CENTRAL SAN GABRIEL MOUNTAINS *continued*			
95. Devils Canyon	5.8 miles	3	•
96. Cooper Canyon Falls	3.1 miles	3	
97. Will Thrall Peak via Buckhorn	11.2 miles	5	
98. Mount Williamson	5 miles	3	
99. Waterman Mountain	6.5 miles	3	
100. Twin Peaks	9.7 miles	5	
101. Kratka Ridge	1.5 miles	3	
102. Winston Ridge and Winston Peak	4.3 miles	3	
103. Mount Islip	6.9 miles	4	
104. Throop Peak	4.4 miles	2	
105. Mount Hawkins	6 miles	3	
106. South Mount Hawkins from Crystal Lake	11.6 miles	4	
107. Lewis Falls	1 mile	2	•
108. Smith Mountain	6.8 miles	4	•
109. Mount Baden-Powell	8 miles	4	
110. The Bridge to Nowhere	10.1 miles	5	•
MOUNT BALDY AREA			
111. Sunset Peak	7.9 miles	3	•
112. Timber Mountain via Icehouse Canyon	8.8 miles	3	
113. Bighorn and Ontario Peaks	13.9 miles	4	
114. Cucamonga Peak	11.7 miles	5	
115. Thunder Mountain	9.4 miles	3	
116. Telegraph Peak	11.8 miles	4	
117. Mount Harwood and Mount San Antonio (Mount Baldy)	10 miles	5	
PUENTE–CHINO HILLS			
118. Hacienda Hills	4.7 miles	3	•
119. Worsham Canyon	4.2 miles	3	•
120. Turnbull Canyon	4.3 miles	2	•
121. Sycamore and Dark Canyons	4.6 miles	3	•
122. Powder Canyon	4.8 miles	3	•
123. Telegraph Canyon	12 miles	4	•
124. San Juan Hill	6 miles	3	•
125. Carbon Canyon Redwoods	2.6 miles	1	•

HIKES AT A GLANCE   15

KID-FRIENDLY	DOG-FRIENDLY	WATERFALL	HISTORICAL	SHADE	RIVERS & STREAMS	VISTAS	ALPINE
	•			•	•		
•		•		•	•		•
	•			•		•	•
	•					•	•
	•		•				•
						•	•
			•			•	•
	•		•	•		•	•
	•			•		•	•
	•			•		•	•
	•		•			•	•
•	•	•		•	•		
						•	
•	•			•		•	•
			•		•		
	•					•	
	•		•		•		•
	•		•		•	•	•
	•					•	•
	•					•	•
	•					•	•
						•	•
	•			•		•	
	•					•	
	•					•	
				•		•	
	•					•	
				•			
						•	
•	•			•	•		

Acknowledgments

Although there is only one author's name on the cover of this book, there are countless individuals who have influenced and inspired its creation in manners both direct and indirect. It is impossible to acknowledge everyone here, but I'll make an attempt.

First, infinite thanks are due to my parents, Bernadette and Richard, for teaching me to read at a very early age and feeding that hunger throughout my life. Thanks also to my many teachers, from elementary school through college, who've shaped and improved my writing and inspired my love of history.

Special thanks to friends who have joined me on the trails over the years, especially those who traveled alongside me as I learned how to hike: Aimee Jones; Rachel Freed; Meryl Friedenthal; Rebecca Melrose; Kolby Kirk; my first hiking partner, Will Hathaway; and my fellow guidebook authors Shawnté Salabert and Scott Turner.

Thanks to those local outdoor writers whose shoulders I stand on, including Jerry Schad and especially John W. Robinson, whose exhaustive and lively histories of the local trails were a primary motivator for both my exploration and my writing.

Staff of local parks, volunteer organizations, and fellow lovers of hiking have been unbelievably helpful during this process and the list of names is enormous, but special thanks goes out to Michael Liang, Zach Behrens, and Kate Kuykendall of the Santa Monica Mountains National Recreation Area; Supervisor Jeffrey Vail and Sherry Rollman of the Angeles National Forest/San Gabriel Mountains National Monument; and Kim Teruya of the Mountains Recreation and Conservation Authority.

Thank you to the readers of *Modern Hiker* for informing me of updated trail conditions during an especially insane year of SoCal weather, and more importantly for their support since 2006. I would not be able to pursue this passion without you.

Of course, thank you to Kate Rogers, editor in chief at Mountaineers Books, for reaching out to me in the first place. Thanks also to managing editor Margaret Sullivan, editor Laura Shauger, project editor Lisa Wogan, and copy editor Janet Kimball, whose attention to detail puts eagles' eyes to shame.

And finally, thanks to my partner, Daniel Lyman, for his limitless support and enthusiasm, for joining me on many of these trails, for never getting bored when I wouldn't stop talking about some ill-fated historical figure, for tolerating deadline-adjacent panics, and for keeping me fed during the writing process. There is a very high chance I would have starved without you.

Opposite: Daniel investigates the Devils Punchbowl.

Bear Canyon is a spectacular introduction to the San Gabriel Mountains.

Preface

Unlike most people who run hiking websites and publish books about hiking, I did not grow up spending a whole lot of time in the outdoors. I grew up in a small town in New England and was very much a skinny, allergy-ridden, indoor kid. I strongly preferred reading books, playing video games, and watching worn VHS tapes of British comedies to camping, hiking, or even just spending time in the sun.

I've now lived in Los Angeles for over a decade but I honestly think that if I hadn't stumbled into the world of hiking (and believe me, "stumbling" is the best way to describe many of my early hikes), I would have left California a long, long time ago. I love living in cities, but for me hiking has been an invaluable pressure-release valve from the madness of urban life. Only after I established my weekly routine of walking meditation, spending entire days away from screens and monitors and emails and text messages, could I take a breath, step back, and really understand what is important in life.

Among peaks in the Front Range above Altadena and Pasadena, I would sit, exhausted, and gaze out over the endless tangle of traffic and freeways wondering why more people didn't know this incredible resource was here for them. I could feel the effects that time on the trail here had on me, and more than anything I wanted to share this peace with others.

In recent years, psychologists have begun to discover what hikers have known all along. Hiking is not just good for staying physically fit, it's also good for your mental health. Studies have found that hiking can increase creativity and focus while reducing stress, anxiety, and depression. Spending time in nature can also increase feelings of empathy and altruism. In a culture that seems to manufacture anxieties only to sell you an expensive remedy, isn't it nice to know there's a cure for some of our ills that doesn't require a pricey co-pay?

No matter who you are or where you came from, whether you're plotting a Pacific Crest Trail thru-hike or just looking for a place to exercise in the morning or unwind after the office; whether you grew up camping with your family or have never worn hiking boots before, know this: These trails are here for you.

Now let's go hike them.

The Western Town at Paramount Ranch is still used in film and television today.

Introduction

Los Angeles literally manufactures images, so it makes sense that you'd get some pictures in your head when you think about the city. Unfortunately, they're usually not the good ones. You think of smog. You think of sprawl. You think of strip malls, urban decay, traffic, decadence amid poverty, plastic surgeons, celebrity scandals, earthquakes, wildfires, and maybe a line of people with too much money and not enough common sense in front of a mile-long salad bar of different kinds of vegan kosher gluten-free ethically raised kale.

I used to think that way, and let's be honest, there's a bit of truth in those stereotypes, but if you spend some time in the City of Angels you start to see beyond them. My perspective changed one day, while I was driving home from work after a winter storm. Giant mountains seemingly appeared out of nowhere, standing behind the tall buildings of downtown. Where did these rugged peaks come from? And how hadn't I ever noticed them before? I looked at a map, followed the Angeles Crest Highway into the San Gabriel Mountains, and that was that.

From an elevated perch, the city has an entirely different look. From there, you can see the enormous belt of rugged hills and mountains that surround and bisect the sprawl, offering nearly limitless opportunities to those tired, nerve-shaken, over-civilized people John Muir wrote about. Los Angeles isn't just a good hiking city; it's a great hiking city. It took me years to figure that out, but now you know it, too.

This book covers a range of day hikes from easy strolls to full-day backcountry adventures, and most trailheads can be reached in less than an hour's drive from downtown (on a weekend morning when everyone else is sleeping or brunching). I've included trails from Ventura County across the Transverse Ranges and into Orange County, so no matter where you live, you should be able to find something nearby.

Following the hikes in this book will take you to places you never knew existed in the L.A. area. You'll hike from the bottom of canyons where tar still seeps from the ground to barren peaks more than ten thousand feet in the sky. You'll explore the world's largest urban national park, stand beside thousand-year-old trees clinging to windswept ridgelines, feel the mist of gently cascading waterfalls, and gaze at huge slabs of rock bent into impossible shapes by tectonic action.

Contrary to the belief that L.A. has no history, you'll also visit movie sets from the Golden Age of Hollywood, the site of the first gold rush in California (sorry, '49ers), towering concrete bridges abandoned deep in the wilderness, hotels built on mountaintops, white-knuckle stagecoach passes cut into cliffsides, Nazi-sympathizer compounds, old mines, and yes . . . you'll also get up close and personal with the Hollywood sign.

Welcome to the outdoorsy Los Angeles. You're going to enjoy it.

USING THIS GUIDE

Look, I'll be honest, I could write (and in some cases have written) several thousands of words on these trails. However, the physical limitations of a convenient, backpack-sized

Purple sage in bloom. Smell this!

for determining each of these ratings, but I can't—they're totally subjective. The **star rating** is loosely based on the personality of the trail, its scenic beauty, historic nature, potential for solitude, and a bunch of other intangible qualities that you may have good grounds to argue with me about. Think of it this way: The higher the rating, the more likely you are to stop hiking, look around, and say, "Whoa!"

The **difficulty rating** is based on the length of the hike, the steepness and condition of the trail, whether or not routefinding is required, or whether altitude may be an issue. Generally, 1s and 2s are going to be pretty easy, 3s are solid hikes that will make most hikers break an occasional sweat, 4s will feel like good work, and 5s are the ones that will make you walk funny at the office on Monday.

guidebook mean that sometimes descriptions have to be streamlined a bit. You should have enough of the turn-by-turn nuts and bolts of the trails to effectively find your way, as well as some flavor text to let you know what's worth noting along your hike, whether that's a rare plant or interesting history about the trail. If that sounds like a lot, don't worry. We've got a system here.

What the Ratings Mean

Each trail in this guide begins with a list of information to help you get a better feel for the route, find the trailhead, and know whom to get in touch with if you have any questions.

Every hike begins with two ratings—a star rating for the overall awesomeness of the route and an assigned number to signify its general difficulty. I'd like to tell you I've devised a purely scientific method

Distance and Elevation

Of course, each trail has some hard numbers to help you find the one that's right for you, including **roundtrip mileage**, **elevation gain**, and the **high point**. These numbers are as I have measured them and are as accurate as possible, but keep in mind that sometimes GPS devices can be finicky beasts and these numbers may differ from other sources of information. Oftentimes, official trail signs are incorrect, too. I think the only way to get a true reading is to take a bunch of measuring sticks on the trail, and even then that would be accurate only as long as the trail didn't change or erode.

A quick moment here to talk about elevation gain. People measuring elevation gain tend to fall into two camps: those who just give you the difference between the trail's highest and lowest points and those who measure the cumulative gain along the way.

Neither system is perfect. If you're using the cumulative method, a trail that meanders along some ridgeline bumps but stays relatively level will have a deceptively high elevation gain. If you're using the difference method, an out-and-back route that drops into a canyon and rises to a peak will have a deceptively small elevation gain. Over time, I have found that using the difference between the high and low points tends to give a number that more accurately portrays the hike, so that's what I'm using. On trails where this method gives some deceptively easy numbers, I've placed some warnings in the descriptions. The high point is, as you would expect, the elevation of the highest point on the trail. I've never found this terribly useful myself, but there you go.

Best Season

As Los Angeles is in a mostly temperate Mediterranean climate (please don't call it a desert; you'll look foolish), the majority of the trails here can be hiked year round. Whether or not you should hike them year round is another story, though. I'll go into the "Seasons of Los Angeles" a bit later, but hikes that have a "best" time to hike will be described in their **season** listing. Some hikes technically may be hikeable all year round but are potentially miserable (Vasquez Rocks in the summer) or dangerous (high San Gabriels after some winter storms) during certain times of the year. Those trails will not be labeled as year-round options. In certain situations, hikes may be hikeable all year round but really are best during certain times, and in those cases the generally recommended months will be noted as well. In most of these instances, you'll notice that the best time to hike is usually late winter to early spring. This is generally the best time

to hike in the lower elevations throughout the region (see "Seasons of Southern California").

Maps and Contacts

If you're the type of hiker who follows the Boy Scouts' "Be Prepared" motto, you'll enjoy knowing which maps to use for each trail and whom to contact for the most current trail information. The maps I've used are the **USGS topographical maps**, which are a bit old-school and often woefully out of date when it comes to city streets, but they are the gold standard of paper maps for most areas that include hiking trails, and generally have excellent data on the landscapes. These days there are myriad online mapping services and ways to print your own topo maps as well, not to mention excellent local and regional maps. Although they are limited in their geographic scope, I have always found the Tom Harrison Maps series to be exceptionally clear and accurate. The company has great coverage of the Santa Monica and San Gabriel mountains and Its maps are available at most local outdoor stores as well as at www.tomharrisonmaps.com.

For **contact** info, I have listed the primary agency responsible for handling the majority of land on each hike. Keep in mind that in some cases, trails pass through multiple agency boundaries and those boundaries themselves are very subject to change (see "Road and Trail Conditions" for more on that). All agency phone numbers and websites are helpfully arranged for you in Appendix I. Remember that numerous factors may alter trail conditions and you should always check with the land manager before you head out for a hike. They'll know the conditions on their trails better than anyone else.

And finally, now that just about everyone has a GPS receiver built into their phones, I've provided **GPS coordinates** to each trailhead. Be aware, however, that blindly following a GPS may lead to some sad-face events like missing a trailhead or driving off a cliff, so I've also included some more traditional driving directions. Always look at a route to a trailhead before you get in the car, and always bring a paper map along. Cell phone reception among those rugged peaks and canyons is very unreliable.

Hike Descriptions

Icons at the top of each hike description will let you know at a glance what to expect on the trail.

 Kid-friendly denotes a trail that may have some fun highlights for hikers in smaller boot sizes, like fun rock-scrambling areas and nature centers. Most of these trails are a bit on the easier side, but hey, I don't know your kids, so you're going to have to make the call on whether they can handle a 4- or 6-mile hike.

 Similarly, **Dog-friendly** trails are routes that are good for most dogs and are in places where dogs are allowed, but you'll have to gauge your own canine companion's hiking prowess. If your pooch has never hiked before, you probably don't want to start them on a 12-mile trek just because dogs are allowed there.

 Waterfall means, well, that there's a waterfall on the route. Keep in mind that "waterfall" in Southern California means something different than in many other, wetter parts of the world; the falls here are often smaller and shorter than those farther north and, depending on the time of year and the amount of rainfall we've had, they may not exist at all.

 Historical Interest means there's usually a good story involved with the hike. There may be ruins or a museum along the way, or perhaps something important happened there, like an oil strike or scientific experiment.

 Shade denotes trails that have significant stretches of tree cover or are on the north sides of mountains and tend to lie in shadows more often than sunshine. If it's a hot summer day and you're still gung-ho on getting some miles in, you might want to pick one of these trails.

 The **Rivers and Streams** icon signifies that the trail is near or along a—wait for it—river or stream. As with our waterfalls, many of these flowing waters are seasonal arroyos or are dependent on heavy winter rains filling up springs and aquifers, so they may not be there depending on the time of year you're hiking.

Vistas mean a trail has some killer views along the way. I know, most trails have pretty good views, so these are the ones that are stunners (depending on weather and haze). Be sure to take your camera to get those precious Instagram likes!

Alpine indicates that a trail is at a higher elevation and has more of a pine-forest feel than some of the lower-elevation hikes.

As this is a hiking guidebook, most of the words here are dedicated to describing the actual trails you'll be hiking. Each hike begins with a short synopsis that gives you a little taste of what's to come. A more detailed description follows with a mix of on-trail directions, historical asides, fun facts, and the occasional attempt at a joke. I apologize in advance.

SEASONS OF SOUTHERN CALIFORNIA

Transplants to Los Angeles from other parts of the country bemoan the region's apparent lack of seasons, but once you've spent a few years here getting to know the local flora and fauna, you'll recognize our subtler seasonal changes.

Contrary to our perpetual blue-sky image, late spring and early summer are dominated by a phenomenon known as "June Gloom" (or "May Gray," or in lengthier seasons, "No-Sky July" or even "Fogust"). In this season, a marine layer of low clouds from the Pacific blankets the L.A. basin, keeping temperatures cool and the sun hidden. Here's a pro tip for you: If you climb above three thousand to four thousand feet in elevation, you can often get above the marine layer and enjoy full sunshine. A few peaks in the Santa Monica Mountains will put you right above the clouds, while most of the Front Range peaks in the San Gabriels and all of the Central San Gabriels should be nice and sunny.

Our "Endless Summer" usually begins in June or July and can easily last well into November and even December. Usually by the end of July the marine layer weakens, meaning more sun and higher temperatures. If you don't get an early start, you could be in for some serious sweating and risk of sunstroke on exposed trails, especially at lower elevations and inside canyons. The snowpack at higher elevations should melt enough for nontechnical hikes, so most

hikers flee to the high San Gabriels during these months. This is also when most of our native plants go into their dormant phases, so the green rolling hills you were enjoying earlier in the year will slowly become brown. It's okay, they're not dead, they're just pining for the fjords.

Despite a few cooler days and some light rain occasionally sneaking into October and November, our "Winter-Spring" lasts from December to April. L.A. gets 86 percent of our annual rainfall in these months. Temperatures can dip into the forties, giving Angelenos a great excuse to dust off those expensive winter layers that hide in the backs of closets for most of the year (after a few years of living here, you'll think it's cold too). If you can dodge the rainstorms—and rain here is a huge event so you'll have plenty of notice from local news and water-cooler conversations—these are some of the absolute best months to hike here. The higher elevations will be getting snowed in, but the lower elevations begin to come alive again as our native plants get their annual drinks. Sage scrub becomes unbelievably fragrant, and the rain clears the air of our natural haze and occasional unnatural smog, meaning the views are absolutely postcard-perfect stunning. If we got a good amount of winter rainfall, by mid- to late March, you can also expect to see wildflowers starting to bloom throughout Southern California, so make sure you have lots of available memory on your camera when you're hiking.

PERMITS AND REGULATIONS

If visitors are required to pay fees to enter a park—either on foot or in their cars—I've noted it in the hike description. Generally, California state parks charge a daily entry fee for use. You also can purchase annual passes at the parks or online at www.parks.ca .gov, but there are several different tiers and there are some restrictions; the most expensive pass is just under $200, and not all state parks are included. Unless you plan on visiting many state parks or continue to visit the same park multiple times in a year, I have not found an annual pass to be a terribly economical decision.

Southern California's national forests have long been home to something called the Adventure Pass—a day-use program that charged any visitor who parked inside the national forests a daily fee. Since 2012, the system has been challenged in federal courts and drastically reduced from its former range. As of 2016, there are 66 specific sites in Southern California that will require an Adventure Pass, and all of these sites must offer well-marked fee-free areas 0.5 mile away from the improved areas.

This program is still very much in flux and likely to continue to change, but you can purchase a daily Adventure Pass ($5) or make things easier with an annual pass ($30). The annual America the Beautiful Pass ($80) also works here, and it is good for admission to more than two thousand national parks, national forests and Bureau of Land Management sites across the country as well.

As part of a new program that began in 2014, if you have a fourth-grader in your family, you can also get a free Every Kid in a Park Pass, which works exactly the same as an America the Beautiful Pass for one year. Head to www.everykidinapark.gov to apply.

In addition to entry fees, there are five federal wilderness areas in the region covered in this book. Regulations vary among wilderness areas, but the regions that do require day-use permits do not charge additional fees for those permits. Again, I've noted where free permits are required on trails and whom to contact to get them.

ROAD AND TRAIL CONDITIONS

It should go without saying, but I'll say it anyway: Everything in this book—and in life if you want to get philosophical about it—is subject to change. During the course of writing this, California was at the tail end of an historic four-year drought. Almost every river, lake, and arroyo was bone dry, and our waterfalls had been reduced to a trickle. Southern California then braced for what most believed would be the strongest El Niño on record, anticipating many of those same canyon trails or the winding mountain roads used to get to their trailheads would be washed out and inaccessible. The big El Niño turned out to be a dud, but with flash floods, wildfires, and earthquakes all part of the natural order of things in Southern California, it is absolutely vital that you check road and trail conditions before setting out for your hikes. As our climate warms and weather patterns shift and become more intense, it's best to expect the unexpected.

Caltrans (www.dot.ca.gov) and the Department of Public Works (www.dpw.lacounty .gov/roadclosures/) should be your go-to resources for road closures and repairs. Both the Angeles Crest and Angeles Forest highways are regularly closed during winter months and occasionally more often for landslides in the higher elevations.

The contacts listed for each trail should be able to give you helpful boots-on-the-ground observations. Even these may change, however. In 2014, the San Gabriel Mountains National Monument was carved out of a large chunk of the Angeles National Forest, and a finalized, comprehensive

A hiker explores rock formations in the Santa Monica Mountains.

land-use plan for the new designation is still a few years off. Efforts are also underway to expand the monument's borders and although the Forest Service still manages the monument, its districts are about to be redrawn. Parks within the Santa Monica Mountains National Recreation Area have been known to swap managers, and the ambitious "Rim of the Valley" plan aims to expand that overlay's boundaries around the San Fernando Valley and complete a comprehensive connector trail system.

AN URBAN WILDERNESS

While Los Angeles is blessed with an impressive ring of local, county, state, and federal lands for outdoor recreation, the city also places an enormous amount of pressure on those lands. Each year, more than three million people visit the San Gabriel Mountains and over six hundred thousand visit the Santa Monica Mountains; combined, that's more annual visitors than Yellowstone, Zion, Olympic, or Rocky Mountain national parks.

While it is exciting that more and more people in Los Angeles are enjoying our public lands, unfortunately when some visitors come from the city, they bring the problems of urbanized life with them. Graffiti, theft (including theft of trail signs!), vandalism, littering, noise pollution, and just plain overuse are sadly commonplace on some of the more popular trails. In recent years, illegal marijuana grow farms have been found in both mountain ranges. These are not only dangerous to hikers who stumble upon them in the backcountry, but are also incredibly destructive to the sensitive habitat.

As you have purchased and are reading this book, we'll go ahead and assume that you're a responsible hiker who cares about protecting and preserving our green spaces for the future—or at the very least that you're willing to learn how to do that. By far, the best way to teach people how to responsibly enjoy our parks is to do so by example. Speaking from experience, there are few greater joys than taking someone who's never been hiking before to your favorite trail and sharing it with them. You can watch their face light up as they experience their city in an entirely new light. Note that spark, then fan the flame with more hikes. Read some of the recommended books or join one of the volunteer or advocacy groups listed in the appendixes here, share what you learn, and watch the inspirational fires grow. Over time, those flames will spread through the citizens of the region, and we can pressure our elected representatives to give our parks and green spaces the resources they need and deserve.

So how do you enjoy these parks responsibly? Well, wouldn't you know it, it's the next section of the book.

HOW TO BE A GOOD HIKER

There are no codified rules or instruction manuals for how to be a good hiker, but the principles of Leave No Trace come pretty close. You can read the original rules at the Leave No Trace Center for Outdoor Ethics website (www.lnt.org), but they basically boil down to "leave things the way you found them" and "be considerate of people, wildlife, and plants." Some helpful specifics are as follows:

Leave a Plan. Get yourself into the habit of leaving an itinerary with someone at home. Let them know where you're going, when you expect to be back, and whom to call in case you don't check in. Most hiking guidebooks and experts will tell you to never hike alone. While it is true there is safety in numbers, I personally find solo hiking to be an incredibly rewarding experience—but always, always make sure you let someone know where you are. While you're making that plan, be sure you're also checking current road, trail, and weather conditions

before you leave. If conditions look iffy, make sure you have the proper gear (and know how to use it) or have a backup trail instead. Remember that when a storm comes through the region, it may be fairly pleasant in the cities, but the weather in the mountains will likely be totally different. Search and rescue groups already spend more time dragging unprepared hikers off the trails than they should, so don't give them any more work.

Follow the Rules. The hikes in this book encompass a wide variety of landscapes, some more fragile than others. Local parks and land agencies have posted park-specific rules, and in some cases certain trails or sections of trails may be closed for restoration, safety, or other reasons. It's important to respect and follow these rules wherever you are, whatever they may be.

Stay on the Trail. Look, I know sometimes switchbacks are annoying and it seems like it would be easier to just walk straight up the hill to cut some time off your climb. The problem is that those trails are designed to withstand erosion from hikers and water flow during rainstorms, and when you cut a new path you can greatly increase that erosion, which leads to damaged trails, which leads to closed trails, which leads to unhappy hikers. Stay on the established trails wherever they are. In many hikes in this book, I refer to "use-trails," which are unofficial routes or firebreaks that have received enough traffic to become semi-official hiking routes. For the most part, staying on these unofficial trails is far less invasive than cutting a new path on your own. Sometimes, park staff will close off use-trails to prevent erosion, but they will also usually give you another option of travel.

Know When to Yield. Many routes described in this book are multi-use trails, open to hikers, equestrians, and cyclists. Generally, the expectations to yield are as follows: Cyclists yield to hikers and hikers yield to equestrians. In practice, however, it is usually easier for hikers to yield to everyone else. When letting a cyclist or equestrian pass you, do your best to safely step off the trail to give them a wide berth. Horses are more likely to run uphill when spooked, so stand to the downhill side of them if possible. Remember that in all cases, politeness and courtesy go a long way.

Know the Right-of-Way. When you're meeting other hikers, those going uphill have the right-of-way. You'll appreciate this when you're trudging up a steep hill and have just hit a good rhythm. If you're going uphill and you do need a breather, though, feel free to wave the downhill hikers on. If you're hiking slower than the person behind you, let them pass. If you're the faster hiker and the person ahead of you isn't letting you pass, there's a good chance they may not even know you're there. In that case, just say hello or announce a friendly "on your left" or "on your right." For good hiking karma, flash a smile as you pass. Bonus karma for high fives.

Hike Responsibly with Your Dog. There is only one trail in this book where dogs are allowed off leash. If dogs are allowed on your hike, keep them on leash and under your control at all times. Be sure to pack enough food and water for them on the hike and re- member that not all people like dogs, so you may want to hold on extra tight if your pooch just loves to say hello to everyone.

Don't Bother the Wildlife. Remember that these trails are not a petting zoo nor are they your private gardens. Don't pick flow- ers and don't feed or harass animals. Now that said, coastal sage scrub has some of the best-smelling plants on earth and as an

A cyclist enjoys the view from Henninger Flats. Remember to share the trail when hiking.

L.A. hiker you owe it to yourself to have some up-close-and-personal time with them. The good news is that the scent stars of that community—California sagebrush and various species of sage—can all be enjoyed just by gently rubbing your hands along their leaves. No need to pick, trim, or crush! For even less effort, just hike in the Santa Monica Mountains after a good rain. The smell of fresh rain mixes with the aromas of dozens of different native plants, creating the finest perfume you'll ever experience.

Don't Take Souvenirs. The old saying "Take only photographs, leave only foot-prints" rings true here. Leave the natural and historic features as you found them so that others can enjoy them, and don't even think about taking anything home with you. Unless, of course, you're packing out some litter you found along the trail!

Don't Add to the Noise Pollution. Listening to music while hiking is not a new thing, but an unfortunate new trend that seems to be gaining in popularity is sharing that music with others whether or not they want to hear it. Whether it's via your cell phone's tinny speakers or a more powerful wireless device, please, don't do this. One of the primary benefits of spending time in nature is getting away from all the noise of the city. Traffic, car horns, email push noti-fications, and yes, music. I don't care how good your taste in tunes is: leave the speak-ers at home and bring headphones if you can't stand being without constant noise.

Take Care of Business. If an outhouse exists, use it. If not, try to get as far off the trail as possible—at least 200 feet away from campsites and water. For solid waste, dig a cathole six to eight inches deep and cover it when you're done. Pack out any toilet paper or hygiene products, which, I know,

sounds gross—but you also don't want to come across little toilet paper tumbleweeds when you're hiking, do you? Also, don't forget hand sanitizer.

SO WHAT'S GOING TO KILL ME OUT THERE?

In my years of running an outdoor website, the most frequently asked questions I get are variations of "So what's going to kill me out there?" Yes, there are some potentially dangerous animals sharing the trails with you; however, not only are your odds of encountering them extremely low, but almost every instance of injury from animals is preventable. These creatures have far more to fear from us than we do from them.

Mountain Lions

Many people are surprised to learn that mountain lions live so close to a heavily urbanized city like Los Angeles, but the Na-tional Park Service has monitored more than thirty of the big cats in and around the Santa Monica Mountains—with one local celebrity, dubbed P-22, even making his home inside Griffith Park!

Mountain lions are extremely elusive and hunt by stealth, meaning you will likely never, ever see one while hiking. Although they look frightening and can definitely do some serious damage, media coverage of the attacks far exceeds the amount of time you need to spend worrying about them. Between 1986 and 2014, the California Department of Fish and Wildlife tracked just fifteen mountain lion attacks on hu-mans and three fatalities.

These cats are generally opportunistic hunters and aim for prey that's too weak to fight back. If you should encounter a moun-tain lion on the trail:

Don't Run. Running may make you look like prey and trigger the lion's hunting instinct.

Look Big. If you appear like another aggressive predator, the lion may back away. Stand your ground, wave your arms, hold up your jacket—anything you can do to appear larger than you are.

Create Distance. While maintaining eye contact and making noise, slowly back away, giving the mountain lion ample room and opportunity to escape.

Protect Small Children and Dogs. The lion will be more apt to go after what it considers smaller, weaker animals.

Fight Back. If the lion does charge, fight back with whatever is available, protecting your neck and throat. Rocks, branches, trekking poles, ballpoint pens, and even bare hands have been enough to turn lions away.

Bears

Although fearsome grizzlies used to roam throughout California, the few black bears that now live in Southern California were reintroduced from Yosemite in 1933. Like their northern relatives, today's SoCal black bears generally run into trouble with humans when they're looking for food. Skittish and solitary, black bears will usually leave the area long before you arrive. Since 1986, Los Angeles County has had only five black bear attacks and no fatalities. The entire state has not experienced a single fatal attack since that year, even though between twenty-five thousand and thirty thousand black bears now live here.

You can minimize the chances of coming into contact with a black bear by:

Hiking in a Group. Generally, it's almost always safer to hike in a group anyway, but adding more people comes with the added benefit of more people noises and people smells—great ways for bears to know to move along.

Talking as You Hike. You'll want to walk a fine line here between not bothering your fellow hikers by making a ruckus and making enough noise to let big animals know you're in the area. I think this is a little more useful for solo hikers, and I've been known to belt out a few choice tunes to the manzanita while deep in the wilderness. I haven't had any requests for encores yet, but I also haven't heard any complaints. Many stores will sell you "bear bells"—tiny jingle bells you can hang from your backpack to make extra noise. The efficacy of these festive accessories is questionable: many longtime hikers I know who frequent grizzly country refer to them as "dinner bells."

Keeping Scented Items Away from Camp. If you're spending the night on the trail or in a campground, it's important to keep all food, food-related, and scented items (including deodorants and toothpastes) in a bear canister or bear bag hung 4 feet from a tree trunk, 10 feet off the ground, and at least 100 feet away from camp.

Rattlesnakes

Most of the snakes you'll meet on the trail will not be dangerous to you, but unless you're extremely adept at identifying snake species, you should treat them all the same as you would any other wild animal—with a respectful distance.

I won't lie. There are few things as automatically terrifying as cresting a low, sunny hill in the spring and noticing your next step will put your boot directly on top of a coiled rattlesnake, but even these bites rarely kill humans. According to the California Poison Control Center, rattlesnakes account for a little over eight hundred bites per year with only one or two deaths.

Avoid getting a snakebite by:

Wearing the Right Clothes. Don't hike barefoot or in sandals. Although they add extra weight and are falling out of fashion among the ultralight crowd, mid-height boots that cover your ankles and loose, long pants can help prevent fangs from getting into your skin.

Staying on the Trail. Avoid tall-grass areas where snakes may hide out during the day.

Watching Where Your Hands and Feet Go. Always step on top of logs and rocks, not over them, and be especially careful when scrambling or climbing.

Using Trekking Poles. Trekking poles create extra vibrations in the ground that let snakes know something big is coming their way.

If you do happen to encounter a snake on the trail, back away to give it plenty of room. Most snakes have poor eyesight and sense prey only via vibrations on the ground, so stomp to encourage the snake to move along and wait for it to leave before continuing. If the snake doesn't move, try going around it (with lots of room!) or just turn back and have an early snack break somewhere away from the snake. The trail will still be there later, the snake probably won't.

If the unfortunate happens and you do get bitten, the best thing you can do is to remain calm. Remove any watches, bracelets, or rings that might constrict swelling, immobilize the bite area, and wash it gently with soap and water if you can. Try to get to a doctor as quickly as possible and keep the bite below your heart.

Please, don't ever kill a snake you encounter. Not only do several nonvenomous species mimic rattlesnake behavior for protection, but even rattlesnakes are an important part of our ecosystems.

Ticks

Many people forget that ticks are prevalent in California. In meadows, overgrown areas, and in brushy chaparral, ticks hang out at the ends of blades of grass or leaves and wait for a warm-blooded creature to brush them—after which they crawl to a secluded spot on the body and dive in headfirst to drink blood. In other words, ticks suck.

Tick bites may be common if you spend a lot of time bushwhacking or on grassy backcountry trails—especially in the warmer summer and fall months. Although instances are rare, ticks in California are known to carry the agents of Lyme disease and Rocky Mountain spotted fever.

The best way to combat tick bites is to make it more difficult for them to get to your skin and easier for you to see them. Wearing long, light-colored pants tucked into your socks won't win you any fashion awards, but

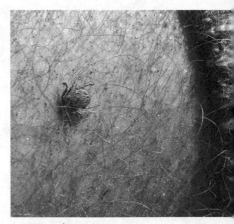

A most unwelcome visitor

it will go a long way toward making sure the little bloodsuckers never get to you. They crawl slowly, so it's a good idea to get in the habit of doing a quick spot check after you hike through overgrown areas of a trail.

If you do happen to spot one, don't panic. Ticks are relatively easy to remove with a simple pair of tweezers or a commercially available tick-removal tool. The process is the same: You grasp the tick near its head and pull upward, away from the skin. If you're too squeamish or don't have tweezers, you can wait until you get home or to a doctor's office. If present, pathogens generally don't enter your bloodstream for twenty-four hours after the bite.

Do not—I repeat—do not attempt to remove the tick by annoying it with rubbing alcohol, petroleum jelly, fire, or anything else. These methods persist in outdoorsy folklore but are almost always more harmful than just leaving the tick alone until a doctor can remove it.

OH GOD, WHAT ABOUT THE PLANTS?

As a hiker, you are far more likely to run into problematic plants than you ever are likely to encounter a truly dangerous animal. There are three main culprits you will probably meet on the trails here: poison oak, stinging nettle, and poodle-dog bush.

Poison Oak

Common and widespread throughout the country, the three-leaved bane of hikers and forest explorers is prevalent in Southern California as both a climbing vine and a shrub. Often occurring in shaded canyons and along arroyos and streams below five thousand feet, every part of this plant—including its leafless branches in the winter—contains oils that can cause itchy

rashes through skin contact or lung irritation if the branches or leaves are burned. The old adage "Leaves of three, let it be" is wise to follow here. Symptoms will usually last one to two weeks and can be treated with topical lotions, aloe vera, and antihistamines. Breathing in poison oak smoke can cause severe allergic reactions. If you're unfortunate enough to have added some branches to your campfire, you should put the fire out and seek medical attention immediately.

Stinging Nettle

If you wander off-trail along a riparian canyon and suddenly notice a tingling sensation on exposed skin that quickly turns to painful itching, congratulations—you've just become acquainted with stinging nettle. This three- to seven-foot-tall plant has long, pointed leaves that, along with the stems, are covered in tiny hairs that act like hypodermic needles, injecting a little cocktail of chemicals that cause a painful reaction. Ain't nature grand? Stinging nettle will often go away on its own, especially if you quickly wash the affected areas and don't touch other parts of your body. If it lingers, you can treat the rash with calamine lotion, oral antihistamines, and cold compresses.

Poodle-Dog Bush

Unless you're a California native plant nerd, you probably haven't heard of this cuddly-sounding plant, endemic to Southern and Baja California. Visually, poodle-dog stands out. It grows to six feet high and blooms with blue, lavender, or purple flowers. It also has a powerful, dank smell reminiscent of a row of Venice pot shops.

Although symptoms may not appear for several days after exposure, touching the tiny hairs of poodle-dog bush can result in

Poodle-dog bush: Do not touch!

severe skin irritation, with painful, itchy blisters that can last for weeks. Antihistamines are not always effective in treating the rash and some topical anesthetics can actually make the rash worse, so if you've been exposed, it's best to seek medical attention. If that's not enough, those tiny hairs can stick to your clothing, so if you've stumbled into this plant, wash your hiking gear separately from other clothes with extreme care.

Poodle-dog bush is a fire-following plant, meaning it tends to thrive after a wildfire. The San Gabriel Mountains have had an explosion of poodle-dog bush since the 2009 Station Fire, and while crews are carefully removing these plants from trails as they rebuild, you are likely to encounter them in the recovering burn zone for at least a decade. Best to admire this one from afar.

GEAR

Few things bum me out as much as meeting someone who wants to hike but never does because they can't afford to get outfitted from head to toe in the latest equipment. Safety, planning, and gear aside, hiking is basically just walking outside—and there are many, many trails that you could easily do in a good pair of sneakers and some gym clothes.

That said, once you've decided that you'd like to move beyond those easy trails, there are some purchases that are worth spending a bit of cash on. When you're hiking, your number-one bodily priority is taking care of your feet and that means proper footwear. A solid pair of well-fitted hiking shoes and a reliable pair of wicking socks can mean the difference between an awesome day of hiking and a miserable week of limping on blisters.

Any good outdoor store will be able to help you find a shoe that's right for where you want to hike and that feels good on your feet. I still prefer the heavier mid-height boots (and have been rocking my favorite pair since 2008), but the trend nowadays is toward lighter trail runners. It's really a matter of preference. A benefit of hiking in Southern California is that for the most part we can get away without waterproof boots. Despite all their claims of breathability, I have yet to find a waterproof boot that doesn't require me to swap sweaty socks multiple times on a hike.

As for socks, you're going to want to ditch the cotton and go for a wicking synthetic fabric or spring for wool. Keeping your feet cool and dry is the key to keeping blisters away, and both fabrics do this admirably. Synthetic fabrics can be cheaper than wool, but wool tends to last longer and—as a bonus—won't get stinky.

As you set out for your hike, you'll want to pack items depending on where you're headed, what time of year it is, and what's predicted in the weather forecast. Over time, you'll learn what you need and what's not as useful. As a community, hikers have settled on a list of important items called the Ten Essentials. First appearing in the third edition of *Mountaineering: The Freedom of the Hills* in 1974, the current list is generally agreed to contain the following:

Navigation: A paper map and analog compass, as well as the ability to read and use them, are the first items that should go in your pack. GPS units are fine and dandy, but you don't want to get lost because a battery dies or you drop an electronic device into a stream, do you?

Sun Protection: Sunscreen is an absolute must here in Southern California, especially on long summer days and at high altitudes. Apply it every few hours, and also include lip balm with sunscreen, a hat, and sunglasses (which are also helpful for keeping bugs and brush out of your eyes).

Insulation: You are likely to experience a number of different weather conditions on your hike. Maybe it's seventy degrees and sunny at your apartment, but on a shaded, northern trail at high elevation it will be much cooler. Bring an extra layer for the coldest possible temperature, keeping in mind that it can get pretty chilly when the sun goes down here, even in the summer.

Illumination: Pack a lightweight LED flashlight or headlamp in case you'll be hiking after sunset or need to spend a night.

First-aid Supplies: You can purchase excellent prepackaged first-aid kits at outdoor stores or build your own. At a minimum, be sure to have bandages, gauze, scissors, tweezers, and pain relievers. Oh, and duct tape. Never leave home without duct tape. It's seriously good for everything.

Fire: Bring a firestarter and waterproof matches in case you need to spend an evening.

Repair Kit and Tools: A multi-tool or Swiss Army knife is perfect for making any quick repairs along the way. You may want some more duct tape here, too.

Nutrition: Always make sure you bring more food than you think you'll eat—ideally enough to get you through a night if necessary. Also, make sure you bring some salty snacks to add electrolytes to your water intake.

Hydration: Many experts recommend three to four liters of water for a full day of hiking in hot weather or at high altitudes. You may find that you need more or less than that over time, but the rule of thumb is if you find yourself thirsty, you're already dehydrated. Another splurge item worth the money is a good day pack with a sleeve for a hydration bladder. I usually bring a two- or three-liter hydration bladder, which gets me through the toughest day hikes, but I should also mention that most of my hiking partners are aghast at how little water I drink. If you plan on drinking any water from springs, streams, or rivers, you'll definitely want to have a treatment method. Iodine tablets are the cheapest and lightest option. Filters are great but they won't remove viruses.

Emergency Shelter: A space blanket is an excellent emergency shelter for an unplanned overnighter and won't take up a lot of room in your pack.

It is important to remember that all the gear in the world will do you no good if you don't know how to use it. Every year, the Sierra Club's Angeles chapter runs a ten-class, hands-on seminar called the Wilderness Travel Course. You will learn a *ton* about outdoor recreation, including how to navigate with a map and compass, buy the right gear, build emergency shelters, perform wilderness first aid, and more. The class also has multiple outings to practice in the field. Registration usually begins in July for classes beginning in January. Head to www.wildernesstravelcourse.org for more info and to sign up.

ARE WE HIKING YET?

I like your enthusiasm! You are about to experience the Los Angeles region in a way many people don't even know is possible. As you leave behind the noise and clamor of city life and hit the trails, I encourage you to slow down and notice the true heartbeat of the region. Hike the same trail at different times of the year to see how the landscape breathes and changes. Burst through the layer of June Gloom and revel in your private sunny sky while the city sleeps below. Eagerly await rain in the forecast so you can chase ephemeral waterfalls and enjoy exquisite views in all directions. Listen to the trails as you hike: for birdsong, for scurrying alligator lizards, for the breezes through oak leaves. Remember that life is not just a rat race, paychecks, promotions, or pictures in magazines. Go into work on Mondays with scratches and bruises and sore legs and killer stories and weird tan lines. Go camping, see the Milky Way at night, and remember how small we all are.

Pick your favorite hikes, learn our history, and care, truly care about this place and its future. Only then, I think, will you be a true Angeleno.

Well, that, and you're gonna need to have a favorite taco joint.

A NOTE ABOUT SAFETY

Safety is an important concern in all outdoor activities. No guidebook can alert you to every hazard or anticipate the limitations of every reader. Therefore, the descriptions of roads, trails, routes, and natural features in this book are not representations that a particular place or excursion will be safe for your party. When you follow any of the routes described in this book, you assume responsibility for your own safety. Under normal conditions, such excursions require the usual attention to traffic, road and trail conditions, weather, terrain, the capabilities of your party, and other factors. Keeping informed on current conditions and exercising common sense are the keys to a safe, enjoyable outing.

—Mountaineers Books

Opposite: Trails like this at Charmlee Wilderness Park provide incredible ocean views.

pacific coast

Aaah, the Pacific Coast. Odds are, seeing the Pacific Ocean is one of the things that brought you out to Los Angeles in the first place.

Immortalized in mid-budget, sixties party flicks and Beach Boys songs, the Pacific Coast hems in the SoCal sprawl from the built-up areas of Long Beach and the Palos Verdes Peninsula to uber-fancy Santa Monica and Malibu and into Ventura County. Most of the good hiking is north of Santa Monica along the rightfully world-famous Pacific Coast Highway (PCH), where an alliance of preservationists and, let's face it, NIMBYs protecting their property from those they felt were unworthy of the views, had the foresight to preserve open space and access for hikers, cyclists, and equestrians.

Most of the hikes contained here are on the ocean-facing side of the Santa Monica Mountains, meaning the great Pacific's influence is a bit more profound. Trails here tend to get more moisture from the marine layer, and the region's coastal canyons can get socked in with fog in the mornings. The hikes are mostly moderate in difficulty and many feature spectacular ocean views and sometimes even beach access—a fantastic way to conclude a hot day on the trails.

1 Mugu Peak

RATING/ DIFFICULTY	LOOP	ELEV GAIN/ HIGH POINT	SEASON
***/3	5.2 miles	1251 feet/ 1267 feet	Year-round

Map: USGS Mugu Peak; **Contact:** Point Mugu State Park; **Notes:** Dogs allowed on leash only on beaches, at the campground, and in day-use areas. No dogs allowed on trails; **GPS:** N 34.091450, W 119.065857

A moderate loop trail from the Pacific Coast to one of the most prominent peaks in the region, this route ignores a direct ascent of Mugu Peak and instead takes you on a beautiful tour of the southern regions of the park near naval bases, through old ranch lands, and into some of the last remaining native grasslands in Southern California.

GETTING THERE

From Santa Monica, head north on the Pacific Coast Highway (CA-1) for 36 miles, crossing into Ventura County. After you pass Decker Road, you'll travel 10.8 miles, passing Mugu Rock before you reach the Point Mugu Naval Air Station on your left. There is a small dirt lot across from a rifle range. If you're coming from Ventura, this turnoff is 2.3 miles south of the intersection of the PCH and Las Posas Road.

ON THE TRAIL

The Chumash Trail begins just across the road from the Point Mugu Naval Air Station, so there's a chance your hike may begin with the sounds of rifles firing or jets flying overhead. There is a much higher chance of your getting a good workout, however, as the trail begins with a no-nonsense 860-foot climb that many hikers have described as "hellish."

Worry not—this is the toughest climb of the hike, and as you complete the incline and crest the coastal ridge you'll get your first views of the surprisingly expansive native grassland in the rolling hills of the interior Santa Monica Mountains. Pass the Mugu Peak Trail at 0.6 mile and just beyond that, ignore the use-trail to your right. Instead, stay left to head into the La Jolla Valley Natural Preserve, an undefined section of the park with exemplary grassland. Just before

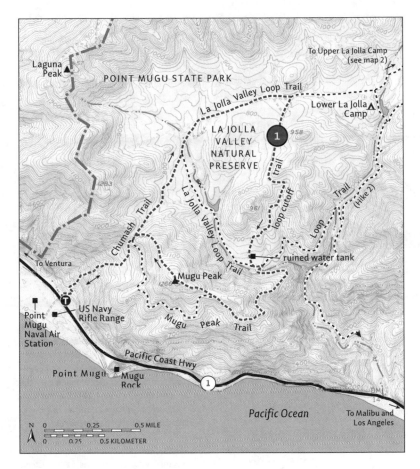

1.2 miles, stay to the left and hike on the La Jolla Valley Loop Trail.

The Loop Trail makes a 3.1-mile path through the valley, skirting several hike-in backcountry campsites, but for this trip, take a right at 1.9 miles on the loop cutoff to head south through the meadow—probably the best place in Southern California to live out your *Sound of Music* opening-shot fantasies.

At 3 miles look for a ruined water tank and continue south on the Mugu Peak Trail as it makes a gradual ascent up the mountain's southern flank.

At 3.9 miles, head right onto a well-worn use-trail that climbs straight up through some fields of prickly pear cacti and heads toward higher ground (the established Mugu Peak Trail doesn't actually reach the peak).

A hiker crests the Chumash Trail and heads into La Jolla Valley.

At 4.2 miles, top out on the summit of Mugu Peak, where the Stars and Stripes fly on a weathered flagpole and the views open up, revealing the gnarled ridge of Boney Mountain to the east and the Channel Islands to the west. Descend another steep use-trail to the northwest and rejoin the Chumash Trail at 4.6 miles to return to the trailhead.

2 La Jolla Canyon Loop

RATING/ DIFFICULTY	LOOP	ELEV GAIN/ HIGH POINT	SEASON
***/3	7.5 miles	1106 feet/ 1120 feet	Year-round

Map: USGS Point Mugu; **Contact:** Point Mugu State Park; **Notes:** Dogs allowed only in campground and day-use areas. No dogs allowed on trails. Camps are walk-in only; **GPS:** N 34.086010, W 119.036689

This large loop in southern Point Mugu State Park provides access to rare native grassland and unique native plants as well as stunning views of the coast and the Santa Monica Mountains, not to mention some reliably eye-catching wildflower shows in the spring. Due to the massive 2013 Springs Fire, there are also ample opportunities to witness fire recovery in a very visceral manner.

GETTING THERE

From Santa Monica, take the Pacific Coast Highway (CA-1) 32 miles west to Point Mugu State Park, passing the Sycamore Canyon entrance and campground to reach the La Jolla Valley entrance on the northern side of the road. Park along the PCH—just be sure to check signage. There is also a parking lot inside the park, but it is somewhat expensive. This hike begins from the park entrance.

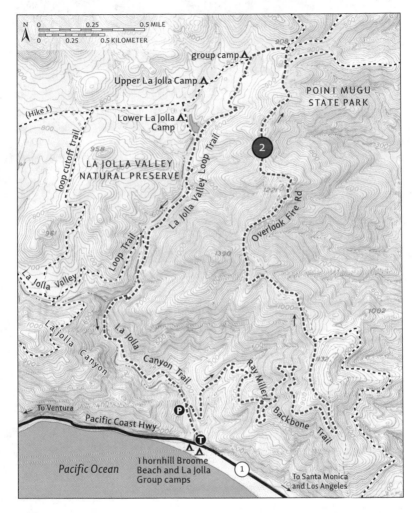

N

| 0 | 0.25 | 0.5 MILE |
| 0 | 0.25 | 0.5 KILOMETER |

group camp ▲

Upper La Jolla Camp ▲

POINT MUGU
STATE PARK

(Hike 1)

Lower La Jolla ▲
Camp

LA JOLLA VALLEY
NATURAL PRESERVE

La Jolla Valley Loop Trail

2

Overlook Fire Rd

loop cutoff trail

Loop Trail

La Jolla Valley

La Jolla Valley

La Jolla Canyon

La Jolla Canyon Trail

Ray Miller / Backbone Trail

To Ventura

Pacific Coast Hwy

P

T

Pacific Ocean

Thornhill Broome
Beach and La Jolla
Group camps

1

To Santa Monica
and Los Angeles

ON THE TRAIL

Begin your ascent on the Ray Miller/Back-bone Trail as it makes a slow but steady climb past the La Jolla Canyon Group Camp and along the edge of the Santa Monica Mountains. On cool days with a bit of coastal fog you might mistake this rugged stretch of coastal mountains for Big Sur... if you squint.

At 2.3 miles go right as the trail turns inland and at 2.7 miles stay left at the junction to continue on the Overlook Fire Road. For the next 2 miles, this road provides some

Monkey flowers liven up the landscape in the spring.

of the best views in the park: to the east, Big Sycamore Canyon and Boney Ridge; to the west, the grassy meadows of La Jolla Canyon. At 4.7 miles, stay to the left at the multi-trail junction to leave the fire road and join the La Jolla Valley Loop Trail.

In another 0.2 mile stay to the left at the group camp to begin your journey south into the canyon (unless you're planning on staying at one of the three primitive trail campsites just to your west). Here you'll hike through thigh-high grasses (Tick check! Tick check!) and past a shady, seasonal pond that's also a home to thick groves of poison oak. Beyond this, the canyon narrows and becomes much more rugged. At 6 miles, veer to the left to stay on the La Jolla Canyon Trail, and on the last 1.2 miles to the trailhead keep your eyes peeled for the giant coreopsis, an odd yellow-flowering native that looks like it wandered into the canyon from a Dr. Seuss book.

EXTENDING YOUR TRIP

Easily lengthen this trip to the west by completing the La Jolla Valley Loop Trail through the meadows, tackling nearby Mugu Peak (Hike 1), or by creating your own loop on Point Mugu State Park's extensive trail network. Just be sure to contact the rangers to make sure your trails aren't closed for fire recovery.

3 The Grotto

RATING/ DIFFICULTY	ROUNDTRIP	ELEV GAIN/ HIGH POINT	SEASON
***/2	3 miles	890 feet/ 1712 feet	Year-round

Maps: USGS Trifuno Pass, Arroyo Sequit; **Contact:** Santa Monica Mountains National Recreation Area; **Notes:** Dogs allowed on leash to Happy Hollow. Group camping available by reservation; **GPS:** N 34.1100, W 118.9374

This out-and-back on the Circle X Ranch, a former Boy Scout property, remains a popular and classic Southern California hike for Santa Monica Mountains explorers of all ages and abilities. A lovely trail takes you into a canyon with exquisite coastal sage scrub, beautiful views of the highest peak in the mountain range, and a fun boulder-scrambling area.

GETTING THERE

Travel north from Santa Monica on the Pacific Coast Highway (CA-1) for about 29 miles, then turn right on Yerba Buena Road (right after the Neptune's Net restaurant). Travel northeast on Yerba Buena Road for 5.3 miles and park in the Circle X Ranch parking area.

ON THE TRAIL

The small Circle X Ranch building near the parking area has flush toilets, a water fountain, and a lot of helpful information on trails and activities throughout the Santa Monica Mountains. Stop inside to say hello or just begin your trip hiking down the road to the group campground. At 0.1 mile, leave the dirt road behind and start hiking on the Grotto Trail—a very well-maintained footpath that begins in some shady brush and chaparral. This is a great place to spot wildflower blooms in the spring, especially from showy ceanothus bushes.

The trail skirts the edge of the often-dry West Fork Arroyo Sequit and crosses it at 0.5 mile at a junction with the Canyon View Trail. Stay on the Grotto Trail and descend

Sandstone and Exchange peaks from the Grotto Trail

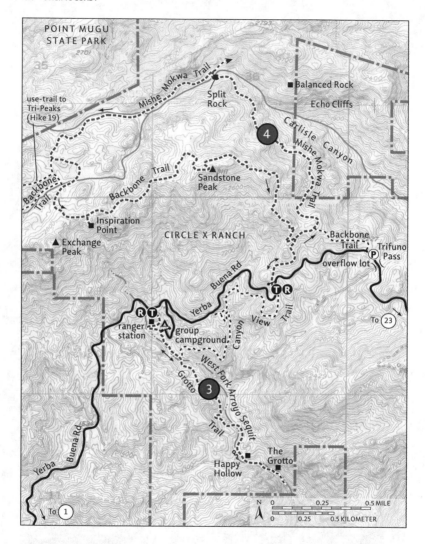

into the canyon as meadows give way to a denser riparian canopy. At around 1.3 miles, the trail reaches Happy Hollow—a small streamside clearing surrounded by old, twisted sycamores and canyon live oaks. The established trail ends here, but the route continues east on a well-traveled use-trail along the arroyo.

With a bit of boulder hopping, at 1.4 miles you'll reach the Grotto—a large collection of rocks in the arroyo that provides plenty of opportunities for scrambling and beginner-level rock climbing. This is a great place for a picnic or just to get your hands dirty. If it's too crowded here, there is another Grotto-like boulder collection farther down the canyon. Continue south 0.1 mile on the use-trail (and across the rocks). After this, the use-trail vanishes and any further exploration will require bushwhacking—and excellent poison oak–spotting skills. Return back to the trailhead the way you came, enjoying the majestic views of Sandstone and Exchange peaks as you climb out.

Maps: USGS Trifuno Pass, Newbury Park; **Contact:** Santa Monica Mountains National Recreation Area; **Notes:** Dogs allowed on leash; **GPS:** N 34.111420, W 118.926747

🦴 🐾 *Perhaps the single best day hike in Southern California, this loop to the highest point in the Santa Monica Mountains offers a little bit of everything that makes hiking here great: coastal views, spring blooms, shaded canyons, sunny slopes, and easy scrambling. On clear days, hikers have commanding vistas stretching from Ventura and the Channel Islands past the Palos Verdes Peninsula and sometimes even to the San Gabriels. An absolute must-do.*

④ Sandstone Peak

RATING/DIFFICULTY	LOOP	ELEV GAIN/HIGH POINT	SEASON
*****/3	6.1 miles	1656 feet/3111 feet	Year-round

GETTING THERE

From Santa Monica, take the Pacific Coast Highway (CA-1) north for about 29 miles and take a right onto Yerba Buena Road (just past the Neptune's Net restaurant). Continue northeast on Yerba Buena Road for 6.4 miles

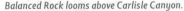

Balanced Rock looms above Carlisle Canyon.

to a dirt parking area on the left side of the road, just after a sharp bend.

ON THE TRAIL
This trail begins at a gate and kicks off with a moderately steep ascent to the first junction at 0.3 mile. It is possible to hike directly to Sandstone Peak from here (a 3-mile out-and-back), but take a right to head east on the Backbone Trail for this much more interesting loop. At 0.5 mile, stay to the left to start north on the Mishe Mokwa Trail while the Backbone Trail continues east toward an overflow parking area and Trifuno Pass, an historic regional trading route.

The trail continues to the north, and at the 1-mile mark it turns to the west, hugging the edge of Carlisle Canyon. Across the canyon rises Echo Cliffs, an area popular with climbers, and the massive, seemingly perilously perched Balanced Rock, popular with fans of Road Runner cartoons. At 1.8 miles the trail dips into a riparian grove along a seasonal creek with a lovely picnic table and the aptly named Split Rock. Follow in the footsteps of countless Boy Scouts before you and pass through the rock before continuing.

Ignore the use-trail to Echo Cliffs and stay left to start a gradual ascent on an old ranch road. Keep an eye out for soaring hawks above as the prominent, bouldered summit of Tri-Peaks (Hike 19) comes into view. At 2.9 miles, stay to the left on the Mishe Mokwa Trail and do the same at 3.2 miles. At 3.4 miles, take a left back onto the Backbone Trail and—to truly soak in the views of the Pacific Ocean—keep an eye out for the short spur trail to Inspiration Point, where a small memorial to a Boy Scout is perched on an exposed ledge. Return to the Backbone and at 4.5 miles look for a sign marking the summit trail to Sandstone Peak.

The established trail basically dissolves into a series of use-trails here, all of which converge on the barren, rocky slope that you'll scramble up to reach the summit of Sandstone Peak. Here you'll be met with a sweeping panorama of the landscape and the watchful eyes of W. Herbert Allen, whom the Boy Scouts unsuccessfully tried to rename the mountain after.

Scramble back down to the Backbone Trail and head east. At 5.8 miles, take a right to return to the trailhead.

EXTENDING YOUR TRIP
You can hike on rough use-trails to the back of Tri-Peaks from the junction at 2.9 miles. You can also continue hiking west at 3.2 miles on the Backbone Trail into Point Mugu State Park.

5 Charmlee Wilderness Park

RATING/ DIFFICULTY	LOOP	ELEV GAIN/ HIGH POINT	SEASON
***/2	2.8 miles	646 feet/ 1395 feet	Year-round

Map: USGS Trifuno Point; **Contact:** Charmlee Wilderness Park; **Notes:** Open 8:00 AM–sunset. Dogs allowed on leash. Parking fee required; **GPS:** N 34.058223, W 118.879328

Lovely, mostly easy trails dot this former ranch. Old buildings survive in the meadows and woodlands, many trails feature phenomenal coastal views, and the park staff leads guided hikes and events from the excellent nature center. In the spring, the combination of rolling green hills, bursts of wildflower color, and the long line of the Pacific Coast is not to be missed.

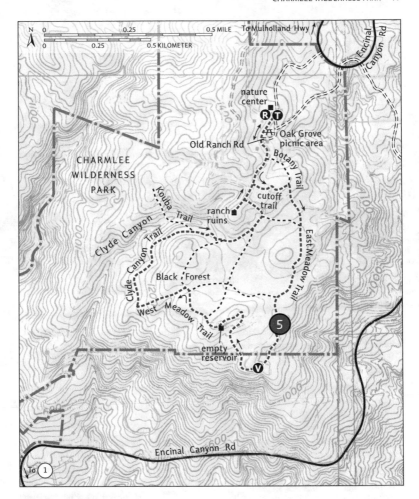

GETTING THERE

From Santa Monica, travel north on the Pacific Coast Highway (CA-1) for 24.2 miles, passing Zuma and Robert H. Meyer beaches. Turn right onto Encinal Canyon Road. The entrance to the park is 3.8 miles down the road on your left. Park near the nature center.

ON THE TRAIL

Head south on the Old Ranch Road, which passes the Oak Grove picnic area in just 450 feet. Keep right to stay on the Old Ranch Road and at 0.2 mile, turn left onto a short cutoff trail heading east and then turn right onto the Botany Trail at 0.4 mile. Continue

Looking toward Point Dume

hiking south as the Botany Trail skirts the perimeter of the park, passing through a dense grove of native oaks just before 0.5 mile.

From this point, the Botany Trail becomes the East Meadow Trail, and now you'll be hiking through some truly gorgeous Southern California grassland. In spring, the meadows here explode with colorful fireworks of monkey flowers and elegant clarkias—and no matter what time of year you're hiking, you'll have the mighty blue Pacific as a backdrop. Stay to the left at every junction and the trail will drop down a coastal bluff for a million-dollar Malibu beachfront view at 1.1 miles. On this part of the coast you're oriented more east–west than north–south: to the east lies the promontory of Point Dume, while to the west you may spot surfers at Leo Carrillo State Beach.

Past this overlook, the East Meadow Trail bends to the north and climbs back upward. At 1.4 miles, pass an empty concrete reservoir and stay left at the junction just beyond the reservoir to hike on the West Meadow Trail. At 1.6 miles, turn left onto the Clyde Canyon Trail and pass through a small grove of oaks known as the Black Forest. This rugged section drops down onto the eastern side of its namesake canyon before turning east toward the meadows. Stay straight at the junction with the Kouba Trail at 2.1 miles and stay to the left at the next few trail junctions. At 2.4 miles, visit the ruins of the former ranch house, which burned down in a wildfire in 1978. When you're done, head north from the ranch back to the trailhead—and give thanks that this area wasn't turned into a golf course like a previous owner was planning to do.

6 Escondido Falls

RATING/ DIFFICULTY	ROUNDTRIP	ELEV GAIN/ HIGH POINT	SEASON
***/2	3.6 miles	204 feet/ 348 feet	Year-round

Map: USGS Point Dume; **Contact:** Santa Monica Mountains Conservancy; **Notes:** Park closed sunset–sunrise. Dogs allowed on leash; **GPS:** N 34.0260545, W 118.7797319

The multi-tiered, 150-foot-tall Escondido Falls is the tallest waterfall in the Santa Monica Mountains. Although its level of watery majesty is subject to the whims of precipitation, the hike to the falls is a reliably lovely trek through a shaded canyon with an opportunity for some tough scrambling and even climbing for the more adventurous types.

GETTING THERE

From Santa Monica, travel 17.7 miles north on the Pacific Coast Highway (CA-1). Take a right onto Winding Way. There is a sign for the Winding Way Trail on the west side of the street that leads to a very small parking area. If parking is unavailable, you can park on the PCH, just watch out for "No Parking" signs. There is no parking on Winding Way itself. Metro bus 534 stops at PCH/Paradise Cove, about 0.5 mile west of the trailhead.

ON THE TRAIL

The Winding Way Trail is located in well-heeled Malibu, which means the local landowners have put the parking far away from their manicured lawns and the actual trailhead. Begin your hike on the paved surface of Winding Way. You'll pass expansive mansions and dilettante ranches before the road turns into a partial cul-de-sac at 0.75

Native oaks and sycamores provide shade en route to Escondido Falls.

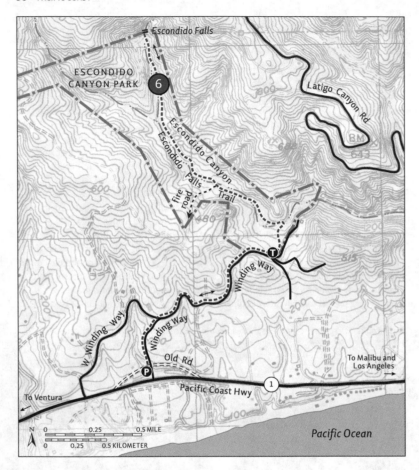

mile. Continue toward the equestrian ranch and look for a small wooden sign on the left hand side of the road at 0.8 mile to finally start hiking on a trail.

The trail drops into Escondido Canyon and hops the usually wet bottom to enter Escondido Canyon Park proper. Keep left at 0.9 mile to head north on the Escondido Falls Trail. The undeveloped canyon is a refreshing contrast to the super-sized homes you passed to get to it; canyon live oaks and twisted sycamores line the trail, providing a surprising amount of shade along the way. Ignore the faint old fire road at 1.2 miles and stay to the right as the trail rises slowly, occasionally leaving the riparian shade for some sunny sage scrub. You may be able to spot the top of the falls from here.

You'll hear the song of falling water before you reach the base of the lower falls at 1.8 miles, where the tiered, moss-covered rocks of the falls seem to drip like candle wax along the cliff. A beautiful grove sits at the bottom of the cascade, where a shallow pool is ringed by ivy and ferns. When you are done enjoying the refreshing ambiance, return the way you came.

EXTENDING YOUR TRIP
There is a very unofficial use-trail that climbs about halfway up the waterfall to a second grove, as well as an even more rugged climbing route to the very top. The scramble is moderately challenging and should be attempted only by those with experience (and no fear of heights); this holds even more true for the climbing route.

7 | **Solstice Canyon**

RATING/ DIFFICULTY	LOOP	ELEV GAIN/ HIGH POINT	SEASON
****/2	3.1 miles	535 feet/ 721 feet	Year-round

Maps: USGS Malibu Beach, Point Dume; **Contact:** Santa Monica Mountains National Recreation Area; **Notes:** Dogs allowed on leash but are not allowed at the waterfall; **GPS:** N 34.0378580, W 118.7501870

One of the most popular trails in the Santa Monica Mountains, this route passes what is rumored to be the oldest tree in Malibu, as well as the ruins of its oldest stone structure. At the end of the canyon lie the ruins of a 1950s ranch house and a small, cascading waterfall.

GETTING THERE
From Santa Monica, head north on the Pacific Coast Highway (CA-1) for 15.5 miles and turn right onto Corral Canyon Road. In 0.2 mile, turn left onto Solstice Canyon Road. There is a large parking area in 0.3 mile with restrooms, water, and informational kiosks, and there are several smaller overflow lots along the way. Metro bus 534 stops at PCH/ Corral Canyon, about 500 feet from the park entrance.

ON THE TRAIL
If you want an easy, (mostly) stroller-friendly hike, head directly onto the paved Solstice Canyon Trail. For this trip, however, head

A small cascade near the Roberts Ranch House

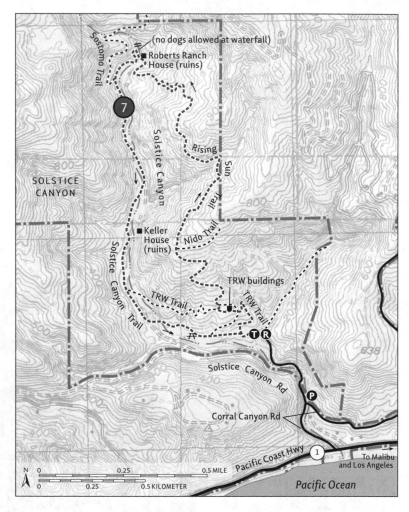

Sostomo Trail

(no dogs allowed at waterfall)

■ Roberts Ranch House (ruins)

7

Rising Sun Trail

SOLSTICE CANYON

Solstice Canyon

Nido Trail

■ Keller House (ruins)

Solstice Canyon Trail

TRW Trail

TRW buildings

TRW Trail

T R

Solstice Canyon Rd

P

Corral Canyon Rd

Pacific Coast Hwy

1

To Malibu and Los Angeles

Pacific Ocean

N
0   0.25   0.5 MILE
0   0.25   0.5 KILOMETER

north from the parking area on the TRW Trail, which climbs up a ridge just above the parking area. At 0.2 mile, cross an old paved road that leads to the remnants of buildings used to test satellite equipment from 1961 to 1973 (the TRW stands for Thompson Ramo

Wooldridge, the company that leased the land to space program research).

At 0.3 mile, take a right onto the Rising Sun Trail, which continues a steep, shade-less ascent up the eastern side of Solstice Canyon. Be sure to occasionally look back for some unique views of the Pacific Ocean framed by the canyon walls. At 0.7 mile, stay straight at the junction with the Nido Trail. You'll get a short respite from the incline before it picks back up again. At 1.3 miles, the trail makes a series of tight switchbacks down to the canyon floor.

At 1.8 miles, the trail dips into the refreshing shade near the ruins of the Roberts Ranch House, built in 1952 by the prolific and pioneering African-American architect Paul Revere Williams. Despite some innovative fire-prevention techniques built into the design and landscaping, the house burned down thirty years later. Many foundations and walls remain, as does a natural waterfall feature on the east side of the property that now serves as a popular picnic destination.

When you're done exploring, head west on the Solstice Canyon Trail, keeping left at the junction with the Sostomo Trail at 1.9 miles. Although damaged in the 2007 Corral Fire, the canyon here is bouncing back and offers plenty of cool shade and (mostly) year-round running water. At 2.5 miles, note the impressive oak tree just to the west of the trail, thought by many to be the oldest tree in Malibu. Across the creek lie the ruins of the Keller House, a stone cottage built by former landowner Matthew "Don Mateo" Keller in 1865. This was the oldest still-standing stone structure in Malibu until the Corral Fire. Continue on the Solstice Canyon Trail to return to the trailhead.

EXTENDING YOUR TRIP

Gain extra mileage and distance by adding the Sostomo Trail and Deer Valley Loop Trail to your hike. This route climbs through more coastal sage scrub to the western ridge of the canyon, passing the ruins of a few other cabins from the area's ranching past.

8 Corral Canyon

RATING/ DIFFICULTY	LOOP	ELEV GAIN/ HIGH POINT	SEASON
***/2	2.5 miles	525 feet/ 539 feet	Year-round

Map: USGS Malibu Beach; **Contact:** Santa Monica Mountains Conservancy; **Notes:** Dogs allowed on leash. Parking fee at trailhead. Access to Dan Blocker Beach seasonal only; **GPS:** N 34.033995, W 118.734698

A small and lightly visited park that protects the only remaining undeveloped canyon in Malibu with a creek flowing freely into the Pacific, Corral Canyon features stellar views of the coast and a unique estuary salt marsh. Hungry hikers will appreciate its proximity to a solid seafood joint, too.

GETTING THERE

From Santa Monica, head north on the Pacific Coast Highway (CA-1) for 14.7 miles. You'll see a sign for the trailhead just before the parking lot for Malibu Seafood. There's a small parking area adjacent to the seafood restaurant ($5 fee), or you can park on the PCH for free. Metro bus 534 stops directly at the trailhead.

ON THE TRAIL

Ignore the prominent beach-access walkway beneath the Pacific Coast Highway and head to the northeast corner of the lot, where you'll find the Sara Wan trailhead near a parking spot reserved for loading. As you begin on the Corral Canyon Loop Trail, the route quickly drops into a richly fragrant stretch of trail—California sagebrush and purple sage compete with the salt air of the ocean for your

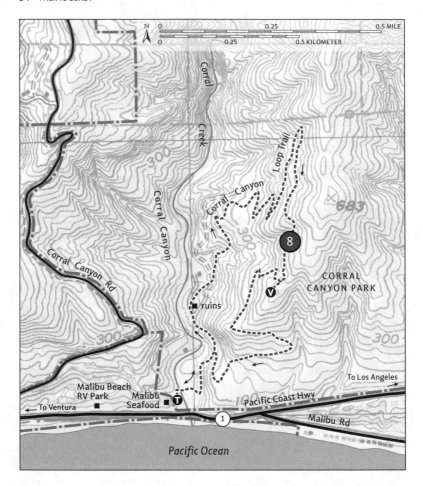

olfactory attention (with hints of fried fish wafting in from the west). The trail quickly hops over Corral Creek and turns north. At 0.2 mile, keep left to begin the loop section.

Pass the remnants of a former ranch house just before the 0.3-mile mark and get ready for a climb. The trail leaves the creek's riparian zone with its mature coast live oaks,

alders, and sycamores and begins a steady, switchbacking climb. There is plenty of coastal sage scrub here but nothing in the way of shade, so try to time this hike for the morning or late afternoon if you're exploring during the summer. To the north, only a few pockets of development mar the view of Corral Canyon's wilderness.

Beautiful coastline views (and fried seafood accents) await hikers at Corral Canyon.

By 1.2 miles your elevation gain is behind you. The trail turns south and as it gently descends you'll get one of the best hiking views of the coastline near L.A.—and likely a cooling ocean breeze, too. Just past the 1.5-mile mark, look for a short use-trail to a firebreak that follows the ridge to your southwest for a spectacular viewpoint where you can soak it all in. Return to the trail, turn left, and follow it downward to close the loop at 2.3 miles, then return to the trailhead the way you came.

9 Castro Crest

RATING/ DIFFICULTY	ROUNDTRIP	ELEV GAIN/ HIGH POINT	SEASON
***/4	7.6 miles	1237 feet/ 2386 feet	Year-round

Maps: USGS Point Dume, Malibu Beach; **Contact:** Malibu Creek State Park; **Notes:** Park open dawn–dusk. Parking at trailhead not available during red flag fire warnings; **GPS:** N 34.0788600, W 118.7554690

A challenging hike in the southwestern corner of Malibu Creek State Park, this route offers coastal ridgeline views, unique rock formations, and panoramic vistas of the Goat Buttes and rugged Trifuno Canyon.

GETTING THERE
From Santa Monica, head north on the Pacific Coast Highway (CA-1) for 15.5 miles. Turn right onto Corral Canyon Road and stay on this road for about 5.5 miles. Pass the first gate at Mesa Peak Motorway and park at the end of the road after it turns from Corral Canyon Road to Castro Peak Motorway (unsigned).

ON THE TRAIL
Head east on the unsigned Backbone Trail from the trailhead—look for a rocky firebreak heading toward some jagged, pinnacle-like rock formations. The rugged single-track follows the north side of the ridge through tilted layers of warped sedimentary rock, evidence of the region's

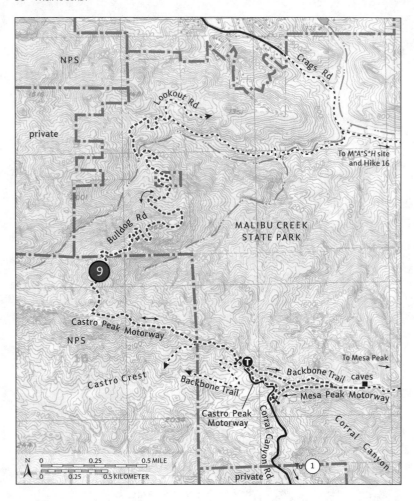

tectonic activity. Evidence of the region's more recent human history can be found in the rusted, half-buried car bodies.

Continue east as the Backbone Trail doubles up with Mesa Peak Motorway and the rock pinnacles grow larger and more complex. Look for caves carved by wind and

water in the odd folds around 0.7 mile. When you're done exploring the caves, backtrack to the west. At the junction where the Backbone Trail breaks off right, stay left on Mesa Peak Motorway for great views of the north end of Corral Canyon (Hike 8). Rejoin Castro Peak Motorway at 1.2 miles and keep right.

THE BACKBONE REALIZED

Did you know Los Angeles has its very own long-distance hiking trail? First proposed in the 1960s, the 67-mile-long Backbone Trail grew slowly, along with the Santa Monica Mountains National Recreation Area. The final easements for the trail were secured in 2016, and an official opening ceremony was held in June, celebrating a route that runs from Will Rogers State Park to Thornhill Broome Beach. The trail is still being improved (you cannot legally camp anywhere on the route right now), but National Park Service rangers do lead annual section hikes of the route. Head to www.nps.gov/samo/planyourvisit /backbonetrail.htm for the latest info.

Return to the trailhead and shake off the déjà vu by heading onto Castro Peak Motorway past the gate. At 1.8 miles, stay on Castro Motorway as the Backbone Trail drops to the south. You soon leave the state park and hike onto the high ridge of Castro Crest on a parcel of National Park Service land just beyond this boundary. To your left, the Pacific Ocean; to your right, a view of Malibu Creek State Park that stands in stark contrast to your views along Malibu Creek (Hike 16).

Unfortunately, the summit of Castro Peak sits on private land, so you won't be able to reach it. But turn right onto Bulldog Road at 2.3 miles and get your legs ready—in the next 2.3 miles, this dirt road drops 1226 feet. The scenery on the road itself isn't much, but the views of the interior of Malibu Creek State Park are worth the journey.

The unusual rock formations along Castro Crest

Stay to the right at 3.2 miles, then left at 3.7 and 3.9 miles, and right at 4.4 miles to continue on Bulldog Road. This route ends at the junction with Lookout Road at 4.6 miles. You can continue farther if you wish. Just remember: it's all uphill on the way back out.

EXTENDING YOUR TRIP

There are a lot of ways to extend this hike. To the east, you can continue a ridgeline trek from the junction of the Backbone Trail and Mesa Peak Motorway to Mesa Peak itself (2.9 miles to Mesa Peak, one way). From the junction with Lookout Road, it's 1 mile to Trifuno Canyon, where you can join the route described in Hike 16. All these trails connect, and it is possible to build your own giant loop around the entire Malibu Creek State Park. Depending on which trails you choose, you could expect as much as a long, 15-mile day in plenty of sun.

10 Zuma Ridge

RATING/ DIFFICULTY	ROUNDTRIP	ELEV GAIN/ HIGH POINT	SEASON
***/2	5.3 miles	1401 feet/ 1817 feet	Year-round

Map: USGS Point Dume; **Contact:** Santa Monica Mountains National Recreation Area; **Notes:** Park open sunrise–sunset. Dogs allowed on leash; **GPS:** N 34.033763, W 118.818109

This relatively mild out-and-back is popular with locals, and for good reason. The Zuma Ridge hike has a steady but approachable incline, and the sweeping views of the Pacific coastline start out almost immediately. If you're feeling energetic, there are many other trail options in this area to extend your time outdoors.

The ocean views are plentiful on the Zuma Ridge Trail.

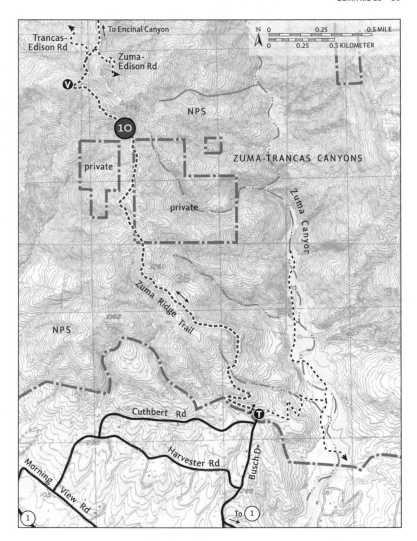

GETTING THERE

Take the Pacific Coast Highway (CA-1) about 20 miles west from Santa Monica and turn north on Busch Drive near the main parking area for Zuma Beach. A small parking lot and the trailhead are at the end of the road in 1.4 miles.

ON THE TRAIL

At the north end of the parking lot, look for the wider Zuma Ridge Trail, which heads west; heading east on the narrower trail will take you into Zuma Canyon itself. The Zuma Ridge Trail passes a gate and very quickly rises above the tony backyards and private horse ranches of Malibu. Even before the 0.1-mile mark, you'll start to get views of the Pacific Ocean, Zuma Beach, and the Channel Islands—large Santa Catalina lies to your south, while the significantly smaller Santa Barbara and San Nicolas islands are off to the southwest.

Staying on this route is pretty easy—you just remain on the main fire road and ignore the very few side trails and dirt roads. Enjoy the sage scrub along with the brilliant coast and canyon views as you continue climbing upward. At 2.4 miles, there's a particularly nice overlook on the west side of the road with fantastic views of rugged Encinal and Trancas canyons. To the west lie Anacapa and Santa Cruz islands, while to the northwest you'll be able to see the jagged, sandy-colored out-croppings of Boney Mountain and Sandstone Peak (Hike 4). Trancas-Edison Road heads west at 2.5 miles, and Zuma-Edison Road heads east just 0.1 mile farther. Turn around here and hike back the way you came in.

EXTENDING YOUR TRIP

It is possible to hike all the way to Encinal Canyon Road on this route. This is 6 miles one way and best done with a car shuttle. Alternatively, you could make a 10-plus-mile loop following Zuma-Edison Road east to Kanan-Edison Road and the Ocean View Trail, which would eventually return you to the trailhead. These routes are all completely shadeless and should not be attempted on hot, sunny days.

11 Nicholas Flat

RATING/ DIFFICULTY	LOOP	ELEV GAIN/ HIGH POINT	SEASON
****/4	6.9 miles	1644 feet/ 1685 feet	Year-round

Map: USGS Trifuno Pass; **Contact:** Leo Carrillo State Park; **Notes:** Park gate locked 10:00 PM–8:00 AM. Dogs allowed only in day-use areas, campgrounds, and North Beach. Parking fee inside state park. No overnight parking on street. Visitor center hours vary. Beach access available; **GPS:** N 34.046200, W 118.932149

One of the most challenging and rewarding hiking experiences in the Santa Monica Mountains, this trail rises from the coast through four different plant communities to spectacular secluded grasslands. Along the way, you'll be treated to some of the best views of the Santa Monicas you'll get on any hike.

GETTING THERE

This trail is located just inside Leo Carrillo State Park, near the intersection of Mulholland Highway and the Pacific Coast Highway (CA-1), 19.9 miles south of Oxnard and 28.3 miles west of Santa Monica. There is paid parking inside the state park or free parking along the PCH. If you plan on parking on the street, get there early, especially on weekends as beachgoers will by vying for those same spots.

ON THE TRAIL

East of the entry gate, look for a sign for the Camp 13 Trail. Less than 200 feet past this, head onto the Nicholas Flat Trail at the junction with the Willow Creek Trail. This route wastes no time in starting its ascent through thick groves of purple sage, which often blooms here into the late spring and early summer. At 0.9 mile, stay to the left at the four-way junction to begin your long, hard slog to Nicholas Flat.

This ridgeline trail is steep, shadeless, and relentless; start early to take advantage of the cooling marine layer until the impressive views of Boney Mountain can further motivate you. By 2.3 miles you've done most of the uphill work. Stay left at the first junction with a short Ridgeline Trail spur to the south and right at the next junction at 2.5 miles, where the Ridgeline Trail heads north. Continue east as coastal views begin to open

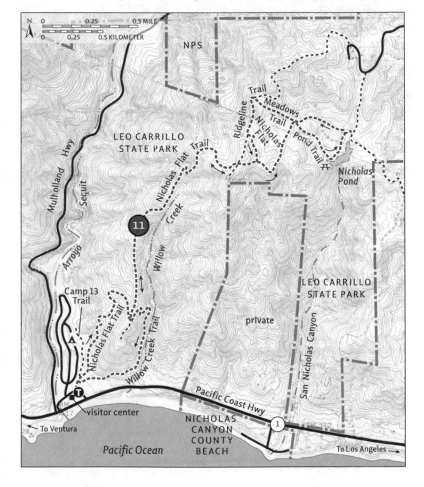

Meadows near Nicholas Flat

up in the chaparral. At 2.8 miles you'll spot the first open grassland on the hike—often chock-full of wildflowers in the spring. At 2.9 miles, stay to the right to take the Pond Trail to the seasonal Nicholas Pond—an exceptionally peaceful spot for a picnic lunch.

Continue northeast from the pond's shore and take a left at 3.4 miles, enjoying a rare bit of shade and some fragrant hummingbird sage ground cover. At 3.7 miles, take a right onto the Meadows Trail for some good walking-through-the-meadows time and at 4 miles take a sharp left to return south on the Ridgeline Trail, where you'll have some of the best views of the Santa Monica Mountains you'll get anywhere. Continue on the Ridgeline Trail or save yourself some elevation by staying left on a more level stretch of trail at 4.2 miles. Turn right when you reach the Nicholas Flat Trail and follow it downhill to the four-way junction at 6 miles. For a change in scenery, stay to the left to descend to the trailhead on the Willow Creek Trail.

12 Serrano Canyon

RATING/ DIFFICULTY	LOOP	ELEV GAIN/ HIGH POINT	SEASON
****/3	8.6 miles	864 feet/ 888 feet	Year-round

Maps: USGS Point Mugu, Trifuno Pass; **Contact:** Point Mugu State Park; **Notes:** No dogs allowed on trails. $12 fee required for day-use areas and parking; **GPS:** N 34.072285, W 119.014290

Extremely pleasant and not too tough, the Serrano Canyon loop ventures through one of the rare areas in Point Mugu State Park spared the worst of the 2013 Springs Fire, then opens up onto old ranch land with expansive grasslands and tremendous views of Boney Mountain. When you're done with this trail you can also walk under the Pacific Coast Highway (PCH) for a dip in the Pacific Ocean!

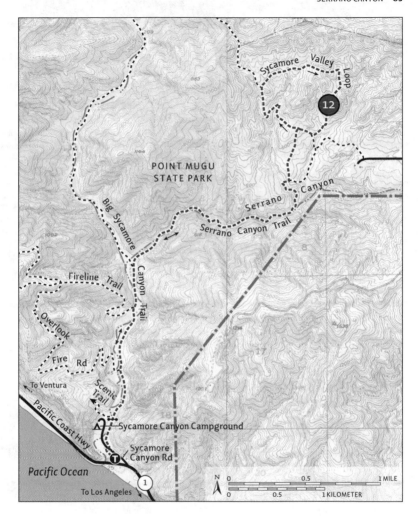

GETTING THERE

The trailhead is inside the Sycamore Canyon Campground of Point Mugu State Park, about 32.3 miles west of Santa Monica on the Pacific Coast Highway (CA-1) or 14.3 miles south of the CA-1/Rice Avenue exit off US Highway 101 in Ventura. There is a day-use fee inside the park, but if you can beat beach traffic and don't mind a bit of an extra walk you can also park along the PCH for free during the day.

Old ranch equipment with Boney Mountain in the background

ON THE TRAIL

Walk north along Sycamore Canyon Road through the campground. Pass the gate at 0.3 mile and mind the cyclists on the broad fire road. The Springs Fire did a number on this section of the park back in 2013—and a landslide shortly after didn't help—but although the scars are still visible, the canyon is definitely on the road to recovery. As you hike along Big Sycamore Canyon Trail, ignore the Scenic Trail just past the gate, the Overlook Fire Road at 0.7 mile, and the Fireline Trail at 1 mile. Veer right at the junction at 1.3 miles to head onto the Serrano Canyon Trail.

The contrast in Serrano Canyon is remarkable—not only is the trail much narrower and significantly less traveled, but as you progress farther you may be surprised to see surviving sycamores, cottonwoods, and oaks. The canyon walls narrow and the trail bobs and weaves through the canyon's

wash, providing an excellent taste of what places like Upper Sycamore Canyon (Hike 18) used to and will look like again.

At 2.8 miles the trail turns north and leaves the canyon and at 3 miles it crests a hill and spits you right into the thick of that iconic grassland the park is known for. Stay left to head north here, passing some moodily rusted ranch equipment at 3.2 miles. At 3.4 miles, turn left to proceed clockwise along the Sycamore Valley Loop. From here, you'll have some truly killer views of Boney Mountain to the east and the rolling hills inside Point Mugu State Park. At 4 miles, take a right onto a slightly less-defined trail to close the loop. This section of the route is on looser ground (an aftereffect of the fire that will ease with time) and has some steep sections, but nothing that should cause worry. At 5 miles, stay to the right and you'll close the loop at 5.2 miles. Return the way you came in.

Opposite: Hikers trek along one of the region's many dusty fire roads toward Calabasas Peak.

inland santa monica mountains

The Santa Monica Mountains stretch about 40 miles from the Hollywood Hills to Ventura County's Point Mugu as part of the region's Transverse Ranges—a series of mountain ranges that lie east-to-west instead of the more general north-to-south direction of most of the rest of the mountains in the state. Hike here and you'll be treated to historic ranches, old movie sets, secluded meadows, and rustic creeks in rugged and rocky canyons that sometimes feel like they're still enjoying life in the 1960s (in a good way!).

The trails in this section have a bit less coastal influence than those in the previous Pacific Coast section. Weak marine layer cloud cover may not make it into these areas as often, so expect the trails to be a bit sunnier and warmer.

13 Rocky Oaks Park

RATING/ DIFFICULTY	LOOP	ELEV GAIN/ HIGH POINT	SEASON
**/1	1.4 miles	135 feet/ 1846 feet	Year-round

Map: USGS Point Dume; **Contact:** Santa Monica Mountains National Recreation Area; **Notes:** Park open 8:00 AM–sunset; **GPS:** N 34.096725, W 118.814051

Rocky Oaks Park is a small but diverse park in the Santa Monica Mountains with easy trails suitable for beginner and young hikers. Trails here are very picturesque but they won't take you long to do, so do this as part of a larger day trip in the mountains. Highlights include coastal

Lots of shade and picnic areas await visitors to Rocky Oaks Park.

sage scrub, an artificial pond, and a picnic area beneath a cathedral of beautiful, mature canyon oaks.

GETTING THERE

From US Highway 101 in Agoura Hills, take the Kanan Road (County Road N9) exit and head south. In 6.2 miles, turn right onto Mulholland Highway. The entrance to Rocky Oaks Park will be on your right.

ON THE TRAIL

From the west end of the parking area, head north about 180 feet on the Rocky Oaks Loop Trail, passing a shed from the land's former ranch days. Take a left to begin the loop clockwise as the trail leaves the shade of oak trees and traverses a small meadow.

At 0.2 mile, take a very slight left, then continue north. The loop trail heads east and makes a gradual but noticeable climb through dense coastal sage scrub filled with California buckwheat and some of the densest black sage growth you'll find in the Los Angeles region. Keep an eye out for blooming phacelias and cardinal larkspur in the shadier sections here, even into the late spring. At 0.4 mile, stay to the right or take the short spur trail to an overlook. The trail heads northeast and reaches a locked gate at 0.7 mile.

Take a sharp right turn onto the Pond Trail as it dips into the seasonal streambed that—in wet years—fills the old ranch pond. Note the change in vegetation from sage scrub to oaks and invasive Spanish brooms. At 0.8 mile, take a slight left. At another unsigned junction just past this, stay to the right to take the Pond Trail around the east and south banks of the pond and back to the Rocky Oaks Loop Trail, or head straight to take the Glade Trail through the oak-covered picnic area back to the parking lot.

If you take the route along the southern lip of the pond, stay to the left at 1.2 miles and return to the trailhead the way you came in.

14 Paramount Ranch

RATING/ DIFFICULTY	LOOP	ELEV GAIN/ HIGH POINT	SEASON
***/2	2.8 miles	125 feet/ 863 feet	Year-round

Map: USGS Point Dume; **Contact:** Santa Monica Mountains National Recreation Area; **Notes:** Park open 8:00 AM–sunset. Dogs allowed on leash; **GPS:** N 34.115905, W 118.754992

This easy hike takes you through three native plant communities and more than eighty years of Hollywood history on a former ranch turned studio backdrop. Perhaps one of the most

Equestrians also enjoy the mellow trails at Paramount Ranch.

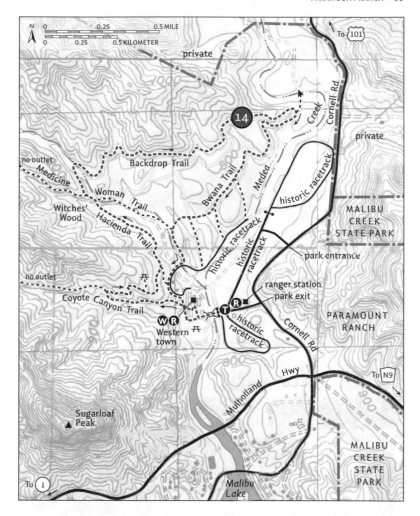

unusual hikes in the region and considered by some historians to be the best remaining example of a production facility from the Golden Era of motion pictures, Paramount Ranch is the only unit of the National Park System dedicated to interpreting filmmaking.

GETTING THERE

From US Highway 101 in Agoura Hills, take the Kanan Road exit and head south for 0.5 mile. Take a left onto Cornell Road. In 1.9 miles, look for Paramount Ranch which will be on your right.

ON THE TRAIL

From the parking area, cross the bridge over the surprisingly lush Medea Creek to be instantly transported back in time to the Wild West—in the form of a permanent Western village built in 1953 from the prop sheds of earlier Hollywood productions dating back to 1927. The "Western town" is only about a block long, but these buildings have served in hundreds of films and television shows even up to today. Take a right about 300 feet from the parking lot to walk counterclockwise through the town, taking note of a huge valley oak in its center. To the west of the town stands a faux train station that also doubles as a shaded picnic area. Look for the signed Coyote Canyon Trail to its west and leave the town behind.

This trail follows a narrow ribbon of riparian habitat but is mostly through chaparral. Look for California buckwheats and tarweeds blooming late into the spring. At 0.4 mile, keep right and at 0.5 mile stay to the right again at the junction with a short trail to a picnic area. At 0.6 mile turn left onto the Hacienda Trail. This trail splits around two low hills and joins the Medicine Woman Trail at 0.9 mile. Climb a very small hill past an oak grove known as Witches' Wood (named for fortune-tellers who prognosticated here during renaissance fairs in the 1970s) and stay to the right to join the Backdrop Trail.

This route hugs the edge of the huge grassy field that showcases the rare oak savanna plant community. Ignore the very faint use-trails at 1.6 miles and make a sharp turn right at 1.8 miles to join the Bwana Trail. Rejoin the Medicine Woman Trail at 2.4 miles and take a right at the historic racetrack to return to the Western town.

15 King Gillette Ranch

RATING/ DIFFICULTY	LOOP	ELEV GAIN/ HIGH POINT	SEASON
***/1	1.8 miles	253 feet/ 860 feet	Year-round

Map: USGS Malibu Beach; **Contact:** King Gillette Visitor Center; **Notes:** Park open

A matilija poppy (or "fried egg poppy") warms the native gardens near the botanical center.

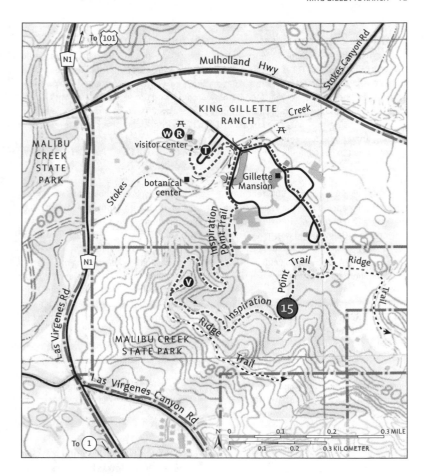

8:00 AM–sunset. Visitor center open daily 9:00 AM–5:00 PM. No dogs allowed. Free parking for two hours (fee afterward); **GPS:** N 34.103121, W 118.706541

🚶🏠♿ *An easy 1.8-mile loop trail provides stellar views of the Malibu Creek watershed, as well as explorations of the historic King Gillette Ranch and the brand-new Anthony C. Beilenson Interagency Visitor Center, an innovative and modern headquarters for the Santa Monica Mountains National Recreation Area.*

GETTING THERE

From US Highway 101 in Calabasas, take the southbound exit for Las Virgenes Road (County Road N1). In 3.3 miles, turn left onto

A WARM WELCOME TO THE SANTA MONICA MOUNTAINS
The Anthony C. Beilenson Interagency Visitor Center resides in a former ranch horse stable that was renovated in 2012 as a beautiful home base for the many agencies that cooperate in the Santa Monica Mountains National Recreation Area. (The site is managed as a partnership of the National Park Service, Mountains Recreation and Conservation Authority, Santa Monica Mountains Conservancy, and California State Parks.) The center does an exemplary job of showcasing the country's largest urban national park and often hosts events and rotating arts and history exhibits and is not to be missed—especially for newcomers who are still trying to get a handle on how, exactly, this unit of the National Park Service works.

Mulholland Highway and in 500 feet, turn right into the ranch. From the Pacific Coast Highway (CA-1), turn north onto Malibu Canyon Road (County Road N1). In 4.6 miles it becomes Las Virgenes Road. In another 2.7 miles, turn right onto Mulholland Highway and take another right into the ranch parking lot.

ON THE TRAIL
Walk through the visitor center's picnic area and behind the restrooms to begin the trail at the Mountains Recreation and Conservation Authority's (MRCA) botanical center. Here, MRCA naturalists grow native plants for restoration projects in their parks throughout the Los Angeles area, and you can walk through some incredible examples—including some seven-foot-tall matilija poppy bushes. At 0.2 mile, take a right onto the paved road and cross the bridge over Stokes Creek, keeping right again to stay on the west bank of the pond that sits in front of the historic King Gillette Ranch—built for razor magnate King Camp Gillette in 1926.

At 0.3 mile, turn right off the maintenance road to begin on the Inspiration Point Trail. This trail begins with a bit of shade but opens up quickly (and gains a bit of elevation, too). At 0.7 mile, take a sharp left on the spur trail to Inspiration Point for 360-degree views of the Santa Monica Mountains and especially great views of Malibu Creek State Park's Goat Buttes to the west. Head back down and stay to the far left to continue heading east on the Inspiration Point Trail.

At 1.3 miles, stay left at the junction with the Ridge Trail to head back to the King Gillette Ranch House. Wander around the grounds and cross the bridge to return to the visitor center.

16 Malibu Creek

RATING/ DIFFICULTY	ROUNDTRIP	ELEV GAIN/ HIGH POINT	SEASON
****/2	8 miles	181 feet/ 709 feet	Year-round

Map: USGS Malibu Beach; **Contact:** Malibu Creek State Park; **Notes:** Park open dawn–dusk, visitor center open noon–4:00 PM on weekends only. Dogs allowed on leash in campgrounds and day-use areas, no dogs on trails. Parking fee required; **GPS:** N 34.097057, W 118.716240

 *Visit an old set from M*A*S*H, stroll along ponds on land that was formerly a hunting*

Climbers practice their craft in the rock pools near Century Lake.

and fishing club for millionaires, get your hands dirty alongside rock climbers, and take a kayak into the water if you're in the mood.

GETTING THERE

Travel north from Santa Monica on the Pacific Coast Highway (CA-1) for 13.2 miles. Turn north onto Malibu Canyon Road (County Road N1), which becomes Las Virgenes Road in 4.6 miles. At 6.1 miles, turn left into the Malibu Creek State Park entrance station. From US Highway 101 in Calabasas, take the Las Virgenes Road (County Road N1) exit and head south. Continue on Las Virgenes Road for 3.4 miles and turn right into the entrance station. You may also park your car near the intersection of Las Virgenes and Mulholland Highway and hike into the park, although break-ins have been reported there.

ON THE TRAIL

Enter the park from the main parking area on the dirt Crags Road Trail, which crosses Las Virgenes Creek and then hugs the north bank of Malibu Creek in a surprisingly dense riparian corridor. Ignore the Grassland Trail and at 0.3 mile where the trail splits, stay to the right to hike on the High Road and continue enjoying the plentiful shade of canyon oaks. At 0.9 mile, stay to the right to continue on Crags Road. The trail makes its one major climb into the rocky territory of the Goat Buttes and drops back down toward the shore of artificial Century Lake. Ignore the side trails at 1.3 and 1.6 miles and at 1.8, stay right at the junction with the Forest Trail (you'll hike this on your way out).

West of this junction, the trail narrows into a rocky single-track and at 2.4 miles it reaches the remnants of the outdoor set of *M*A*S*H*, one of the highest-rated and most critically acclaimed TV programs ever made. Hawkeye, Radar, and the rest of the 4077th Mobile Army Surgical Hospital worked here from 1972 to 1983, and there are still some remnants left behind—including old vehicles. A renovation in 2007 restored a replica signpost and added informational plaques and a shaded picnic area.

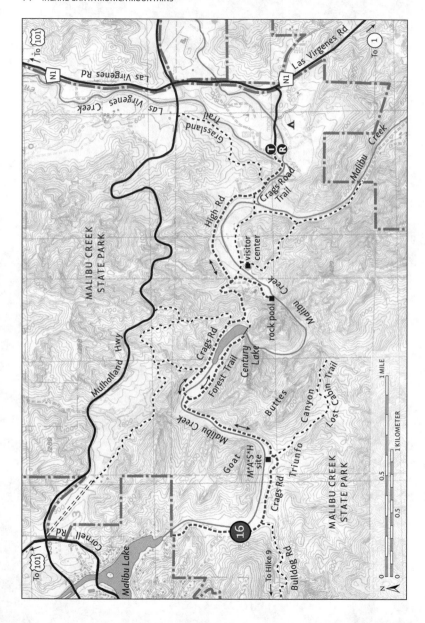

Continue west along Crags Road. At 2.7 miles, stay right at the junction with Bulldog Road, and then reach the trail's end at the park's boundary and Malibu Lake. For more highlights, backtrack to the Forest Trail at 4.7 miles and hike beneath the decidedly nonnative pine trees to reach an overlook of the Century Dam. Retrace your steps back toward the trailhead but stay right at the intersection with the High Road. At 6.5 miles, take a right to head toward the visitor center and a short spur trail that leads to a rock pool popular with climbers and scramblers. To return to the trailhead, go back to the intersection with the High Road, and turn right.

OTHER OPTIONS

Extremely ambitious hikers can join the Castro Crest trail (Hike 9) from Bulldog Road. You can also break this route up into smaller sections for easier hikes. An out-and-back to the M*A*S*H set is about 5 miles roundtrip; to Century Lake it's 2.6 miles roundtrip; and to the rock pool it's about 2.2 miles roundtrip.

17 Old Boney Trail

RATING/ DIFFICULTY	LOOP	ELEV GAIN/ HIGH POINT	SEASON
***/3	11.4 miles	1535 feet/ 1834 feet	Year-round

Maps: USGS Newbury Park, Trifuno Pass;
Contact: Santa Monica Mountains National Recreation Area and Point Mugu State Park;
Notes: Main parking area open 8:00 AM–sunset. Satwiwa Native American Indian Cultural Center open weekends 9:00 AM–5:00 PM. No bicycles allowed on trails. Dogs allowed on leash only on developed

California buckwheat blooms last almost the entire year.

trails inside National Park Service land, not on trails inside the state park; **GPS:** N 34.152869, W 118.965624

Old Boney Trail is a long, pleasant, and mostly secluded loop through the rolling mountains and wide grasslands of northern Point Mugu State Park. This is a *great full-day trek, especially when spring wildflowers show up.*

GETTING THERE

From US Highway 101 in Thousand Oaks, take the Lynn Road exit and head south. Continue for 5.6 miles. Just past Via Las Brisas, where Lynn Road turns into Potrero

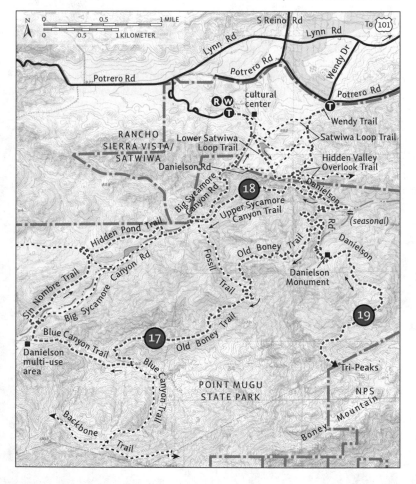

Road, look for the large gate for Rancho Sierra Vista on your left. The parking area is at the end of the road.

ON THE TRAIL

Head southeast past the restrooms and along a dirt road to enter the Rancho Sierra Vista/Satwiwa area. Pass old ranch buildings on your left and at 0.4 mile, stay straight to head to the southeast on the Lower Satwiwa Loop Trail, which cuts across some of the best straight-on views of Boney Mountain in the entire Santa Monica Mountains National Recreation Area. The trail crosses a meadow area considered sacred to the Chumash, and at 0.75 mile reaches the northern edge of Big Sycamore Canyon.

Head east into Point Mugu State Park on Danielson Road and stay to the right where the Hidden Valley Overlook Trail enters from the left at 0.9 mile to descend, watching out for eroded sections of trail.

At the junction with the Upper Sycamore Canyon Trail at 1.3 miles, go straight to stay on Danielson Road. At the 1.5 mile mark, there's a short spur to a seasonal waterfall (really only present following a good rainy season). Visit the falls and backtrack to where Danielson Road begins climbing up the southern wall of Big Sycamore Canyon. At the junction with the Old Boney Trail at 2.5 miles, continue straight on Danielson Road to the Danielson Monument, an old cabin foundation and lovely wrought iron gate commemorating Richard Ely Danielson, the former owner of Rancho Sierra Vista who sold his land to California State Parks, forming the foundation for much of Point Mugu State Park. The rough backcountry route to Tri-Peaks (Hike 19) continues from here. Return to the Old Boney Trail at 3.3 miles and turn left.

Climb a short, steep ascent and stay straight at the junction with the Fossil Trail at 4.6 miles (which is also a good cutoff if you're in the mood for a shorter route). At 6.7 miles, turn right onto the Blue Canyon Trail to descend to the Danielson multi-use area (group camp reservations required). Head north on the paved Big Sycamore Canyon Road at 7.6 miles and look for the Sin Nombre Trail on the left at 7.8 miles. Make a short backtrack south before taking a hard right at 8 miles. The Sin Nombre Trail and the Hidden Pond Trail, which you reach at 8.9 miles, are roughly parallel to Big Sycamore Canyon Road but meander through wide, open grasslands with lovely views and are a much nicer option than hoofing it along the paved incline of the road. Keep an eye out for snakes and keep left at 10 miles to follow Big Sycamore Canyon Road back to the trailhead.

18 Upper Sycamore Canyon

RATING/ DIFFICULTY	LOOP	ELEV GAIN/ HIGH POINT	SEASON
***/2	4.1 miles	427 feet/ 1068 feet	Year-round

Map: USGS Trifuno Pass; **Contact:** Santa Monica Mountains National Recreation Area and Point Mugu State Park; **Notes:** Main parking area open 8.00 AM–sunset. Satwiwa Native American Indian Cultural Center open weekends 9:00 AM–5:00 PM. No bicycles allowed on trails. Dogs allowed on leash only on developed trails inside National Park Service land, not on trails inside the state park; **GPS:** N 34.152869, W 118.965624

🏠 🎽 *Offering a unique opportunity to see Southern California's fire ecology up close and personal, this route takes you*

A barren Point Mugu State Park after the 2013 Springs Fire. Don't worry, it will look better now.

through a riparian canyon badly damaged in the 2013 Springs Fire that is on the mend, giving you a chance to participate in some groundbreaking citizen science.

GETTING THERE

From US Highway 101 in Thousand Oaks, take the Lynn Road exit and head south. Continue for 5.6 miles. Just past Via Las Brisas, where Lynn Road turns into Potrero Road, look for the large gate for Rancho Sierra Vista on your left. The parking area is at the end of the road.

ON THE TRAIL

Head southeast past the restrooms and along a dirt road to enter the Rancho Sierra Vista/Satwiwa area. Pass old ranch buildings on your left and at 0.4 mile, stay straight to head to the southeast on the Lower Satwiwa Loop Trail, which cuts across some of the best straight-on views of Boney Mountain in the entire Santa Monica Mountains National Recreation Area. The trail crosses a meadow

area considered sacred to the Chumash, and at 0.75 mile reaches the northern edge of Big Sycamore Canyon.

Head east into Point Mugu State Park on Danielson Road, and stay to the right where the Hidden Valley Overlook Trail enters from the left at 0.9 mile to descend, watching out for eroded sections of trail. At 1.3 miles make a sharp right onto the Upper Sycamore Canyon Trail. This route follows the upper reaches of a canyon where the forest was nearly burned to the ground in 2013 but it's already showing hopeful signs of recovery. The trail meanders to the southwest mostly along an intermittent streambed and will provide exceptional views of nearby Boney Mountain as well as longer views down Big Sycamore Canyon toward the Pacific Ocean.

At 2.6 miles, stay right at the junction with the Fossil Trail and at 2.7 miles turn right on the paved Big Sycamore Canyon Road for a long, shadeless uphill back to the trailhead.

FROM THE ASHES

On May 2, 2013, the Springs Fire burst into life near the 101. Unusually early in the traditional fire season, the Springs Fire took advantage of hot winds and drought-weakened chaparral to burn more than 24,000 acres by the time it was finished—about 12 percent of the entire land area in the Santa Monica Mountains National Recreation Area. Unlike after the 2009 Station Fire, which closed huge sections of the San Gabriel Mountains for years, the Springs Fire burn zone was reopened to the public just a few weeks after the last flames were extinguished, providing a unique opportunity for people to experience the effects and aftermath of a wildfire on the Southern California landscape. Today, various park authorities are using the fire as an opportunity to restore native habitat and to gather some of the most comprehensive data ever collected on fire recovery. There are ten photo stations set up all over the burn zone, and visitors are encouraged to snap photos and share them with the parks on social media. Visit www.nps.gov/samo/learn/management/springs-fire-photo-monitoring.htm to see the constantly updated photos and even watch time-lapse video of the region in recovery.

EXTENDING YOUR TRIP

There is an extensive network of trails in this region of the Santa Monicas. For less boots-on-the-pavement time, consider a return trip along the Old Boney Trail (reverse of Hike 17). Very adventurous hikers can also trek to Tri-Peaks (Hike 19) and Sandstone Peak (Hike 4) to the east, Serrano Canyon (Hike 12) to the south, and even connect with routes in the La Jolla Valley to the west.

19 Tri-Peaks via Satwiwa

RATING/ DIFFICULTY	ROUNDTRIP	ELEV GAIN/ HIGH POINT	SEASON
***/5	10.2 miles	2157 feet/ 3010 feet	Year-round

Maps: USGS Newbury Park, Trifuno Pass; **Contact:** Santa Monica Mountains National Recreation Area and Point Mugu State Park; **Notes:** Dogs allowed on leash only on developed trails inside National Park Service

land, not on trails inside the state park; **GPS:** N 34.154405, W 118.950244

Here you'll find a challenging and very steep, unmaintained route to a prominent coastal peak with exceptional views. If you're in the mood for an adventure in the Santa Monica Mountains but don't want to travel a well-beaten path, this is the hike for you—just make sure you're ready for it. Pack extra food and water and be sure to give yourself extra time too!

GETTING THERE

From US Highway 101 in Newbury Park, take the Wendy Drive exit and follow Wendy Drive south until it ends at the intersection with Potrero Road. There is a wide dirt lot on the south side of the road and a signed trailhead.

ON THE TRAIL

Hike southwest along the Wendy Trail. At about 0.3 mile, veer left to head south on

A mountain view from the summit of Tri-Peaks

the eastern edge of the Satwiwa Loop Trail, stay straight at a junction near an old ranch windmill at 0.6 mile, take a left at the Hidden Valley Overlook Trail at 0.9 mile and a sharp left onto Danielson Road at the mile mark.

At the junction with the Upper Sycamore Canyon Trail, stay straight on Danielson Road. At the junction with the Old Boney Trail, continue straight on Danielson Road to the Danielson Monument (see Hike 17 for details). Just to the left of the old cabin foundation, look for a well-worn use-trail through the chaparral at the 3-mile mark. Tracing the remnants of an old ranch road, this steep, unmaintained route wastes no time in gaining elevation. Although you may feel at times like this is more of a climb than a hike, the breaks in the chaparral provide you with ever-widening views along the way. Take your time and exercise caution here. The trail makes a sharp turn south at 3.3 miles and climbs along the edge of the canyon. By 4.1 miles most of the tough elevation gain is out of your way and you'll have views of the volcanic rock outcroppings of Boney Mountain straight ahead to the southwest.

The trail roughly follows this ridge, hitting several mini-peaks along the way (2640 feet at 4.2 miles and 2920 feet at 4.8 miles). The bump at 2920 feet will provide you with phenomenal views of Boney Mountain and Sandstone Peak (Hike 4) to the southeast.

The final push to Tri-Peaks takes a significant amount of scrambling and bushwhacking, including some extremely faint routes through narrow boulders and thick chaparral. Tri-Peaks is an odd-looking summit that appears to be a pile of boulders sitting atop sagebrush, and you'll reach it at the 5.1-mile mark.

EXTENDING YOUR TRIP

It is possible to take a slightly better-traveled use-trail south from Tri-Peaks to the Mishe Mokwa/Backbone Trail near Inspiration Point (Hike 4) if you arrange a car shuttle at the trailhead for that hike. Alternatively, from the intersection with the Backbone Trail, you can head west on the Chamberlain Trail/Backbone Trail to the Old Boney Trail (Hike 17) for an exceptionally long day (but at least the trail going back will be established!).

20 Calabasas Peak

RATING/ DIFFICULTY	ROUNDTRIP	ELEV GAIN/ HIGH POINT	SEASON
**/2	4.6 miles	1076 feet/ 2163 feet	Year-round

Map: USGS Malibu Beach; **Contact:** Santa Monica Mountains Conservancy; **Notes:** Dogs allowed on leash. Self-service parking fee; **GPS:** N 34.105932, W 118.637269

This moderately graded ascent outside Topanga Village has some of the best views of the interior of the Santa Monica Mountains—and is a great place to watch the marine layer flowing over the coastal peaks. There are fascinating caves and rock formations on display here and intriguing spur trails if you want to spend a bit more time exploring.

GETTING THERE

From US Highway 101 at Topanga Canyon Boulevard (CA 27), exit onto Topanga Canyon Boulevard heading south. In 1.4 miles, turn right onto Mulholland Drive and in another 0.5 mile, take the third left onto Mulholland Highway (that part can get a little confusing, so go slowly). From there, continue 1.7 miles and take a left onto Old Topanga Canyon Road. Stay on Old Topanga for 3.8 miles and take a right onto Red Rock Road. Follow Red Rock Road for 0.8 mile (the last 0.2 mile is an unimproved dirt road) to reach two parking areas. There are iron rangers near both parking lots with envelopes for parking fees. If you're coming from the Pacific Coast Highway (CA-1), travel 5.3 miles from Santa Monica, turn north onto Topanga Canyon Boulevard (CA-27) and drive for 4.3 miles before taking a left onto

Old Topanga Canyon Road. Continue on Old Topanga for 1.9 miles and take a left onto Red Rock Road.

ON THE TRAIL

Hike past the gate at the end of Red Rock Road to pass the remnants of Camp Slauson, a former Boy Scout camp that became Santa Monica Mountains Conservancy land in 1986. There is no camping here anymore, but you'll find a drinking fountain, restrooms, and a small picnic area. This early section of the trail is well-shaded. Kids (and those young at heart) will enjoy scrambling and exploring the cave formations on the south side of the road on the first 0.3 mile. Be on the lookout for marine fossils embedded in some of the rocks.

At 0.4 mile, stay straight at the junction with the Red Rock Canyon Trail to continue on the dirt road. The trail gains slow but

Look for marine fossils in Red Rock Canyon.

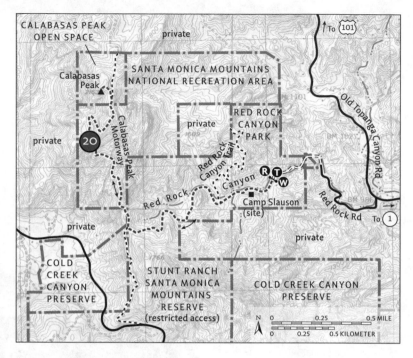

noticeable elevation here as it winds its way toward Calabasas Peak Motorway. You won't have many views before you reach that junction, but be sure to look behind you to soak in the region's strange, angular rock formations.

Keep right at 1.1 miles to continue your climb upward on Calabasas Peak Motorway. On clear days you can see the Pacific Ocean from here—and on those June Gloom afternoons you can sometimes experience the thick blanket of the marine layer dissolving over the coastal range in a moody, extremely photogenic slow-motion display. Just before 2.1 miles, look for a faint use-trail leaving a

ridge on the western side of the road. This short firebreak climbs two steep slopes before turning back toward Calabasas Peak. Return the way you came.

EXTENDING YOUR TRIP

If you're looking for a more rugged add-on experience, explore the Red Rock Canyon Trail 0.4 mile from the trailhead on the north side of the fire road. This winding, sometimes-faint single-track spur will take you through some more interesting geology and up to an overlook of the rippled canyons, adding up to 1.4 miles roundtrip, depending on how far you feel like exploring.

Opposite: The Santa Monica Mountains and suburban sprawl from Simi Peak

san fernando valley/
simi hills

Ask people what comes to mind when they hear "the Valley" and if you hear "hiking" first, I'll treat you to a Double-Double at In-N-Out.

Known more for suburban sprawl and strip malls, the Valley is definitely a hidden gem when it comes to hiking in the L.A. region. Its low but imposing peaks hide hair-raising old wagon passes, stunning mesas, several endangered and endemic plants, and secluded ranges of mostly untouched oak scrub that not only give you a chance to see a California of a bygone era but also provide some of the most beautiful views in the entire state (in my very unbiased opinion, of course).

The protected swaths of land in the western valley are also an important wildlife corridor in the Santa Monica Mountains, which are otherwise hemmed in by enormous freeways. A movement is underway to construct a wildlife crossing over the ten-lane 101 in Agoura Hills, which would not only provide connections for the wildlife, but also increase trail connections for hikers.

21 Wildwood Park

RATING/ DIFFICULTY	LOOP	ELEV GAIN/ HIGH POINT	SEASON
****/2	4.5 miles	626 feet/ 924 feet	Year-round

Year-round Paradise Falls is a pleasant surprise for SoCal hikers.

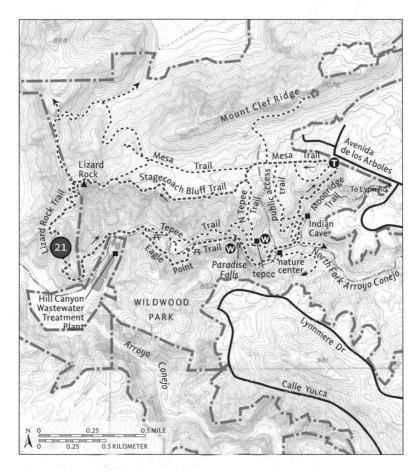

Map: USGS Newbury Park; **Contact:** Conejo Open Space Conservation Agency; **Notes:** Park open sunrise–sunset except during inclement weather. Dogs allowed on leash only. Tours of the Hill Canyon Wastewater Treatment Plant (see Appendix I) are free but must be scheduled ahead of time; **GPS:** N 34.219926, W 118.902336

One of the most diverse regional parks in Southern California, this 1765-acre gem holds sweeping grasslands, inspiring mesas, caves, a year-round riparian canyon, a waterfall, picture-perfect picnic areas, and a state-of-the-art water treatment plant that's open for tours.

GETTING THERE
From US Highway 101 in Thousand Oaks, take the exit for Lynn Road and head north. In 2.5 miles, turn left onto Avenida de los Arboles. Trailhead parking is at the end of the street.

ON THE TRAIL
Look for the prominent information board and head west on the straight-shot Mesa Trail, which tops a broad, low hill before opening up to some stunning grassland, mountain, and mesa views. Stay straight on the Mesa Trail until just before the 0.4-mile mark, where you'll take a left onto the North Tepee Trail, and then just past 0.5 mile, head west on the Stagecoach Bluff Trail—a rugged, rocky route that rises through prickly pears and cholla cacti. At 1.2 miles, stay to the far left to hike up a steep incline to the prominent southern face of Lizard Rock. Look for a well-worn use-trail at 1.4 miles to scramble to the peak itself for some killer views of the park and the Santa Monica Mountains to the south.

Scramble back down to the Lizard Rock Trail and head south along a series of broad switchbacks to the canyon floor. Keep an ear open for cyclists here, as there are plenty of blind corners. At 2.4 miles, the trail basically skirts the western edge of the Hill Canyon Wastewater Treatment Plant, a high-tech treatment plant that runs entirely on renewable energy. Just past the facility, the trail enters the dense riparian canyon of the North Fork Arroyo Conejo. At 2.8 miles, cross the arroyo to the majestic Skunk Hollow picnic area and tackle the rough Eagle Point Trail for some extra elevation gain. After a steep drop, the trail deposits you at the Oak Grove picnic area at 3.3 miles. Cross the arroyo again and head east, reaching the spur trail for Paradise Falls at 3.5 miles. Soak in the cool breezes but not in the water—it's mostly untreated urban runoff—and rejoin the trail heading east above the falls, staying straight at 3.8 miles to head toward the nature center (or climb up the side trail to an unusual giant tepee structure). At 4 miles, head toward Indian Cave, a diminutive slash in the rock that provides a bit of fun for young scramblers. A narrow but well-traveled use-trail next to the cave's entrance will take you to the Moonridge Trail and back to the trailhead.

22 China Flat and Simi Peak

RATING/ DIFFICULTY	ROUNDTRIP	ELEV GAIN/ HIGH POINT	SEASON
****/3	5.5 miles	1128 feet/ 2405 feet	Year-round

Map: USGS Thousand Oaks; **Contact:** Rancho Simi Recreation and Park District and Santa Monica Mountains National Recreation Area; **Notes:** Dogs allowed on leash. Trails may be closed during inclement weather and other emergencies; **GPS:** N 34.193543, W 118.775467

A fun, moderate hike to the highest point in the Simi Hills, this route features some interesting rock formations, a decent elevation gain, and a beautiful stretch of native oak grassland.

GETTING THERE
From US Highway 101 in Agoura Hills, take the exit for Lindero Canyon Road heading north. Stay on this road for 3.8 miles and park between King James Court and Wembly Avenue. Park on the street.

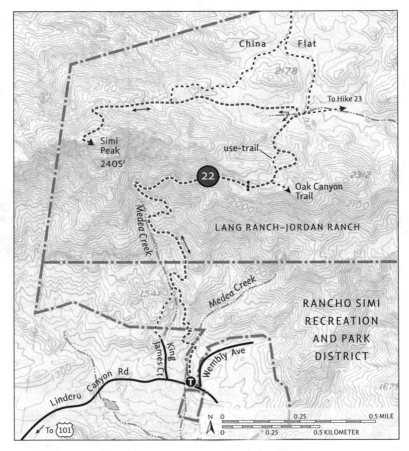

ON THE TRAIL

The trail begins in a narrow strip of parkland surrounding the banks of one of the upper branches of Medea Creek as it meanders behind some suburban backyards. After passing through some dense fields of yerba santa and California buckwheat, keep right at 0.4 mile to continue climbing the rough, rocky route. At 1.5 miles, the trail levels out and passes two rusted gates, remnants of the area's former ranch days. Just beyond this, stay to the left at the junction with the Oak Canyon Trail to follow a road into China Flat—either staying on the old road grade or taking the steeper use-trail through the chamise bushes.

Here, you'll transition from sage scrub to the large oak savanna that's hidden in the

Native oak savanna near China Flat

surprisingly hilly China Flat. Stay to the left at 1.8 miles and head west behind the long ridge of Simi Peak. In the spring, the grass glows emerald and is punctuated by bursts of wildflower color; in hotter months, its gold stands in contrast to the dark oaks above it. At 2.3 miles, stay straight at the junction with a longer loop trail that circles the edge of the flat.

The trail becomes narrower and rougher as it makes its way up the north side of Simi. At 2.7 miles, look for a prominent rocky section with a short metal pole and you've reached the summit. Enjoy the commanding views of the Santa Monica Mountains to the south and return the way you came.

23 Cheeseboro and Palo Comado Canyons

RATING/ DIFFICULTY	LOOP	ELEV GAIN/ HIGH POINT	SEASON
****/4	10.4 miles	755 feet/ 1756 feet	Year-round (best Feb–Mar)

Map: USGS Calabasas; **Contact:** Santa Monica Mountains National Recreation Area; **Notes:** Dogs allowed on leash; **GPS:** N 34.156380, W 118.730814

 This beautiful trail in the Simi Hills is an oasis amidst the sprawl of the

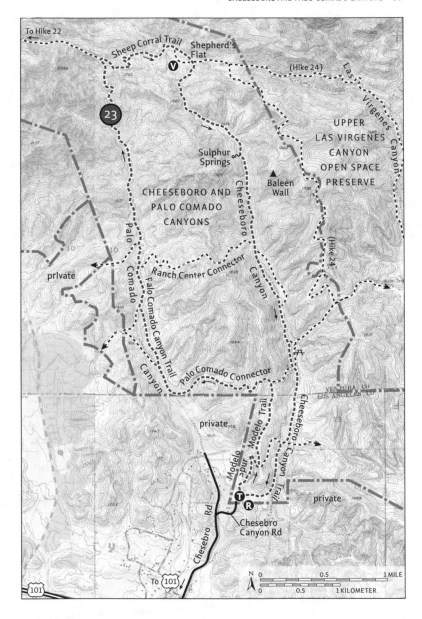

To Hike 22

Sheep Corral Trail

Shepherd's Flat

(Hike 24)

Las Virgenes Canyon

23

UPPER LAS VIRGENES CANYON OPEN SPACE PRESERVE

Sulphur Springs

Baleen Wall

CHEESEBORO AND PALO COMADO CANYONS

Cheeseboro Canyon

(Hike 24)

Water Tank

Palo Comado

private

Ranch Center Connector

Cheeseboro Canyon

Palo Comado Canyon Trail

Palo Comado Connector

Canyon

VENTURA CO.
LOS ANGELES CO.

private

Modelo Trail

Cheeseboro Canyon Trail

Modelo Spur

private

T

R

Chesebro Canyon Rd

Chesebro Rd

To 101

N   0   0.5   1 MILE
    0   0.5   1 KILOMETER

101

Solitary oaks and solitude are both plentiful in these canyons.

San Fernando Valley. Similar in scope and feel to neighboring Las Virgenes Canyon (Hike 24), this lengthy journey will make you feel like you're a million miles away from the city. In spring, you can snap photos of emerald meadows that could easily fool people into thinking you've booked a flight to Ireland.

GETTING THERE

From US Highway 101 in Agoura Hills, take the Chesebro Road/Agoura Hills exit and head north, following signs for Chesebro Road. In 0.7 mile, go right on Chesebro Canyon Road (and yes, it's spelled differently than the canyon!). The trailhead is at the end of the road.

ON THE TRAIL

From the trailhead, leave the main trail and head north on the Modelo Spur Trail. This trail climbs along a ridge and meets the Modelo Trail at 0.5 mile. Keep left to head north and at 1.2 miles, turn left to hike along the Palo Comado Connector on a slowly widening ridgeline. The trail turns north and drops into a wooded area and at 2.4 miles, stay to the right to join the Palo Comado Canyon Trail. Here, you'll enter an exemplary slice of classic California oak woodland, with lush coast live oaks and their more gnarled-looking relatives, the valley oaks, which can live for up to six hundred years.

The Palo Comado Canyon Trail continues north, slowly transitioning to tougher sage scrub and chaparral. Ignore all trails heading west and at 3.3 miles, skip the eastbound Ranch Center Connector and keep trudging north. The trail follows the entire length of Palo Comado Canyon and can be used to hike to China Flat and Simi Peak (Hike 22), but for the route described here, take a right at 5.1 miles onto the single-track Sheep Corral Trail. At 5.9 miles, an optional use-trail to the south leads to a nice view of the canyons and a spot to eat a lunch or snack. Continue east, passing an old sheep corral and a major trail junction at Shepherd's Flat at 6.2 miles.

Head south on the Cheeseboro Canyon Trail. At 7.2 miles, you'll pass (and may be able to smell) the aptly named Sulphur Springs on your right and the distinctive Baleen Wall formation to your left. Keep heading south on this trail and ignore the parallel access road and all other spur and connector trails to return to the trailhead.

OTHER OPTIONS

There are many options to turn this large loop into smaller ones using the connector trails. In addition, you can hike north along the Palo Comado Canyon Trail to China Flat and Simi Peak (Hike 22) or head east on the Sheep Corral Trail or Palo Comado Connector Trail to join the Las Virgenes Canyon Loop (Hike 24).

24 Las Virgenes Canyon

RATING/ DIFFICULTY	LOOP	ELEV GAIN/ HIGH POINT	SEASON
****/3	8.6 miles	963 feet/ 1850 feet	Year-round

Map: USGS Calabasas; **Contact:** Santa Monica Mountains Conservancy; **Notes:** Dogs allowed on leash; **GPS:** N 34.168493, W 118.703332

This loop deep in the quiet beauty of Las Virgenes Canyon will take you through old ranch property in rolling hills dotted with dozens of mature native oaks, along rugged former sheep trails through

In the spring, ceanothus bushes grace the canyon with showy floral accents.

fragrant sage groves and poppy fields, and back along a ridge with views that will transport you to a time before the invention of the strip mall. Quite simply, it's one of the best hikes in the San Fernando Valley.

GETTING THERE

Just west of Calabasas on US Highway 101, take the exit for Las Virgenes Road and head north. Drive until the road dead-ends in 1.4 miles. There is free street parking on both sides of the road, but note that one side has street cleaning from 8:00 AM to 11:00 AM on Mondays.

ON THE TRAIL

Hike north on Upper Las Virgenes Canyon Trail, passing the information kiosk. The

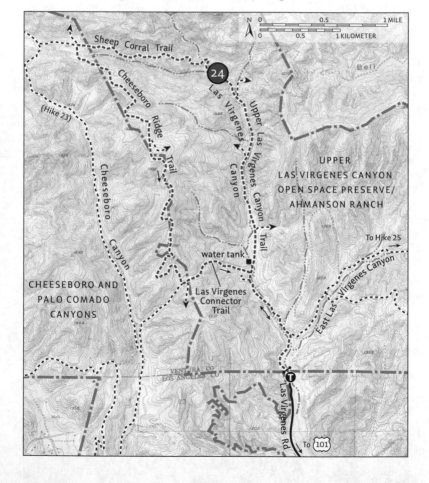

trail skirts by a large patch of California sagebrush and some huge valley oaks. Just before 0.4 mile, hop across a seasonal creek bed (and take a whiff of the nearby sulfur spring) and take a left at the unsigned junction to stay on the Upper Las Virgenes Canyon Trail. At 0.9 mile, ignore the dirt road leading toward a fenced-off area and stay to the right. At 1 mile, stay to the right again at the unsigned junction with the Las Virgenes Connector Trail (sensing a theme about signage here?) and continue heading north, passing an old water tank from the land's former ranch days.

There is more rusting ranch equipment along the trail before the junction at 1.3 miles. Stay straight as the old ranch road dissolves into wheel ruts through the grassland on the canyon floor and insanely fragrant purple sage appears on the hillsides. Stay to the right at the faint junction at 2 miles. By 2.4 miles, you may be bored with the pleasant but semi-monotonous scenery. Look for the well-worn but unsigned Sheep Corral Trail leaving the fire road's west side and soak in the new views as it passes through a meadow, a lovely oak grove, several huge ceanothus bushes, and a sizable colony of person-sized black sage. Begin a sharp climb through rocky terrain filled with blooming wildflowers in the spring, and at 4.1 miles, take a left at the signed (!) junction with the Cheeseboro Ridge Trail.

From here, the trail returns to the fire road, and you're likely to share the route with mountain bikers as it climbs the ridge between Las Virgenes and Cheeseboro canyons. Crest the high point of this trail at 5.1 miles and stay straight at the junction at 5.3 miles as the terrain returns to the "rolling hill" variety. Ignore the various use-trails and old ranch roads to stay on the Ridge Trail.

At 7.1 miles, take a left on the Las Virgenes Connector Trail. Pass through a partial chain link fence, ignore the narrow use-trail at 7.4 miles, and keep right at the junction at 7.7 miles to return to the trailhead.

EXTENDING YOUR TRIP
For an extra-long day in the canyons, this trip can be connected to the Lasky Mesa Loop (Hike 25) at the Canyon Trail or to Cheeseboro Canyon (Hike 23) at the Cheeseboro Ridge and Las Virgenes Connector trails.

25 Lasky Mesa Loop

RATING/ DIFFICULTY	LOOP	ELEV GAIN/ HIGH POINT	SEASON
****/2	5.1 miles	418 feet/ 1408 feet	Year-round

Map: USGS Calabasas; **Contact:** Santa Monica Mountains Conservancy and Mountains Recreation and Conservation Authority, Ranger Services; **Notes:** Park closed sunset–sunrise. Dogs allowed on leash only. Parking fee ($3) at Victory trailhead; **GPS:** N 34.180907, W 118.686691

A beautiful open space preserve in the western San Fernando Valley filled with rolling grasslands and mature live oaks and sycamores, Lasky Mesa offers a relatively easy way to experience the valley's not-too-distant past— and it's drop-dead gorgeous after a few good winter rains.

GETTING THERE
From US Highway 101 in Hidden Hills, take the Valley Circle Boulevard exit and head north for 2.1 miles. Take a left onto Victory Boulevard and park at the Victory trailhead

Lasky Mesa in spring

at the end of the street (note the fee above). There is also limited street parking available outside the trailhead.

ON THE TRAIL

Hike west past the information kiosk and follow the East Las Virgenes Canyon Trail as it turns to the southwest. Straight ahead, verdant valley views (depending on winter rain, of course) unfurl before your eyes with rolling hills dotted by majestic, tangled live oaks. Just past 0.2 mile, take a sharp left onto the Joe Behar Trail, which loops around a low hill on the park's eastern border before continuing to the southwest. Ignore all the use-trails and old ranch roads and at 1.2 miles, stay left at the junction to hike the Mary Weisbrock Loop Trail clockwise around Lasky Mesa—a large, grassy flat named for one of the first movie producers in Hollywood, who favored the area for

epic scenes in films like *Gone With the Wind* and *They Died With Their Boots On*. This large grassland is home to the diminutive, endangered, endemic San Fernando Valley spineflower. Its discovery here was a major motivation for protecting the land from a planned housing development.

Just before the 1.5-mile mark, pass the Ahmanson Ranch on the left (closed to the public but available for weddings) and continue west on the Weisbrock Trail. In another quarter mile, the Weisbrock Trail loops north. You can take this route just over 0.6 mile back to the Joe Behar Trail and return to the trailhead—but the canyon has so much more to show you! Instead, head straight onto the old ranch roads. At 2.1 miles, take the second road from the left, which curves around a hill and begins a dramatic descent to the canyon floor.

Around 2.8 miles, cross the seasonal

creek bed on a use-trail near some towering live oaks and join the East Las Virgenes Canyon Trail shortly thereafter. This wide, well-traveled path will take you back to the trailhead as long as you can navigate the maze of trails: Stay to the right at 3.1 miles and again at 3.2, then left at 3.6 miles, and just ignore the narrow use-trails until you return to the Victory trailhead.

EXTENDING YOUR TRIP

You can extend your hike into neighboring Las Virgenes Canyon by continuing west instead of crossing the creek bed at 2.8 miles. You'll reach the Las Virgenes Canyon Trail in about 0.4 mile and can tackle the lengthy trek in that canyon (Hike 24). Or you can visit the closer Cave of Munits to your north (Hike 26), forming a large figure-eight loop.

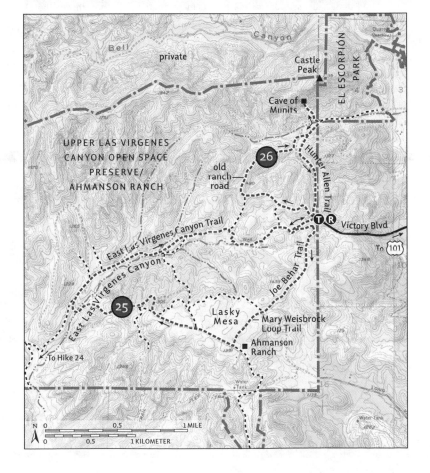

26 Cave of Munits

RATING/ DIFFICULTY	LOOP	ELEV GAIN/ HIGH POINT	SEASON
***/2	2.6 miles	451 feet/ 1480 feet	Year-round

Map: USGS Calabasas; **Contact:** Santa Monica Mountains Conservancy; **Notes:** Park closed sunset–sunrise. Dogs on leash only. Parking fee ($3) at Victory trailhead; **GPS:** N 34.184932, W 118.668168

This is a relatively easy hike to an impressive, cathedral-like cave that was used by the Chumash tribe for spiritual rites and, according to oral history, was the former home of a shaman killed after murdering the son of a powerful chief. The cave is reachable via a moderate scramble, while those feeling extra adventurous can climb all the way out one of its chimney exits.

GETTING THERE

From US Highway 101 in Hidden Hills, take the Valley Circle Boulevard exit and head north for 2.1 miles. Take a left onto Victory Boulevard and park at the Victory trailhead at the end of the street (note the fee above). There is also limited street parking available outside the trailhead.

ON THE TRAIL

Pass the information kiosk and look for a use-trail that makes a beeline up the nearest hill to the west as the East Las Virgenes Canyon Trail heads to the southwest. This section of trail finishes the steepest hiking incline of

Hikers enter the surprisingly cavernous Cave of Munits.

the trip right away, cresting this hill before beginning a slight decline on the other side. At 0.3 mile, stay right at the junction with other use-trails to continue heading west.

Hike past small colonies of purple sage and take a right onto an old ranch road worn down to near-single-track size at 0.6 mile. Here, the trail descends a picturesque ridgeline through several groves of California buckwheat, whose tough foliage and showy flowers provide a nice burst of color in the dry months. As you descend, the ridge of Castle Peak (a corruption of the Chumash *Kas'elew*) looms ahead. Look beneath the peak closest to you and you'll see the entrance to the cave.

At 1.4 miles, make a short scramble and take a left onto the Hunter Allen Trail. The road splits around a mature canyon live oak at 1.5 miles. Veer left here, and at another, more gnarled live oak nearby, climb up the sandy use-trail to the mouth of the cave at almost 1.7 miles. Get your hands dirty with a quick scramble inside the surprisingly expansive cave to see if you can sense any leftover shamanistic vibes. When you're done, slowly scramble out of the cave and return to the Hunter Allen Trail, which will take you back to the Victory trailhead.

EXTENDING YOUR TRIP

You can easily add the Lasky Mesa Loop (Hike 25) either before or after this trail for a fuller day in the Upper Las Virgenes Canyon region. Experienced climbers or scramblers can also climb up through the chimneys in the Cave of Munits to get to the ridge of Castle Peak, where they can bushwhack a rough use-trail to the peak itself and descend a trail into El Escorpión Park (at their own risk, of course).

27 Santa Susana Pass

RATING/ DIFFICULTY	LOOP	ELEV GAIN/ HIGH POINT	SEASON
***/3	5.3 miles	654 feet/ 1627 feet	Nov–Apr

Maps: USGS Oat Mountain, Canoga Park, Calabasas, Simi Valley East; **Contact:** Santa Susana Pass State Historic Park; **Notes:** Park open 8:00 AM–sunset. Archeological resources exist within the park—do not remove, excavate, or deface them; **GPS:** N 34.249548, W 118.619647

Santa Susana Pass State Historic Park contains a beautiful, boulder-strewn landscape of recently preserved land that offers hiking options of varying difficulties, a challenging climb, and a lot of human history—from ancient Chumash, Tongva, and Tataviam sites and trading routes to the Old Santa Susana Stage Road, an active railroad tunnel, and even a slice of L.A.'s dark past with a bit of helter-skelter.

GETTING THERE

From CA-118, head south on Topanga Canyon Boulevard (CA-27) for 1 mile and turn right onto Andora Avenue. (Note: This right hand turn is not allowed 6:00 AM–9:00 AM on weekdays. During this time frame, keep south on Topanga Canyon Boulevard and turn right on Devonshire Street.) Continue on Andora Avenue as it becomes Valley Circle Boulevard. In 0.6 mile, turn right on Lassen Street, then take a quick left on Andora Avenue and look for the southeast entrance of Santa Susana Pass State Historic Park on your right. Park on the street.

It's hard to believe it, but stagecoaches used to drive on these boulders.

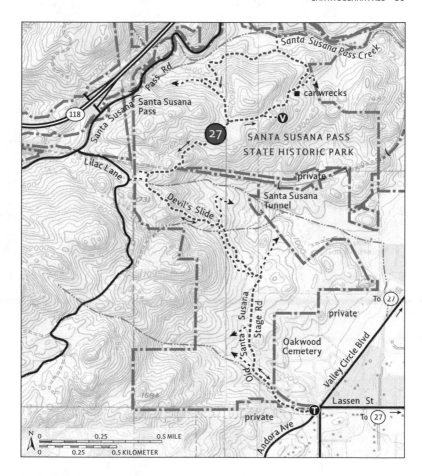

ON THE TRAIL

Head northwest on a wide fire road that follows the route of the Old Santa Susana Stage Road—part of the primary stagecoach traffic route between Los Angeles and San Francisco until a rail connection was built in 1876. The trail here squeezes through some private property lined with live oaks before stretching out into a wide, classic western landscape: the boulder-pile Simi Hills hem in the valley to the northwest while gently sloping into the San Fernando Valley below. Trails here are named on the official park brochure and map, but the trails on the ground don't always line up (and aren't marked at all). Stay to the right at 1.3 miles to finish up the incline and turn right at the connector trail to Lilac Lane at 1.4 miles and again at the T junction just to the north. At 0.8 mile, take a sharp left and ascend a rough, eroded footpath through the brush to another left at 1.1 miles.

Here, the hard sandstone trail gets noticeably steeper—and now you are on the section of the stagecoach road known affectionately to past travelers as the Devil's Slide. Coach riders here were often asked to walk alongside their vehicles carrying large rocks to throw in front of the wheels in case the driver lost control.

Pass a commemorative mosaic sign and keep your eyes open for worn wagon wheel ruts in the sandstone and for the diminutive (and fragrant to the touch) Santa Susana tarweed, an endangered yellow-flowering shrub endemic to the area. Stay to the right at 1.3 miles to finish up the incline and turn right at 1.4 miles and again at the T junction just to the north. Follow the trail northeast as it makes a quick, steep descent and climbs back up to a junction at 1.9 miles. There are many use-trails here, so start this northern loop section counter-clockwise and stay on the widest path. At 2.1 miles, stay to the left for a steep descent.

An optional use-trail heads east here, where you can scramble up a tall rock formation for excellent views (just watch out for the poison oak). Climb down a steep trail, passing some car wrecks beneath oak trees, and stay to the left at 2.4 miles to continue the loop. You're now in the outskirts of the former Spahn Ranch—the site of another Hollywood moviemaking ranch that is much more well-known as the former headquarters of the Manson Family. Nothing of that old ranch remains, so steer clear of charismatic maniacs and follow the trail as it loops back toward the west. Stay to the left at 2.7 miles and again at 3.1 miles. Close the loop at 3.4 miles and return to the trailhead the way you came in.

Opposite: City life is often still in sight from trails in the Hollywood Hills.

eastern santa monica mountains/hollywood hills

Even people who regularly enjoy spending time in the great outdoors of Los Angeles often don't realize the rugged Santa Monica Mountains extend eastward among the multimillion-dollar homes of fancy Brentwood and Beverly Hills (and even farther into Griffith Park).

The trails here are frequently visited by locals (sometimes even the ones you've seen on screen) and offer some of the best accessible hiking to those in Santa Monica or in L.A.'s Westside neighborhoods. This is where L.A.'s unique city-wilderness interface really comes to light as pampered Pomeranians walk the same trails as wild coyotes, and hikers' beat-up Hondas park on trailheads near gated driveways stocked with Teslas.

The trails in this region are often on the easy side of moderate but still offer some beautiful views and tree cover, making this a perfect place for people who are just learning how to lace a hiking boot properly to get some mileage in before tackling some of the bigger peaks.

28 Parker Mesa via the Los Liones Trail

RATING/ DIFFICULTY	ROUNDTRIP	ELEV GAIN/ HIGH POINT	SEASON
***/3	7.3 miles	1286 feet/ 1525 feet	Year-round

Map: USGS Topanga; **Contact:** Topanga State Park; **Notes:** No dogs allowed; **GPS:** N 34.047050, W 118.560048

Popular with fitness enthusiasts and hikers of all stripes, this route begins in a surprisingly lush riparian canyon (in the cooler months at least) and climbs to the small, flat summit of Parker Mesa for sweeping views of Santa Monica Bay and the cities below. It's definitely one of the best trails on the west side.

Hikers enjoy commanding views of Santa Monica Bay from atop Parker Mesa.

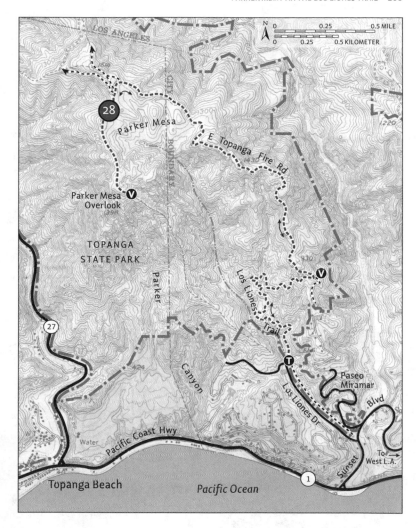

GETTING THERE

From the Pacific Coast Highway (CA-1), 2.4 miles east of CA-27, turn inland onto Sunset Boulevard and left onto Los Liones Drive after 0.3 mile. The trailhead is clearly marked about 0.6 mile down Los Liones Drive. Park on the street. Metro bus 2/302 has a stop at Sunset/Paseo Miramar, where a trail runs parallel to Los Liones Drive for about 0.7 mile.

ON THE TRAIL

The Los Liones Trail starts out looking like any old coastal sage scrub hike, but after a few short hills this single-track really begins to take on a unique character. In the winter and spring, the trail is incredibly—almost impossibly—lush. Ivy and vines cover the narrow canyons like kudzu, and wildflower blooms are intoxicating. In the summer, however, as in most places in this range, the green turns to gold and brown, and the lower reaches may be somewhat less picturesque.

At 1.3 miles, the trail opens up at a view-point near a junction with the East Topanga Fire Road. Make a sharp left onto the fire road to begin a relentless ascent. The bulk of the route is on this wide, shadeless path. Under the summer sun, it can feel especially tough—so be sure to get an early start if it's going to be hot out.

Continue on the fire road and at 3.2 miles stay to the left to continue south to the Parker Mesa Overlook. Your reward for all that uphill work awaits at the vista point at 3.7 miles: benches provide welcome rest for your legs as the views open up before you. Enjoy the view and return the way you came.

29 Temescal Canyon

RATING/ DIFFICULTY	LOOP	ELEV GAIN/ HIGH POINT	SEASON
***/3	4.6 miles	1131 feet/ 1404 feet	Year-round

Map: USGS Topanga; **Contact:** Topanga State Park; **Notes:** Dogs allowed on leash in Temescal Gateway Park only. Parking fee inside state park; **GPS:** N 34.049875, W 118.530551

The oddly shaped Skull Rock makes an impression.

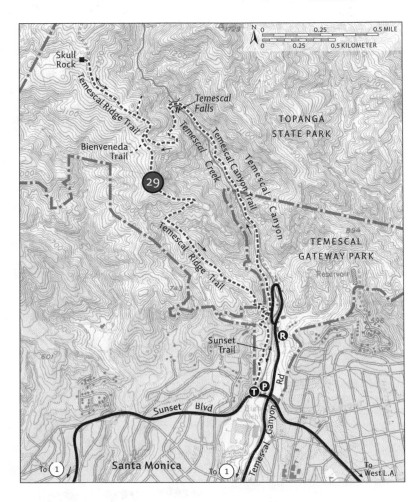

Featuring a challenging and well-traveled trail with a generous amount of shade, great views from the oddly shaped Skull Rock, and a small but calming creek cascade in the upper canyon, this rates as one of the L.A. area's best short day hikes.

GETTING THERE

From the Pacific Coast Highway (CA-1), 3.2 miles north of Interstate 10, turn onto Temescal Canyon Road and follow it 1 mile to the entrance of Temescal Gateway Park at the intersection with Sunset Boulevard. You may park inside the park gates for a fee or you can park for free on the street on either Sunset Boulevard or Temescal Canyon Road. If you do choose to park inside the gate, beware of the legally questionable stop-sign camera inside the park—it's notoriously trigger-happy. Metro bus 2/302 and Santa Monica Big Blue bus 9 both stop outside the park entrance.

ON THE TRAIL
Head toward the southwestern corner of the parking area and look for a green gate near a metal debris dam. The hike starts on the unsigned Sunset Trail, which drops down next to the dam and into a shady riparian canyon near Temescal Creek. There are many unsigned use-trails leading to Temescal Gateway Park from here, so keep to the left until you reach a junction at 0.4 mile. To the left, the Temescal Ridge Trail makes a gradual ascent but spends more time in the sun, while the Temescal Canyon Trail to the right has a steeper climb but more shade. For this route, stay to the right.

The clear, well-maintained trail passes another debris dam and some buildings from the area's days as a conference center for various churches from 1922 to 1994. At the 0.7-mile mark, the trail enters Topanga State Park (no dogs allowed) and it gets significantly more rugged. At 1.5 miles, the trail crosses the creek on a bridge near the generously named Temescal Falls, at most times just a trickling cascade. Continue up the steep but shaded switchbacks and keep to the far right at 1.9 miles to join the Temescal Ridge Trail.

Views really open up here and they only get better. Ignore the firebreak trail at 2 miles, and at 2.4 miles look for a short use-trail to the very scramble-able Skull Rock.

(Hint: It's the rock that looks like a giant, elongated skull.) Views of the Santa Monicas and the bay below are pretty epic from here. Before you get jealous of this rocky disembodied head's perpetual view, return the way you came. At 2.9 miles, veer right to stay on the Temescal Ridge Trail, passing the Bienveneda Trail. Continue on this trail until it reenters the Gateway Park at 4.2 miles and return to the trailhead.

30 Eagle Rock and Temescal Peak

RATING/ DIFFICULTY	LOOP	ELEV GAIN/ HIGH POINT	SEASON
**/2	7.4 miles	856 feet/ 2126 feet	Year-round

Map: USGS Topanga; **Contact:** Topanga State Park; **Notes:** Parking open 8:00 AM–sunset. Trippet Ranch nature center open Sundays 10 AM–3 PM January through July. No dogs allowed. Parking fee; **GPS:** N 34.093015, W 118.588550

This moderate hike in the largest state park inside L.A. city limits takes you to the prominent viewpoint of Eagle Rock and the less-traveled Temescal Peak just off the Backbone Trail. Hike through chaparral and native oak communities—and maybe find some marine fossils along the way.

GETTING THERE
Take the Pacific Coast Highway (CA-1) north from Santa Monica to Topanga Canyon Boulevard (CA-27). Head north on Topanga Canyon Boulevard for 4.7 miles. Just past the village of Topanga, bear right onto Entrada Road and follow the signs for Topanga State Park for 1.1 miles. Parking inside the park

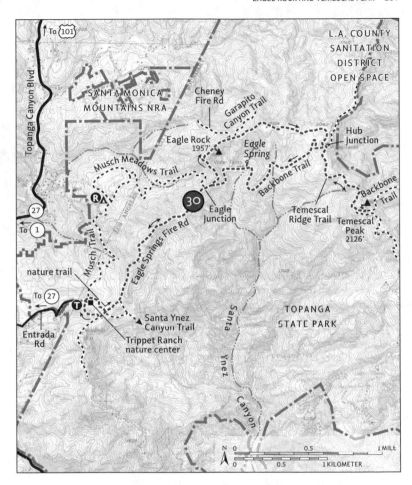

itself requires a fee, but there is also limited free parking on the roads outside.

ON THE TRAIL

From the southeast corner of the parking lot, follow the dirt Entrada Road to the east. Turn left onto a short nature trail that winds through some gorgeous live oaks and sycamores. Topanga is a popular shooting location for commercials and music videos, and it's very likely you've seen these trees standing in for forests all over the world. At 0.2 mile, take a left onto the Eagle Springs Fire Road. There is no shade on this route as it makes a steady climb to the northeast, but the lack of trees allows plenty of good

Eagle Rock rises out of the chaparral in Topanga State Park.

views of Santa Ynez Canyon and the rest of the Santa Monicas.

At 1.4 miles stay straight at Eagle Junction to continue gaining elevation on the fire road. At 1.8 miles, take a short spur trail to the top of prominent Eagle Rock, a pock-marked sandstone formation covered in tiny handholds and miniature arches. Continue east on the fire road, staying right at the Cheney Fire Road at 2.1 miles and again at the Garapito Canyon Trail shortly afterward. At the 3-mile mark you'll arrive at the aptly named Hub Junction. Four major fire roads meet here, and you'll often find hikers and cyclists resting on a small, shaded bench. Head south on the Temescal Ridge Trail (also the Backbone Trail here) and at 3.6 miles, follow the Backbone on a narrow single-track to the left. Look for a rugged use-trail on the left hand side and follow this to Temescal Peak.

From Temescal Peak, you'll have exemplary views of the Santa Monicas to the west—as well as a great angle on Eagle Rock emerging from the waves of brush- and chaparral-covered ridges below it. Backtrack to Hub Junction and this time head west on the lower Backbone Trail at 4.6 miles. Stay left at 5.9 miles and continue on the Eagle Springs Fire Road to the trailhead.

EXTENDING YOUR TRIP

For a change in scenery, at 5.9 miles continue on the Backbone Trail by heading west on the Musch Meadows Trail, and then head back to Trippet Ranch on the Musch Trail. This route will take you through a series of grassy meadows that are especially lovely in the late winter and spring. There is a first-come, first-served backcountry campground along this route—and you're very likely to see browsing deer in the mornings and evenings.

31 Murphy Ranch

RATING/ DIFFICULTY	LOOP	ELEV GAIN/ HIGH POINT	SEASON
***/2	3.8 miles	326 feet/ 825 feet	Year-round

Map: USGS Topanga; **Contact:** City of Los Angeles Department of Recreation and Parks and Topanga State Park; **Notes:** This park seems to be under constant threat of closure and demolition. Areas may be fenced off or otherwise inaccessible, often without notice; **GPS:** N 34.061015, W 118.503599

Just above posh Brentwood and isolated within Topanga State Park you'll find the ruins of an abandoned Nazi-sympathizer compound. The self-sufficient ranch was to be Hitler's sunny California getaway after World War II ended with a German victory.

GETTING THERE

From Interstate 405 at Sunset Boulevard, head west on Sunset for 3.1 miles and take a right onto Capri Drive. Follow this road through a roundabout and a few oddly angled intersections until it ends at Casale Road. The trail is to the left, but there's no parking on that part of the street. Turn right onto Casale Road and park where you can, being mindful of the residents.

ON THE TRAIL

Head west on Casale Road past the intersection with Capri Drive. The road turns into the dirt Sullivan Fire Road as it turns north and passes through a gate to enter Topanga State Park at 0.4 mile. To your west, the early stretches of the Backbone Trail rise into view from nearby Topanga and Will Rogers state parks. As you venture farther along the dirt road, you'll notice that a chained, barbed wire fence separates

HITLER'S HIDEAWAY?

According to a mix of hazy oral history, building records, and local memories, the secluded 55-acre Rustic Canyon Ranch was purchased by a widow named Jessie M. Murphy in 1933. But there is no further record of a Murphy—instead, locals remember a man known only as "Herr Schmidt," who built a complicated irrigation system, functioning powerhouse, machine shop, and bomb shelter, and planted more than three thousand fruit and nut trees in the canyon. Schmidt claimed to have metaphysical powers (not unusual for Southern California) and supposedly ran a chapter of the pro-Hitler American fascist organization the Silver Legion of America here. The Silver Shirts patrolled the ranch's barbed wire borders, and Schmidt had plans underway to add a four-story mansion and libraries designed by the prominent African-American architect Paul Revere Williams, who also designed the house in Solstice Canyon (Hike 7). After Pearl Harbor, the property was seized and later became the Hartford Artists' Colony until 1973, when the City of Los Angeles took it over. Today, this beautiful canyon with a mind-bogglingly rich history isn't getting the preservation treatment like Paramount Ranch (Hike 14) or Solstice Canyon. The city only seems interested in occasionally threatening to tear everything down, while vandals and graffiti taggers slowly dissolve what history remains. Hopefully this weird little slice of California can get an owner who cares about it before everything is vandalized into oblivion.

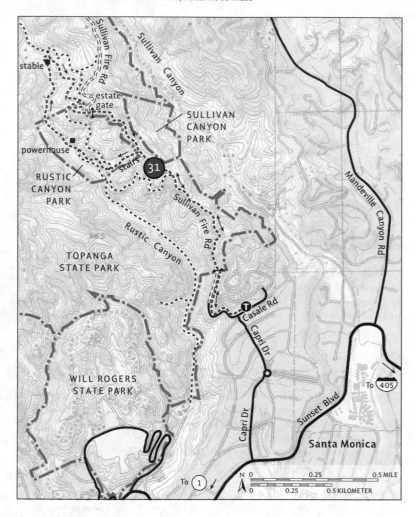

the road from Rustic Canyon. Just past the mile mark, look for a break in the fence and a long, cement staircase heading down into the canyon. Follow these steep, narrow, and shallow steps 260 feet down to Murphy Ranch, a favorite haunt of oddball historians, photographers looking for moody, ruined backdrops, and, unfortunately, seemingly every tagger and vandal in Los Angeles County.

At the bottom, a sprawling system of old ranch roads, secret staircases, and use-trails

The long, narrow staircase to Murphy Ranch

can make this region fairly confusing, although it is possible to wander around the area on your own without getting too lost. Stay to the left at the end of the staircase and continue descending. You'll pass the ranch's diesel powerhouse at 1.3 miles and the remnants of the machine shop at 1.4 miles. Past the shop, the ranch road dissolves into a single-track trail that dips into the bed of Rustic Canyon Creek at 1.5 miles. The old road reappears at 1.6 miles. Follow it north past an old stable at 1.8 miles as it turns around and heads back to the southeast. Stay to the left at the fork at 2.2 miles to ascend and exit back onto Sullivan Fire Road past the compound's surprisingly ornate gate at 2.3 miles. Follow the road back to the trailhead.

32 Franklin Canyon Reservoir

RATING/ DIFFICULTY	LOOP	ELEV GAIN/ HIGH POINT	SEASON
***/2	1.4 miles	95 feet/ 877 feet	Year-round

Map: USGS Beverly Hills; **Contact:** Mountains Recreation and Conservation Authority, Franklin Canyon Park; **Notes:** Park open sunrise–sunset. Dogs allowed on leash. Be aware of very sensitive motion-detecting cameras at stop signs within the park; **GPS:** N 34.11578, W 118.413826

 *Hike around a historic reservoir that's served as the backdrop in countless movies and*

television shows, from The Andy Griffith Show to Salute Your Shorts and Twin Peaks. This beautiful, shaded stroll above the heart of Beverly Hills sits near the geographic center of the city of Los Angeles—which just so happens to be part of the world's largest urban national park.

GETTING THERE

From CA-2 in Beverly Hills, head north on North Beverly Drive until you reach Coldwater Canyon Park at about 1.3 miles. Take a left at the intersection to continue on North Beverly Drive. In 0.9 mile, veer right onto Franklin Canyon Drive. In 1.1 miles, take a

A shaded section along the Ranch Trail

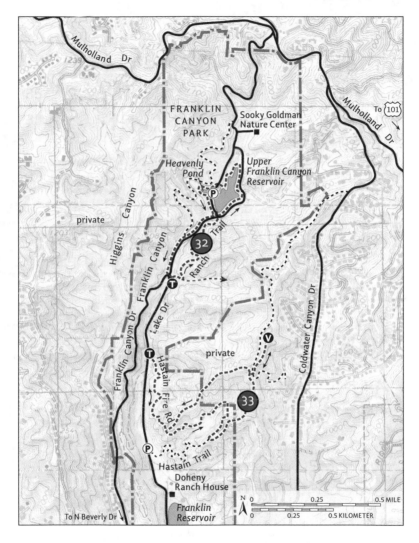

slight right onto Lake Drive and park. From the north, you can enter the park at a somewhat complicated intersection at Mulholland Drive and Coldwater Canyon Avenue. Head

south on Franklin Canyon Drive for 1.3 miles and park just south of Lake Drive. Parking is very limited near this trailhead, but starting here will give you a more rugged hiking experience and a bit more solitude than the generally busier loop around the reservoir itself.

ON THE TRAIL

Cross Lake Drive on a short wooden footbridge and begin your hike heading east. After a little over 200 feet, make a sharp left onto the Ranch Trail heading north. This trail levels out a bit as it meanders toward Upper Franklin Canyon Reservoir. You'll be hiking through some of the densest, most beautiful oak woodland in the region. The shade is especially lovely on warmer days and although you're close to some of the most ostentatious mansions in the country, this trail feels miles away from the hustle and bustle of city life. Ignore the side trail at 0.3 mile and cross Franklin Canyon Drive at 0.4 mile. Here, a lovely route hugs the perimeter of Upper Franklin Canyon Reservoir. Head counterclockwise, passing through tall reeds and grasses that feel more like a marsh than a Southern California canyon.

At 0.8 mile, cross Franklin Canyon Drive for a short, stroller-friendly side loop around Heavenly Pond. Both water features are favorites with waterfowl and migratory birds, and this hike is a great place to spot a wide variety of feathered friends. Follow the trail parallel to Franklin Canyon Drive south and at the 1-mile mark you can either rejoin the Ranch Trail to retrace your steps or walk along Franklin Canyon Drive back to your car. If you take the road, the scenery is especially beautiful in late fall and early winter when leaves are turning colors.

EXTENDING YOUR TRIP

The Sooky Goldman Nature Center has a variety of exhibits on display and often hosts free, informative programs. For a longer trail day, you can hike or take a short drive south to the Hastain Loop (Hike 33).

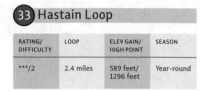

33 Hastain Loop

RATING/ DIFFICULTY	LOOP	ELEV GAIN/ HIGH POINT	SEASON
***/2	2.4 miles	589 feet/ 1296 feet	Year-round

Map: USGS Beverly Hills; **Contact:** Mountains Recreation and Conservation Authority, Franklin Canyon Park; **Notes:** Park open sunrise–sunset. Dogs allowed on leash. Be aware of very sensitive motion-detecting cameras at stop signs within the park; **GPS:** N 34.111373, W 118.415191

A short, rugged loop in the southern half of Franklin Canyon, the Hastain Loop offers a decent workout, lovely canyon scenery, as well as beautiful views of Beverly Hills and Century City.

GETTING THERE

From CA-2 in Beverly Hills, head north on North Beverly Drive until you reach Coldwater Canyon Park at about 1.3 miles. Take a left at the intersection to continue on North Beverly Drive. In 0.9 mile, veer right onto Franklin Canyon Drive. Take a slight right onto Lake Drive. A small parking area will be on your left in 0.4 mile. If this lot is full, there is additional parking 0.3 mile south. From here, you can take an alternate branch of the Hastain Trail to this loop.

ON THE TRAIL

Hike southeast on the Hastain Fire Road. This gently sloping path parallels Lake Drive and offers you only brief moments of shade as it makes its way through some dense oak

Upper Franklin Canyon Reservoir provides a welcome rest stop for migratory birds.

scrub. Note a rugged use-trail at 0.4 mile—this will be your return path—but continue on the fire road.

The trail begins a steady but manageable ascent here, slowly revealing more of the palatial Beverly Hills estates that surround the parkland. At 0.7 mile, pass through an old chain link fence—a remnant of a dispute with a nearby private landholder who was attempting to limit public access before an easement was established. At 0.9 mile, stay left at the junction with the main branch of the Hastain Trail. Heading downhill here will take you to a larger trailhead and a beautiful house formerly used as a private retreat by oil tycoon Edward L. Doheny. Instead, continue ascending, passing open gates at 1 mile and 1.2 miles.

At 1.3 miles, the trail reaches a broad four-way intersection. The easternmost trail will take you out of the park and east toward Coldwater Canyon Drive. Head straight up the center spur for the trail's high point and some beautiful views of the surrounding area, then backtrack and head onto the westernmost spur. This route runs through private land and can eventually get you to the northern parts of the park, but it's a long and not especially beautiful hike. Instead, look for a single-track trail heading west along a ridge at about 1.6 miles and follow this rough and steep (but really fun) route back to the Hastain Fire Road at 2 miles, then follow the fire road back to the trailhead. This section does have some slippery sections toward the end, but it should be manageable for most hikers. If you're looking for an easier route back, just return the way you came.

EXTENDING YOUR TRIP

You can also return via the main Hastain Trail branch to the Doheny Ranch House, then hike north along Lake Drive to the trailhead. If you are in the mood for more time in Franklin Canyon, consider adding the Franklin Canyon Reservoir loop (Hike 32) to your itinerary.

34 San Vicente Mountain via Mandeville Canyon

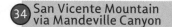

RATING/ DIFFICULTY	LOOP	ELEV GAIN/ HIGH POINT	SEASON
****/3	5.1 miles	705 feet/ 1942 feet	Year-round

Maps: USGS Canoga Park, Van Nuys, Beverly Hills, Topanga; **Contact:** Santa Monica Mountains Conservancy; **Notes:** Park open sunrise–sunset. Dogs allowed on leash; **GPS:** N 34.121236, W 118.506662

This fire road trek rises from a picturesque Westside canyon to a well-preserved Cold War Nike missile site perched on the crest of the Santa Monica Mountains. Few other trails provide such beautiful views while also giving you the chance to ponder the nuke-'em-all military "strategy" of mutually assured destruction.

GETTING THERE

Follow Sunset Boulevard west from Interstate 405 for 2.3 miles. Head north on Mandeville Canyon Road and at 4.8 miles, turn left at Garden Land Road and park on the street. Trailhead parking is very limited, but there is also a small off-road parking area near the Hollyhock Fire Road, 0.3 mile south. A larger lot is available at another alternate trailhead at the intersection of Mulholland Drive and Encino Hills Drive, about 2 miles from the Sepulveda exit of the 405. This provides easier access to the missile site but a much less interesting hiking experience.

The ruins of missile defense base LA96C

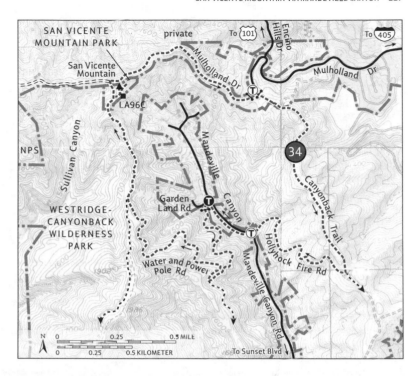

A NUCLEAR SUNSET

By the 1940s, Los Angeles was considered a bona fide military target, and the Department of Defense took steps to protect the burgeoning metropolis. Starting in 1958, it built a ring of sixteen Nike missile defense lookouts, control centers, and launch facilities to guard L.A. from Soviet bombers carrying nuclear weapons. Eventually, we figured out we could just shoot nuclear weapons at people we didn't like on huge rockets well out of the Nike missile's reach, and all the L.A. stations were shut down by 1974. While most have been destroyed, a few stations do remain—and three are reachable by hiking. Mandeville Canyon is the most intact, but you can also visit sites below Oat Mountain (Hike 41) and atop Mount Disappointment (Hike 76). Walk around the ruins and envision these historic places in action, their staffs on constant alert to protect the city from annihilation yet also bored enough to tend to cactus gardens. Just remember, no fighting in the war room!

ON THE TRAIL

From the trailhead on Garden Land Road, walk through the gate and onto Water and Power Pole Road. This path passes under the shade of some mature live oaks and sycamores as it makes a slow climb upward. Keep right at 0.5 mile to continue the climb up, the path winding generally westward. You'll spot the remains of missile base LA96C perched atop the ridge. At 1.4 miles, stay right at the junction and follow the sign toward San Vicente Mountain Park, and at 1.9 miles you'll be at the missile command center's western border. Step through the fence and into the grounds, where newly installed signs do an excellent job of conveying the station's purpose and the tense and lonely lives of those once assigned to work here.

This control center was built because of its clear lines of sight to the Pacific Ocean, coastlines, and downtown Los Angeles. To protect against Soviet bombers, soldiers prepared to spot and track the planes with radar and guide Nike missiles launched from the Sepulveda Basin to their targets before the city could be attacked. Today, you can enjoy the incredible vantage point without quite as much worry about thermonuclear warfare.

Explore the facility and then exit through its front gate and former checkpoint, following dirt Mulholland Drive to the Canyonback Trail trailhead at 3.2 miles. Follow the Canyonback Trail south as the long stretch of Mandeville Canyon draws your eye to the Pacific. At 4.1 miles, turn right onto the Hollyhock Fire Road. Take this back to Mandeville Canyon Road and turn right to walk on the side of the road back to the trailhead, enjoying the ample shade of oaks and sycamores along the way.

35 Wilacre Park

RATING/ DIFFICULTY	LOOP	ELEV GAIN/ HIGH POINT	SEASON
**/2	2.9 miles	453 feet/ 1149 feet	Year-round

Map: USGS Van Nuys; **Contact:** City of Los Angeles Department of Recreation and Parks, Wilacre Park; **Notes:** Parking area open sunrise–sunset. Dogs allowed on leash; **GPS:** N 34.133152, W 118.391672

This route is a peaceful, locally favorite loop in Studio City that offers a respite from some of the crowds of nearby trails, as well as the chance to visit a beautiful park and demonstration garden run by one of Southern California's most influential environmental groups.

GETTING THERE

From US Highway 101 in Studio City, take the exit for Laurel Canyon Boulevard and follow it south for 1.5 miles. Trailhead parking is at the corner of Laurel Canyon Boulevard and Fryman Road on the north side of the Hollywood Hills. Metro bus 218 also stops at the trailhead.

ON THE TRAIL

Head onto the Betty B. Dearing Trail. This roughly paved trail makes a steady but manageable ascent as it meanders to the west. Many unofficial use-trails split off from the main route, but ignore those. At 0.6 mile you'll spot the first of many memorial benches on this route, which are often in shady or picturesque locations. On clear days— especially in the winter and spring—you can get some very nice views across the valley north to the Santa Susanas.

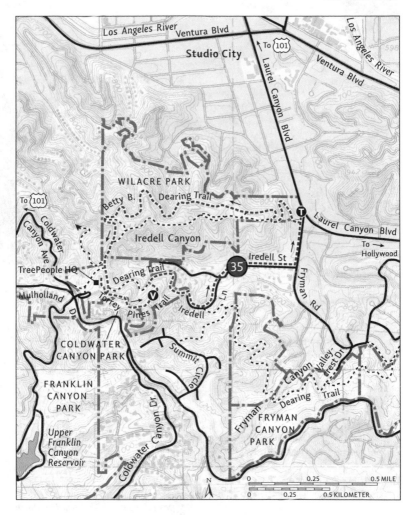

At 1.1 miles the trail bends to the south and at 1.3 miles the trail enters Coldwater Canyon Park. Just to the south of this, look for a well-manicured spur trail that rises to the right. Take a short climb up. Pass some interpretive exhibits about the various rock and soil types found in the Los Angeles area and you'll end up at the TreePeople's Coldwater Canyon headquarters. Spend some time exploring the campus and nursery, head back toward the rock exhibit, and stay to the right for a short trip on the Torrey Pines Trail.

Griffith Park and the San Gabriels from Wilacre Park

At 1.8 miles follow a use-trail on the left to a bench with great (and unusual) side-angle views of Griffith Park. A rough but passable use-trail continues to the northeast past the bench and meets the Dearing Trail at 1.9 miles. (An alternate, easier route would just be to backtrack to the Dearing Trail from the TreePeople headquarters.)

At 2.2 miles, the Dearing Trail meets the paved dead end of Iredell Lane. Follow Iredell east to Iredell Street and take a left onto Fryman Road to return to the trailhead.

EXTENDING YOUR TRIP
Where the Dearing Trail intersects with Iredell Lane, it is possible to continue east on the Dearing Trail. This connects with a series of often-unsigned trails along Mulholland Drive, and you can hike to trailheads at Summit Circle, Mulholland Drive, or Valleycrest Drive. Return to the trailhead is possible from Valleycrest.

36 Runyon Canyon

RATING/ DIFFICULTY	LOOP	ELEV GAIN/ HIGH POINT	SEASON
***/3	3 miles	731 feet/ 1244 feet	Year-round

Map: USGS Hollywood; **Contact:** Los Angeles Department of Recreation and Parks, Runyon Canyon Park; **Notes:** Park open dawn–dusk. Dogs allowed off leash in marked areas. Note restricted parking areas near the trailhead; **GPS:** N 34.103451, W 118.351875

If you've ever opened a glossy gossip rag in the checkout line and seen photos of "Celebrities! Hiking!," they were almost undoubtedly taken in Runyon Canyon. Runyon is short on the wilderness experience, but this surprisingly rugged route in the heart of Hollywood is a haven for those who can't make a longer trip to the more remote trailheads—and it's also one of L.A. County's few off-leash dog parks.

GETTING THERE

The start of this route is at the corner of Vista Street and Franklin Avenue, one block north of Hollywood Boulevard and three blocks west of La Brea Avenue. Metro bus 217 stops about a block away at Hollywood/ Gardner and the Metro Red Line Hollywood/

Highland stop is a 0.8-mile walk. There are alternate entrances on Fuller Avenue and Mulholland Drive, but parking is significantly more difficult.

ON THE TRAIL

Walk up the steep incline of Vista Street and make a sharp right on Runyon Canyon Road, entering the gates of Runyon Canyon Park at 0.2 mile. Head north on the paved road and make a sharp left at 0.3 mile to leave the

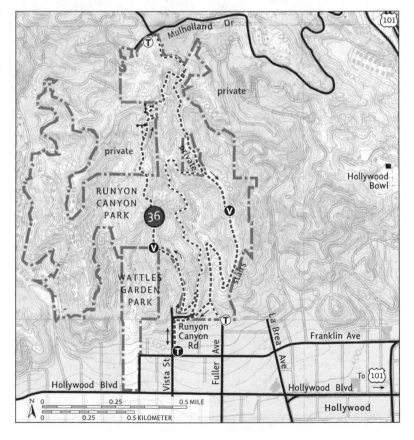

Despite the crowds, Runyon Canyon has some of the best views of Los Angeles.

pavement for the well-worn single-track trail. This trail doubles back above the entrance before turning north, climbing a no-nonsense ascent on a firebreak on the park's western edge. At 0.6 mile, the trail levels for a short distance before making an even steeper climb to a vista point at 0.8 mile. Continue north and make a quick, potentially dicey descent at 0.9 mile. Just past the mile mark, stay to the right on a slightly circuitous staircase built in 2013 after the owner of the long-abandoned mansion in the park cut off access to the more direct fire road route. The stairs rejoin the main trail around 1.2 miles, and at 1.3 miles stay to the right to begin your hike back south.

For the easier descent, stay right at 1.8 miles and follow the road to the trailhead. For better views and more fun, keep to the left to follow a ridge with spectacular views of the Hollywood sign and city below. There's a beautiful vista spot at 1.9 miles—a truly amazing place to watch the sun set over the West Coast—and just beyond it is a steep, slippery section of slides and staircases. The odd metal structure you'll pass at 2.1 miles is all that remains of the circa-1927 Outpost Estates sign, a blazing neon red beacon meant to literally outshine the rival neighboring Hollywoodland housing development's white, wooden sign. Ironically, its showy luminescence was its undoing during World War II, when lights were turned off to avoid giving Japanese bombers easy targets to hit.

Follow the fire road down, keeping right at 2.7 miles to return to the park's western entrance and the trailhead.

EXTENDING YOUR TRIP

At the 1.3-mile mark, it is possible to take a left at the junction to continue climbing up to an overlook above the empty mansion. This route also provides access to the park's Mulholland Drive trailhead.

Opposite: A hiker enjoys the quiet, rugged landscape of the Santa Susanas.

santa susana mountains

The Santa Susana Mountains sit on the northwestern boundary of Los Angeles proper, separating the city from Santa Clarita and the edge of the Antelope Valley. Natural resource extraction has historically played a large role in this region—California's first commercially viable oil well was drilled here, and oil and gas remain big players (and, as is the case with 2015–2016's Porter Ranch natural gas leak, sometimes big polluters).

Geology is the main draw in this range, with all that natural gas, oil, and tar pushed up through the tectonic action of the nearby San Andreas Fault. Trails here often wind their way through narrow canyons surrounded by oddly upturned rocks, making for dramatic adventures and epic photos, while red-tailed hawks and turkey vultures scan the landscape from the skies looking for prey beneath the native oaks and amidst the chaparral.

37 Mentryville

RATING/ DIFFICULTY	LOOP	ELEV GAIN/ HIGH POINT	SEASON
***/3	4.6 miles	922 feet/ 2511 feet	Year-round

Maps: USGS Newhall, Simi Valley East, Oat Mountain; **Contact:** Santa Clarita Woodlands Park; **Notes:** Dogs allowed on leash. Parking fee inside park boundary. Buildings may be closed to the public for restoration. Interpretive tours offered on the first and third Sundays of the month, noon–4:00 PM; **GPS:** N 34.379588, W 118.610621

Explore the remnants of a former boomtown, Mentryville, the site of California's first commercially viable oil-drilling site—and the world's longest-running oil well. Today, hikers enjoy partially restored buildings (and old Hollywood sets) and petroleum history along with a beautifully secluded mountain and canyon loop.

GETTING THERE
From Interstate 5 in Santa Clarita, take the Lyons Avenue/Pico Canyon Road exit and head west. Continue on Pico Canyon Road for 2.3 miles, then take a slight left onto Pico Canyon Service Road, which takes you into Santa Clarita Woodlands Park. Reach

The replica oil derrick at Johnson Park

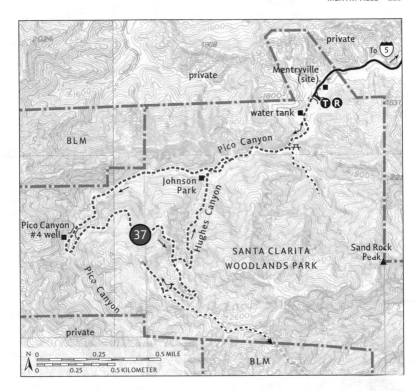

the Mentryville site in 0.5 mile, stay left at the fork for the parking area and pay the self-service fee. You can park outside the park itself, which will add an approximately half-mile hike along the road each way to your journey.

ON THE TRAIL

From the paid parking area, cross the bridge toward the remaining buildings of the boomtown of Mentryville. While some of the structures you see were created by Hollywood production companies, many originals remain—such as Alex Mentry's "Big House." Poke around, then head southwest out of the

town site on the paved road. At 0.3 mile, pass a picnic table and use-trail on the other side of the creek bed but stay on the road. At the 0.6-mile mark, the road splits in two—both grades meet each other at 0.7 mile.

Here you'll come upon Johnson Park, a recreation and picnic area for petroleum workers and their families used from the 1930s through the 1950s. The grounds are in good shape and can still be used for events today. Note the twenty-five-foot oil derrick in the back of the park. Assembled from actual parts, this was a replica built in the 1960s and was never operational here (although it's still a beautiful machine!).

Continue into Pico Canyon. Just before the bridge at 1.6 miles, look for some rusting machinery to your right. This is the site of the Pico Canyon #4 well—the first commercial oil well in the state and a registered National Historic Landmark. Families may turn around here, but for additional beauty and solitude continue on the now-dirt road as it climbs into the Santa Susanas. Continue until 2.7 miles and turn right on another abandoned roadway. Hike through overgrown chaparral to a gorgeous flat at 2.9 miles—a great place for a quiet picnic lunch.

Backtrack to 3.4 miles and take a right to hike a use-trail through Hughes Canyon for some mildly challenging but really fun topography. This trail is significantly steeper and more slippery than the road, but features stunning rock formations, majestic live oaks, and a faint hint of sulfur in the creek. This trail ends at Johnson Park at 3.9 miles.

Turn right and retrace your steps to the trailhead.

38 Towsley Canyon

RATING/ DIFFICULTY	LOOP	ELEV GAIN/ HIGH POINT	SEASON
****/3	5.4 miles	1097 feet/ 2454 feet	Year-round

Map: USGS Oat Mountain; **Contact:** Santa Clarita Woodlands Park and Santa Monica Mountains Conservancy; **Notes:** Park closed sunset–sunrise. Dogs allowed on leash. Parking fee; **GPS:** N 34.358152, W 118.556091

Featuring moderately challenging inclines, natural tar pits and asphalt, and a memorably tight canyon pass, this unique hiking experience is a fun and fascinating loop through an old oil field.

Industrial drilling equipment, not just hikers and wildlife, used to move through Towsley Canyon.

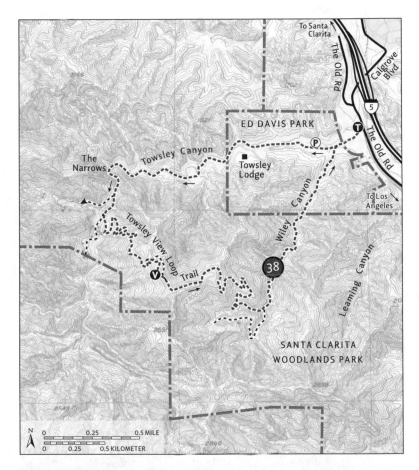

GETTING THERE

From Interstate 5 in Santa Clarita, exit at Calgrove Boulevard and turn west, following the signs for Ed Davis Park/Towsley Canyon as Calgrove becomes The Old Road. In about 500 feet, turn right into Santa Clarita Woodlands Park. There are three parking areas; the main lot and the overflow lot closest to the road are free. There is also a smaller parking lot farther into the park that requires a fee.

ON THE TRAIL

The trail begins on a gravel road that passes a few nondescript old buildings. At 0.2 mile, stay to the right to continue west into

Towsley Canyon, passing the paid parking lot along the way. At 0.6 mile, ignore the spur road that leads to the Towsley Lodge (available for private events) and look for the sign for the Towsley View Loop Trail. Here, the gravel road gives way to a wide dirt trail as the canyon almost instantly becomes more rugged.

At 1.6 miles, the trail makes a sharp turn southward between two large slabs of upturned rock. This area is known as The Narrows and it's a definite highlight of the route. Nearby rock walls beg to be scrambled, and the creek running through The Narrows is occasionally made frothy (and pungent) with naturally occurring tar and asphalt. You'll exit The Narrows by 1.7 miles. Ignore the old oil-drilling roads (and keep your eyes peeled for open tar pits and abandoned drilling equipment), then prepare for the major incline of the route. There's almost no shade here, so get started early during the hot months—but the views of the rugged Santa Susanas are tough to beat.

At 2.8 miles, stay right to climb up to a log bench with an excellent viewpoint of Santa Clarita. The trail levels out through some tall chaparral and the occasional live oak tree before starting its descent. Numerous unnamed use-trails depart from the main trail here, but most rejoin the trail shortly. At 4.1 miles, stay left to make a steep descent down Wiley Canyon's tar-filled creek, keeping right at 5.2 miles to return to the trailhead.

39 Rocky Peak

RATING/ DIFFICULTY	ROUNDTRIP	ELEV GAIN/ HIGH POINT	SEASON
***/3	5 miles	879 feet/ 2715 feet	Year-round

Map: USGS Simi Valley East; **Contact:** Mountains Recreation and Conservation

A cyclist takes a breather in Rocky Peak Park.

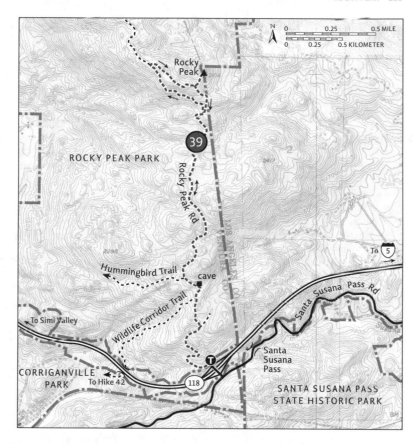

Authority; **Notes:** Park open sunrise–sunset. Dogs allowed on leash, **GPS:** N 34.268156, W 118.635920

🦴🐾 *A rugged hike to the third-highest point in the Santa Susana Mountains on a beautiful, well-traveled trail, this route has spectacular views of the San Fernando Valley, Simi Hills, and Santa Monica Mountains on clear, cool days as well as an unusual, boulder-ridden landscape that's fairly reminiscent of areas farther out in the Mojave Desert.*

GETTING THERE

From the interchange of CA-118 and CA-27, travel 1.8 miles west on CA-118. Take the Rocky Peak Road exit on the eastern edge of Simi Valley and look for parking on the north side of the freeway along Rocky Peak Road. Note that parking on the freeway overpass is prohibited and enthusiastically enforced.

ON THE TRAIL

Any trail that literally starts on a freeway off-ramp might have you skeptical about its wilderness qualities, but once you start hiking up the steep dirt road on the north side of the 118, all your fears will be allayed. As the road climbs up and away from the freeway traffic, you'll instead find yourself surrounded by a dry, boulder-strewn landscape that could make a decent stand-in for Joshua Tree (if you ignore the lack of Joshua trees, of course).

Much of the area here was former ranch land, at one time owned by Bob Hope, so there are a lot of old roads and use-trails. At 0.5 mile stay to the left at a junction of old roads to continue heading north on the main dirt road. Ignore the Wildlife Corridor Trail heading off to the left just past 0.6 mile. At 0.8 mile, the road makes a sharp turn to the west, passing a small cave complex and a junction with the Hummingbird Trail. Stay on the wider fire road heading north, sharing the route with mountain bikers and trail runners and, on clear days, enjoying the wide-open views from the San Gabriels to the Santa Monicas. After a noticeable incline at 1.7 miles, stay left at 1.9 miles, then make a sharp right at 2.3 miles to double-back a bit on another old ranch road.

Just before 2.7 miles, look for a use-trail on your left and scramble up to the prominent pile of boulders known as Rocky Peak. Soak in the views from here, then return to the road along the use-trail. To save a bit of backtracking, turn left and look for a steep but passable use-trail that continues south back to Rocky Peak Road. Return to the trailhead the way you came.

40 O'Melveny Park

RATING/ DIFFICULTY	LOOP	ELEV GAIN/ HIGH POINT	SEASON
****/4	4.5 miles	1440 feet/ 2771 feet	Year-round (best Nov– May)

Map: USGS Oat Mountain; **Contact:** O'Melveny Park; **Notes:** Park open sunrise to sunset. Dogs allowed on leash; **GPS:** N 34.307922, W 118.510965

This surprisingly rugged park on the northwestern city limits is the second-largest city park in Los Angeles. The lower reaches feature some lovely meadows and towering eucalyptus trees, and are a popular destination for locals. The trail network, like that of Griffith Park, is a bit on the unmaintained side: old ranch roads mix with wildlife trails and use-trails, nothing seems to be signed, and there's not a park map in sight. This outer loop utilizes some scrambly use-trails and paths, and will be a challenge for those not accustomed to a stair-climbing workout routine.

GETTING THERE

From Interstate 5 in Sylmar, take the exit for Roxford Street and head west at the off-ramp. The road curves to the north and becomes Sepulveda Boulevard. In 1.1 miles, take a slight left onto San Fernando Road and in 0.5 mile, a left onto Balboa Road. In another 0.1 mile, keep to the right to continue on Balboa Boulevard and in 0.6 mile turn right on Sesnon Boulevard. The entrance to O'Melveny Park and a parking lot will be on your right in 0.5 mile. Street parking is also available.

Expansive views and steep trails are plentiful at O'Melveny Park.

ON THE TRAIL

Cross the bridge at the southwest corner of the parking area and stay on the pavement, passing some tall sycamores and an unexpected citrus grove—remnants of the region's past as the Cascade Ranch (sorry, no fruit picking allowed). About 500 feet into the journey, you'll see a stone marker pointing in different directions for the Nature Trail and Equestrian Trail. If you're looking for a slightly easier journey, follow the Equestrian Trail north to a still-steep but better maintained fire road route. Whether due to a lack of maintenance or bad trail markings, the Nature Trail just sort of disintegrates at a formerly marked junction at 0.2 mile. Veering right here will take you down a steep use-trail back to the citrus grove, while staying straight sends you up an even rougher use-trail that makes a direct assault on one of the park's many steep hills. Get your sense of adventure ready and head straight.

The trail here is basically one steep climb over a hill followed by a steeper climb over an even larger hill. On the second hill, the trail may require a bit of light, nontechnical scrambling. With each climb, the views of the San Fernando Valley and San Gabriel Mountains get more and more spectacular; don't forget to pause to take the occasional photo on your way up. At 0.9 mile, look for a trail heading north through a flat area that connects with the broader fire road trail. Keep left here to continue west on the more "established" hiking route, which is no less

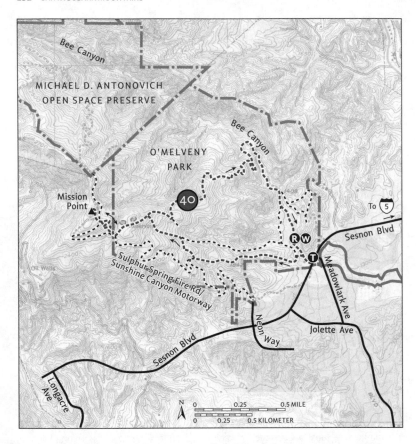

steep than the use-trails you've been on so far but is at least significantly wider.

It's one more big push to a three-way junction at 1.3 miles. Keep left here and follow a mostly level route to 1.5 miles, where the trail skirts a fenced-off border with the Sulphur Spring Fire Road/Sunshine Canyon Motorway. Once again, set your sights upward and follow either the broad, switchbacking route or the direct use-trail to three prominent oak trees at 1.8 miles. Cross the dirt road and

make another beeline straight up the ridge to Mission Point at 1.9 miles, where you'll find a few memorial plaques and benches and a USGS marker at the summit. Taking in the terrain from here, it's easy to imagine the difficulty travelers had entering the Los Angeles region before the 5 was built—to your east, the jagged, upturned peaks of the eastern Santa Susanas lie right in front of the towering San Gabriels, with only the narrow San Fernando Pass as a feasible transit option.

Backtrack to the three-way junction at 2.4 miles and stay to the left at 2.5 miles to continue your descent. While still steep, this route is definitely easier than your climb up. Enjoy the views and a solitary bench at 3.4 miles before the trail drops into Bee Canyon, a shaded, riparian canyon that is a stark contrast to the open-air rolling hills you've been hiking on so far. Enjoy the tree cover and sage scrub on the easy route downward and keep right at 4 miles to return to the trailhead through the more developed end of the park, where a wide meadow is ringed by impressive eucalyptus trees.

41 Michael D. Antonovich Regional Park at Joughin Ranch

RATING/ DIFFICULTY	ROUNDTRIP	ELEV GAIN/ HIGH POINT	SEASON
***/2	3.9 miles	1067 feet/ 2954 feet	Year-round

Map: USGS Oat Mountain; **Contact:** Mountains Recreation and Conservation Authority; **Notes:** Dogs allowed on leash. $5 day-use fee required at trailhead; **GPS:** N 34.307922, W 118.606614

One of the most beautiful valley oaks in the entire Los Angeles region

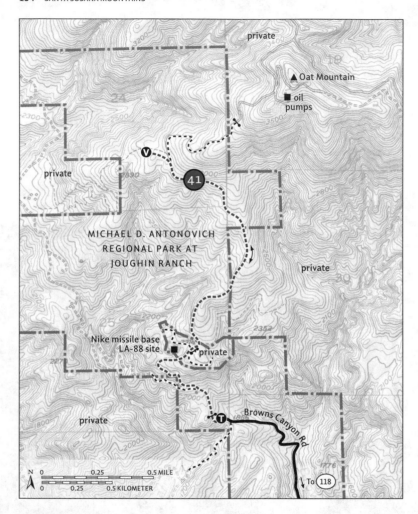

This hike takes you along a nearly abandoned paved road past a historic Nike missile site and up to a flat with fantastic views of the surrounding region.

GETTING THERE

From CA-118, 7.3 miles west of Interstate 405, take exit 35 for De Soto Avenue. At the end of the exit ramp, turn right onto Browns Canyon Road and continue for 3.2 miles, where the road ends at a gate and parking area. There are "No Trespassing" signs along the road, but they are from the area's past as a ranch; Browns Canyon Road is a public thoroughfare until the trailhead.

ON THE TRAIL

Continue west on the paved Browns Canyon Road past the locked gate and keep right at 0.2 mile to continue your slow and steady incline. At 0.6 mile, you'll enter the former grounds of Nike missile base LA-88. Unfortunately, not much of the former grounds remain after a 2008 wildfire gutted most of the surviving buildings—but foundations of the circa-1956 base are visible and some structures still stand. The area had an on-site property manager until the fire, but confusion over the area's multiple land management agencies have left the region unmaintained since then. Vandalism is rampant in these historic structures, and its use as a live-fire L.A. Police Department SWAT training facility isn't helping its structural integrity or its safety. Appreciate this piece of L.A.'s history from a distance.

Continue on the road, the barracks and command center are on your left, while the launch facilities are on your right. Once the Nike site is in your past, the main draw of this hike is the spectacular view of the Santa Susana Mountains. Low grasses cover the rugged, rolling hillsides dotted by the occasional sprawling valley oak. Cattle roam here, too, meaning you'll likely get the chance to have some serious "Wait, where am I?" moments along the way.

At 1.8 miles, turn left onto a spur trail. The paved road continues to the right up to Oat Mountain, the highest peak in the Santa Susanas. Unfortunately, there are active oil

wells along this route, and the public is not currently allowed access to this area. Fortunately, the short side spur takes you to a flat where an absolutely epic valley oak stands watch over the surrounding peaks. The views are just as nice from here as the views from Oat Mountain, and your quiet moment won't be ruined by the sound of oil pumps or angry landowners.

Return to the trailhead the way you came.

42 Corriganville Park

RATING/ DIFFICULTY	LOOP	ELEV GAIN/ HIGH POINT	SEASON
**/1	1.5 miles	125 feet/ 1201 feet	Year-round

Map: USGS Simi Valley East; **Contact:** Rancho Simi Recreation and Park District; **Notes:** Park open 6:00 AM–dusk. Dogs allowed on leash only. Rock climbing and camping allowed by permit only; **GPS:** N 34.263241, W 118.654519

While strolling through the site of an old ranch turned backdrop for hundreds of films and TV shows, aficionados may recognize terrain from well-known Hollywood fare like Fort Apache, How the West Was Won, Gunsmoke, Lassie, and The Fugitive, as well as lesser-known entries like Billy the Kid vs. Dracula.

GETTING THERE

From the interchange of CA-118 and CA-27, travel 1.6 miles west on CA-118. Take the Rocky Peak Road exit on the eastern edge of Simi Valley. Cross the overpass and turn right onto Santa Susana Pass Road heading into Simi Valley. Santa Susana Pass

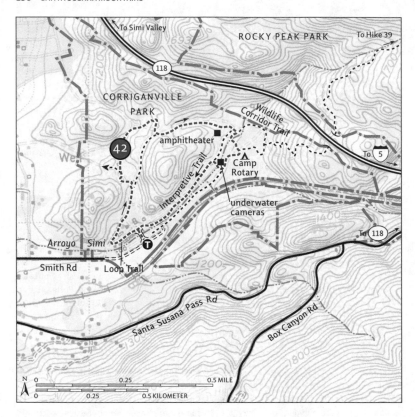

Road becomes Kuehner Drive as it curves north, and in 1.9 miles, turn right onto Smith Road. The park's entrance will be on your left.

ON THE TRAIL

This route follows remnants of the Loop and Interpretive trails inside Corriganville Park. Please note, however, that trail signage and markers are virtually nonexistent.

From the parking area, follow the signs for the Loop Trail, which in this section of the park also doubles as the Interpretive

Trail. Cross a wide bridge and you'll find yourself standing in the open expanse of the moviemaking center/amusement park that stuntman and Tarzan body double Ray "Crash" Corrigan purchased in 1935. Today, just a few ruins and foundations remain, but even seeing these will give you an idea of just how big this place was. Follow the Loop Trail (as much as you can see an actual trail) clockwise along the perimeter of the grounds. Keep an eye out for plaques scattered throughout the property—half of them are interpretive displays about

At its height, Corriganville was one of the most popular tourist attractions in Southern California.

the region's natural features while the rest detail various films and TV shows shot in the locations. At 0.1 mile, the trail heads north along a broad fire road, passing old sets for the John Ford/John Wayne classic *Fort Apache*, and the Howard Hughes–produced flop *Vendetta*. Look for faint paint markings directing you toward the proper trails here, as the prop-erty is riddled with old access roads and use-trails. At 0.3 mile keep left, then make a quick right to stay inside the park and head north, generally following the northern slope of a large rock formation in the center of Corriganville Park.

At 0.5 mile the trail gains a decent amount of elevation climbing into a saddle just north of the rock formation before it heads east and drops down into a shaded canyon. At 0.8

mile, pass an outdoor amphitheater and stay to the right at the junction with the Wildlife Corridor Trail at 0.9 mile. Cross the dry Arroyo Simi (and its concrete edges) to enter into an expansive oak forest with tons of shade and plentiful picnic areas. This is now the site of Camp Rotary, available primarily to Scout and church groups (see Appendix I for contact information). Walk along the eastern shore of the artificial lake and cross the bridge at the 1-mile mark, noting the windows that once allowed for underwater filming.

Follow the Interpretive Trail southwest back to the Loop Trail and old town site, passing some truly beautiful riparian canyon vegetation and enormous, ancient native oaks along the way.

EXTENDING YOUR TRIP

It is possible to continue on the Wildlife Corridor Trail through a tunnel beneath the 118. This trail connects with the Rocky Peak Trail (Hike 39). Visitors interested in the region's history can also stop by the nearby Santa Susana Depot Museum on weekends between 1:00 and 4:00 PM to see a miniature model of what Corriganville looked like in its heyday. Visit www.santasusanadepot.org for more information.

Opposite: A bench on the Bill Eckert Trail provides a nice rest stop with even nicer views.

griffith park

Often compared to Central Park in that other big American city, Griffith Park surprises visitors with how large, diverse, and wild it is. Griffith Park's 4310 acres make it the largest city park in Los Angeles and one of the largest urban parks in the United States.

Griffith is kind of an unusual place—part developed urban oasis and part rugged wilderness park—and the direction of the park seems to oscillate between those two poles. For locals, Griffith Park is one of the most accessible and diverse green spaces in a city notoriously short on parks. For tourists, landmarks like the Hollywood sign and Griffith Observatory are major draws. For many, it can also be a frustrating labyrinth. The park is notoriously poorly signed and even more poorly mapped, and established trails are often accompanied by dozens of use-trails and wildlife routes that can be pretty confusing.

In mid-2016, much-needed (and very welcome) wayfinding kiosks and signs began to appear inside the park at trailheads and major junctions, but it's still best to study maps before you visit so you don't take a wrong turn.

43 Glendale Peak

RATING/ DIFFICULTY	ROUNDTRIP	ELEV GAIN/ HIGH POINT	SEASON
***/2	3.1 miles	327 feet/ 1184 feet	Year-round

Map: USGS Hollywood; **Contact:** City of Los Angeles Department of Recreation and Parks, Griffith Park; **Notes:** Trails open sunrise–sunset. Dogs allowed on leash; **GPS:** N 34.121845, W 118.296782

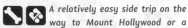 *A relatively easy side trip on the way to Mount Hollywood or a lovely hike in its own right, Glendale Peak is one of the lesser-traveled trails in Griffith Park and can offer some rare solitude for hikers on the southern side of the park. On clear days, soak in sweeping panoramas from the San Gabriels to the Pacific Ocean.*

GETTING THERE

From Interstate 5, take the exit for Los Feliz Boulevard and head west for 1.3 miles. Turn right on Vermont Avenue and drive north through Los Feliz and into Griffith Park. Once inside the park, pass the Greek Theatre on your left and park on the street. The trailhead is on the east side of Vermont Canyon Road, about 1 mile north of the intersection of Los Feliz and Vermont. Metro buses 180 and 181 stop at Hillhurst and Los Feliz, about 0.9 mile from the trailhead.

ON THE TRAIL

The trailhead is at a fire road, sometimes called the Riverside Trail, just north of the Greek Theatre. It begins with a steep incline. Ignore the prominent use-trail at 0.1 mile and continue toward the northeast as the trail levels out; here, you're hiking above the Vermont Canyon Tennis Courts and Roosevelt Golf Course. At 0.5 mile stay straight at the four-way junction. The Riverside Trail follows a southern ridge, vaguely parallel to Commonwealth Canyon Avenue below. At 0.9 mile, the trail drops down to a short connector trail from Aberdeen Canyon to the road. Ignore this route. Stay straight on Riverside and prepare for a sizable incline. If it's clear, you'll start to see some beautiful views toward downtown as you gain elevation.

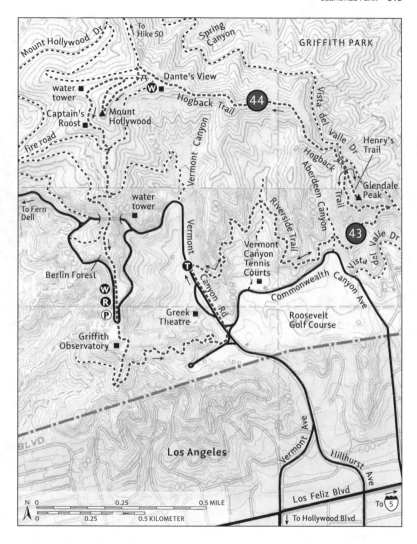

At 1.2 miles, just before the paved Vista del Valle Drive, take a sharp left onto what is sometimes called the Hogback Trail. Heading west, you'll have unique profiles of the Griffith Observatory perched on a nearby ridge, and in the spring this section of trail can get absolutely covered in California poppies.

Downtown Los Angeles from the surprisingly quiet summit of Glendale Peak

At 1.5 miles, take a right onto Henry's Trail, named for the writer and Sierra Club member Henry Shamma, who spent many years leading hikes to Glendale Peak and maintaining trails inside Griffith Park. This short but significantly more rugged trail takes you over a few bumps to Glendale Peak—a beautiful vista point that's criminally overlooked by most Griffith hikers. Return the way you came.

EXTENDING YOUR TRIP

After you visit Glendale Peak, you can return to the junction at the start of Henry's Trail and continue across the bridge along the Hogback Trail to Mount Hollywood (Hike 44).

44 Mount Hollywood

RATING/ DIFFICULTY	LOOP	ELEV GAIN/ HIGH POINT	SEASON
****/3	4.6 miles	856 feet/ 1620 feet	Year-round

Map: USGS Hollywood; **Contact:** City of Los Angeles Department of Recreation and Parks, Griffith Park; **Notes:** Trails open sunrise–sunset. Dogs allowed on leash; **GPS:** N 34.121845, W 118.296782

An accessible highlight loop to the fourth-highest peak in Griffith Park, this trail passes two historic volunteer gardens, a pine forest gift from Berlin, Germany, L.A.'s sister city, and the gorgeous art deco Griffith Observatory and Greek Theatre.

GETTING THERE

From Interstate 5, take the exit for Los Feliz Boulevard and head west for 1.3 miles. Turn right on Vermont Avenue and drive north through Los Feliz and into Griffith Park. Once inside the park, pass the Greek Theatre on your left and park on the street. The trailhead is on the east side of Vermont Canyon Road, about 1 mile north of the intersection of Los Feliz and Vermont. Metro buses 180 and 181 stop at Hillhurst and Los Feliz, about 0.9 mile from the trailhead.

ON THE TRAIL

Follow the route for Glendale Peak (Hike 43). At the junction with Henry's Trail at 1.5 miles, cross the short bridge to continue northwest on the Hogback Trail. This section of the trail climbs about 400 feet in 0.7 mile. It's steep, dusty, and completely shadeless. In other words, don't do this when it's hot and sunny out unless you want your clothes to feel like they've been sitting in a sauna all day. The views are phenomenal, though—on clear days you can see north to the San Gabriels and south to Catalina. At 2.2 miles, take a quick left for some water and much-needed shade at the Dante's View volunteer garden, then return to the Hogback Trail. Take a left at 2.3 miles onto a fire road that takes you to the summit of Mount Hollywood and ignore the short connector trail just past the picnic area that heads west. From here, you'll be looking straight down on the observatory, with the Hollywood sign, Mount Lee (Hike 49), and Burbank and Cahuenga peaks (Hike 48) to the west.

Stay to the left on the descent and take a left at 2.7 miles. Hike on the upper fire road just past this and keep the water tower on your right. At 2.9 miles pass the remnants of the Captain's Roost, another historic volunteer garden badly damaged by a 2007

The rugged terrain of Griffith Park as seen from the central perch of Mount Hollywood

wildfire. At 3 miles reach a four-way junction (ignoring firebreaks) and take a gentle right heading south to take the rugged trail that cuts through some of the chaparral on the south slope of Mount Hollywood. Keep right at 3.1 miles, left at 3.2 miles, and follow the firebreak back to the fire road, crossing over a tunnel at 3.3 miles. Keep left here to rise up to an incongruous pine forest gifted to the city by Berlin in 1990.

At 3.5 miles, cross the large parking lot and head toward Griffith Observatory. Enjoy the views, beautiful art deco sculptures, and free exhibits inside before descending a fire road on the building's eastern side. At 3.8 miles, take a left on another fire road and follow it to Vermont Canyon Road at 4.4 miles. Hike back along the road to your car.

OTHER OPTIONS

If you don't feel like taking the rugged single-track at the four-way junction at 3 miles, the fire road to your far right provides a gentler path to the Berlin Forest—as well as some of the best views of the Hollywood sign in Griffith Park. You may also park near the observatory to access Mount Hollywood on a much shorter direct route. Be aware that parking is often extremely difficult in this part of the park and there are plans to charge for parking here in the future.

45 Beacon Hill

RATING/ DIFFICULTY	ROUNDTRIP	ELEV GAIN/ HIGH POINT	SEASON
***/2	2.9 miles	589 feet/ 1296 feet	Year-round

Maps: USGS Hollywood, Burbank; **Contact:** City of Los Angeles Department of Recreation and Parks, Griffith Park; **Notes:** Trails open sunrise–sunset. Dogs allowed on leash; **GPS:** N 34.118395, W 118.273714

 A relatively secluded hike in the southeastern corner of Griffith Park, Beacon Hill is a great little pre- or post-commute hike or the start of a longer journey inside the park.

GETTING THERE

From Interstate 5, take the exit for Los Feliz Boulevard and head west. The trailhead is close to the William Mulholland Memorial Fountain near the intersection of Los Feliz Boulevard, Riverside Drive, and Crystal Springs Drive just west of the 5. Continue on Los Feliz Boulevard past this intersection and turn right (north) on Lambeth Street. Turn right on Griffith Park Boulevard, which quickly makes a sharp curve before splitting into Shannon Road and Cadman Drive. Park here. Pay attention to street parking signs and be courteous to the residents. Metro buses 180/181, 96, and Rapid Line 780 all stop within a few blocks of the trailhead.

ON THE TRAIL

East Coast refugees will not easily confuse this for Boston's more well-known (and more cobblestoned) namesake, but L.A.'s Beacon Hill has charms all its own, especially in winter and spring when clear skies provide some unique views of downtown and the Eastside's rolling hills. This hike begins by traveling 0.2 mile on the paved portion of Cadman Drive, passing some very nice (but modest for L.A.) houses along the way. At the end of the road, walk through an open chain link fence onto a shaded fire road that parallels a gulch. At 0.3 mile, stay to the right where a use-trail climbs a nearby canyon to Vista del Valle Drive.

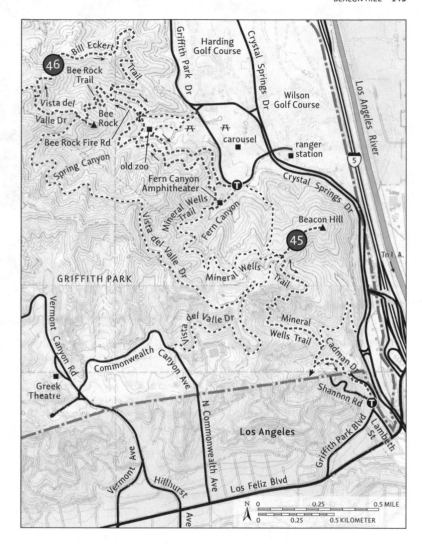

The fire road makes a modest climb, revealing more of the folds and contours of Griffith Park. Look out for the golf courses in the foreground, and the Verdugos and San Gabriels in the background. At 0.4 mile, keep left at the junction with the Mineral Wells Trail and keep climbing up. Just before the mile mark is when the views really start

A morning hike to Beacon Hill provides incredible views of Silver Lake, downtown Los Angeles, and the distant Palos Verdes peninsula.

getting good: visually follow the path of the 5 and you might even be able to make out distant Santiago Peak in Orange County. At 1.3 miles, head east at the junction along a ridge firebreak and ascend one final, short, steep incline to the mostly bald summit of Beacon Hill. Soak in the insanely panoramic views (and hopefully, some solitude), and return the way you came.

EXTENDING YOUR TRIP

From the junction at 1.3 miles, the Mineral Wells Trail will eventually connect with the trail to the Old Zoo (Hike 46).

46 Bee Rock and the Old L.A. Zoo

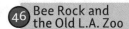

RATING/ DIFFICULTY	LOOP	ELEV GAIN/ HIGH POINT	SEASON
**/3	3.8 miles	573 feet/ 1091 feet	Year-round

Map: USGS Burbank; **Contact:** City of Los Angeles Department of Recreation and Parks, Griffith Park; **Notes:** Trails open sunrise–sunset. Dogs allowed on leash; **GPS:** N 34.131000, W 118.283432

This hike takes you through the remains of an abandoned zoo to a prominent rocky overlook on the eastern side of Griffith Park. Along the way, you'll get some steep, slippery climbs, pass a historic carousel, and even get the chance to climb inside some of the old animal cages. Making your own animal noises is optional but highly encouraged.

GETTING THERE

From Interstate 5, take the exit for Los Feliz Boulevard and head west. At the William Mulholland Memorial Fountain at the intersection of Los Feliz, Crystal Springs Drive, and Riverside Drive, turn right to head north on Crystal Springs into Griffith Park. Around 1.4 miles in, take a left onto the road toward the carousel and park in the large lot. Metro bus 96 stops at the Griffith Park ranger station, about a 0.2-mile walk from the trailhead.

A PARK FOR THE PEOPLE

Entering Griffith Park from the Crystal Springs area, visitors are greeted by a large bronze statue of the redundantly named Griffith J. Griffith, perhaps the city's best-known wife-shooting ostrich farmer. After making his money investing in mining, Griffith purchased Rancho Los Feliz in 1882. Stymied by the rugged, tough-to-develop land, he founded an ostrich farm and built a small railroad to lure tourists in from the then-still-distant city of Los Angeles (and then to show them all the great real estate opportunities nearby, naturally). Perhaps realizing he could probably save some money on property taxes, Griffith donated 3015 rugged acres of his rancho to the city as a Christmas present in 1896, saying, "It must be made a place of rest and relaxation for the masses, a resort for the rank and file, for the plain people." Park development was stalled when the publicly teetotaling Griffith drunkenly shot his wife while vacationing in Santa Monica in 1903. She survived, and the ensuing trial was an early entry in the long line of juicy celebrity scandals in L.A. Griffith spent two years in San Quentin and offered to pay for a Greek Theatre and Hall of Science in his park in 1912, but the city wouldn't touch his money until he died in 1919.

Today that "resort for the rank and file" phrase continues to mean different things to the twelve million people who visit the park each year. Developed tourist attractions like museums, zoos, and miniature railways share space with rugged wilderness trails and rare native species. The two sides don't always see eye to eye, but in a city with notoriously few major parks, it's safe to say that one of the reasons Griffith is such a popular place for locals and tourists is that multifaceted nature. I mean, where else can you walk through TV's Batcave and get the chance to spot a mature mountain lion while the tallest skyscraper on the West Coast is within view?

ON THE TRAIL

Walk south from the parking area and cross the road, looking for a faint footpath heading south next to a usually closed gate. This is the Mineral Wells Trail, and it heads southwest for about 0.2 mile, passing the Fern Canyon Amphitheater along the way. Take a sharp right to head north on the fire road and keep to the left just a few hundred feet later. This stretch of road meanders above the old zoo grounds, but many buildings are visible through the vegetation. Ignore the use-trail at 0.9 mile and stay on the road.

To your west, Bee Rock becomes visible; it's a prominent, bare formation with a small chain link fenced area on its summit. Ignore

all side trails until the 1-mile mark, where the route intersects with the old zoo properly at a gate. Make a hard left to start your ascent on the Bee Rock Fire Road. This steep road continues until 1.3 miles, where it makes a sharp left and abruptly turns into a very steep single-track trail. Climb and scramble through the chaparral until 1.5 miles, when the trail tops out on a ridge. Take a left to follow it to the summit of Bee Rock, where you can soak in spectacular views of Burbank, Glendale, the Verdugos, and the San Gabriels.

Backtrack past the Bee Rock Trail and stay straight to continue on the paved Vista del Valle Drive. Follow this until the 2-mile

Many relics of the old L.A. Zoo remain.

mark, then turn right onto the Bill Eckert Trail. This winding, wide trail is a pleasant and easy descent that also provides some incredible views along the way.

At 3.2 miles, stay right and make a short descent onto a paved path inside the old zoo property. An active zoo from 1912 to 1966, the old zoo grounds are now used for moody photo shoots, apocalyptic movie scenes, haunted hayrides, and as backgrounds to live Shakespeare in the summer months. Stay on the paved path and head south, passing old exhibits and small, definitely not animal-rights-friendly cages on your right. Explore some of the larger housings, and at 3.3 miles take the upper paved path back to the trailhead through additional old zoo structures. When you're done, consider stopping for a ride on the circa-1926 carousel!

47 Hollywood Reservoir

RATING/ DIFFICULTY	LOOP	ELEV GAIN/ HIGH POINT	SEASON
**/1	3.3 miles	23 feet/ 791 feet	Year-round

Maps: USGS Hollywood, Burbank; **Contact:** Los Angeles Department of Water and Power (LADWP); **Notes:** Gates open at 6:30 AM daily. Closing times vary by season. Closed Thanksgiving, Christmas Day, and New Year's Day. No dogs allowed; **GPS:** N 34.128847, W 118.336368

 *Popular with joggers, strollers, and people who just want to get outside, this pleasant and easy walk around the perimeter of the*

Hollywood Reservoir (aka Lake Hollywood) provides some unusual views of the Hollywood sign and lets you walk across the art deco Mulholland Dam, built in 1924.

GETTING THERE

From US Highway 101, about 4 miles north of Santa Monica Boulevard (CA-2), exit at Barham Boulevard and head northeast. In

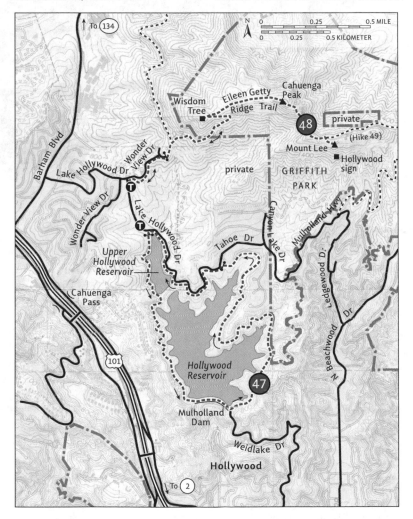

The historic Mulholland Dam

0.3 mile, turn right onto Lake Hollywood Drive and stay on that road as it winds through a hilly residential neighborhood. Just past the stop-signed intersection with Wonder View Drive, turn right to stay on Lake Hollywood Drive and descend down the hill toward the reservoir. Park on the street near the gate to the reservoir path.

ON THE TRAIL

This trail begins at the north gate and makes a counterclockwise journey along the edge of Lake Hollywood. This is a fairly straight-forward loop, as the path is paved and fenced in, preventing any sort of wandering off into LADWP land (this is still a functional reservoir, after all). The western side was long closed to the public after heavy rains in 2005 brought huge mudslides down along all the banks, and it was just reopened in 2013. The lake becomes visible about a half mile into the route and the views are lovely, even though you're looking through a chain link fence. From this trail, you'll be able to get photos of the Hollywood sign with a large body of water in the foreground—a view you're not likely to find on many postcards or vacation albums.

Just before the 1-mile mark, the path runs across the top of the Mulholland Dam, a very picturesque structure from 1924, when L.A. was still an early-stage boomtown. Be sure to note the bear fixtures on the south-facing side of the dam and the elegant typeface on the historic plaques. At 1.2 miles, ignore the gate to Weidlake Drive and stay to the left. At 2.6 miles, exit through the gate at Tahoe Drive and follow the dirt path along Lake Hollywood Drive back to the trailhead. Wave at the tour vans on their way to snap photos of the Hollywood sign, knowing you just got a much more interesting view.

EXTENDING YOUR TRIP

The trailhead to the Cahuenga Peak and the Wisdom Tree hike to the Hollywood sign (Hike 48) is very close-by if you want to add some distance, elevation, and difficulty to your day.

48 Cahuenga Peak and the Wisdom Tree

RATING/ DIFFICULTY	ROUNDTRIP	ELEV GAIN/ HIGH POINT	SEASON
****/4	3 miles	876 feet/ 1821 feet	Year-round

Map: USGS Burbank; **Contact:** City of Los Angeles Department of Recreation and Parks, Griffith Park; **Notes:** Trails open sunrise–sunset. Dogs allowed on leash; **GPS:** N 34.132070, W 118.337866

Not only is this the shortest, steepest, most rugged, and most fun route to the Hollywood sign, but this trail also takes you to one of L.A.'s most famous coniferous celebrities—the Wisdom Tree. This small pine, supposedly planted from a fast-food-giveaway sapling in the 1980s and a lone survivor of a 2007 wildfire, is now home to hundreds of handwritten wishes and prayers from local hikers.

GETTING THERE
From US Highway 101, about 4 miles north of Santa Monica Boulevard (CA-2), exit at Barham Boulevard and head northeast. In 0.3 mile, turn right onto Lake Hollywood Drive and stay on that road as it winds through a hilly residential neighborhood. Just past the stop-signed intersection with Wonder View Drive, turn right on Lake Hollywood Drive and park on the street.

ON THE TRAIL
The first short stretch of this route is along Wonder View Drive. Pass a gate at 0.2 mile and look for the narrow single-track trail

The Wisdom Tree

heading east at the junction at 0.3 mile. A prominent plaque once commemorated the protection of this parcel of land from development in 2010, thanks to an extensive public/private fundraising campaign and last-minute donations from Eileen Getty, the Louis Comfort Tiffany Foundation, and Hugh Hefner (yes, that Hugh Hefner), but sadly, the plaque has since been vandalized. Here, the Eileen Getty Ridge Trail immediately starts a steep, rugged climb through the chaparral. While the elevation gain is intense, so are the views—amazing vistas of the Hollywood Reservoir (Hike 47), Hollywood, the Griffith Observatory, and, on clear days, downtown L.A.

By 0.7 mile, you'll reach the main ridgeline. Head west 0.1 mile to visit the Wisdom Tree and leave your thoughts, then backtrack east along the ridge and keep to the left to continue heading east. Looking north, the charred vegetation is slowly but surely recovering from the 2007 fire that burned 817 acres—one of the largest in the park's modern history. At 1.2 miles, the trail reaches a small clearing at Cahuenga Peak, the highest point in Griffith Park. Past this point, the trail gets even more challenging: there's a short scramble and an epic ridge between Cahuenga Peak and Mount Lee with steep drop-offs on both sides, but nothing difficult enough to worry moderately experienced hikers.

The trail rises and falls over some steep bumps, and at the 1.5-mile mark, the trail unceremoniously spits you out on the paved road to Mount Lee, often to the amusing befuddlement of people who have taken an easier route up. Take a right onto this road to walk behind the Hollywood sign and to the summit of Mount Lee, then return the way you came.

49 Mount Lee via Bronson Canyon

RATING/ DIFFICULTY	ROUNDTRIP	ELEV GAIN/ HIGH POINT	SEASON
****/3	6.5 miles	1068 feet/ 1708 feet	Year-round

Maps: USGS Hollywood, Burbank; **Contact:** City of Los Angeles Department of Recreation and Parks, Griffith Park; **Notes:** Trails open sunrise–sunset. Dogs allowed on leash; **GPS:** N 34.124368, W 118.314464

 Let's face it, eventually someone's going to ask you how to hike to the Hollywood sign, so you might as well know a good, moderate route. This classic hike avoids contentious trailheads in nearby residential neighborhoods, has a relatively moderate climb on its way up, and takes you to visit the original Batcave, too.

GETTING THERE

From US Highway 101, take the Gower Street exit and go north. Turn right onto Franklin Avenue and take the fifth left onto Canyon Drive. Follow Canyon Drive for 1.4 miles into Griffith Park and continue until it ends at a locked gate. Park in the small lot at the gate, along the street, or in the spillover lot just south of the gate.

ON THE TRAIL

At the trailhead, take a sharp turn heading south and proceed up a fire road. In just 0.2 mile you'll reach a cave blasted into the rock that may look very familiar. This tiny corner of Griffith was formerly a quarry operated by the Union Rock Company until the 1920s, when it became a popular backdrop for countless films and television shows,

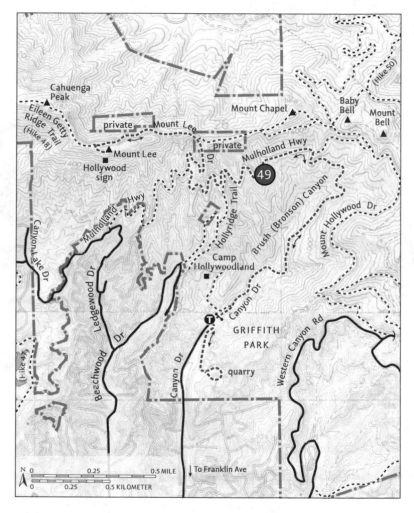

including *The Searchers*, *Army of Darkness*, and, of course, the *Batman* television series. Walk through the cave (stomp around a bit just in case there are any rattlesnakes hiding out) and you'll get a nice view of the Hollywood sign on the other side. Backtrack to the trailhead and turn right to pass the gate and head into Brush Canyon, known as Bronson Canyon. At about the 1-mile mark, the paved road ends and Canyon Drive becomes a wide dirt road, which you'll likely be sharing with joggers, dog walkers, hiking groups, fitness

Someday you will hike to this sign.

GROWING PAINS

Overall, the Los Angeles region is finally waking up to the idea that a major metropolis should also have ample parks with good access for its citizens. But old habits die hard, and there are many places where public access to trails is met with stiff resistance from local residents who are used to the less crowded, less outdoor-minded Los Angeles of yesteryear. Whittier residents near the Turnbull Canyon trailhead (Hike 120) continue to extend permit-parking farther from the trail, homeowners on the Palos Verdes Peninsula are making it more difficult to park near its trails (a major reason that region is excluded from this book), and here in the winding streets below Griffith Park, Beachwood Canyon residents have been engaged in a lengthy battle to block easy trail access to the Hollywood sign. Private security guards have been stationed at trailheads, and residents have agitated for increased permit parking zones and even petitioned a former city councilor to alter the driving directions to the Hollywood sign on Google Maps. Many in the outdoor community are hopeful that a reasonable compromise can be reached, but until that day, we strongly recommend skipping the Beachwood Canyon trailhead and instead hiking to the Hollywood sign via this route or Cahuenga Peak (Hike 48), or snapping photos from the Griffith Observatory, Hollywood Reservoir (Hike 47), or from the Hollywood and Highland shopping complex.

instructors, and equestrians.

At 1.8 miles, take a left at the three-way junction with Mulholland Highway. The sign is at an odd, non-photograph-friendly angle here, but to the east you'll have excellent views of the profile of Mount Hollywood (Hike 44) and the Griffith Observatory. At 2.3 miles, stay right at the junction with the Hollyridge Trail. Just before 2.7 miles, the dirt road ends at the paved Mount Lee Drive. If you're looking for views or photos of the sign, heading left here on the Mulholland Highway will get you some nicer direct views. To reach the summit, turn right and continue on the paved road as it loops around the north side of Mount Lee and passes the Eileen Getty Ridge Trail to Cahuenga Peak (Hike 48) at 3.4 miles. The road ends at the summit of Mount Lee, above and behind the iconic letters. Return the way you came.

50 Northside Loop

RATING/ DIFFICULTY	LOOP	ELEV GAIN/ HIGH POINT	SEASON
****/4	6.8 miles	1190 feet/ 1614 feet	Year-round

Maps: USGS Burbank, Glendale; **Contact:** City of Los Angeles Department of Recreation and Parks, Griffith Park; **Notes:** Trails open sunrise–sunset. Dogs allowed on leash; **GPS:** N 34.152596, W 118.308642

Love Griffith Park but think it's too crowded? This route through the less-traveled northern half of the park provides some incredible views from four different peaks, along with forested trails, steep climbs and scrambles, and park history with a fraction of the foot traffic of other trails.

GETTING THERE
From CA-134, 1.6 miles west of Interstate 5, take the Forest Lawn Drive exit. Heading south on Forest Lawn, make a quick left onto Zoo Drive and a right onto Griffith Park Drive. The parking lot entrance is on the left, before the Skyline trailhead.

ON THE TRAIL
Cross Griffith Park Drive and hike south along the road on a wide equestrian path. This gradually climbing trail narrows under the shade of oaks and at 0.4 mile, the wide road abruptly turns into a rugged, steep single-track affectionately known as the Suicide Trail. Enjoy (?) the views of Forest Lawn Cemetery as you ascend this short but exceptionally steep route, which meets the dirt Mount Hollywood Drive at 0.7 mile. Cross Mount Hollywood to a dirt path on the opposite side of the road. Ignore the many side trails and take a right onto the Toyon Trail at 0.9 mile, skirting the boundary of the decommissioned Toyon Canyon Landfill.

Briefly rejoin Mount Hollywood Drive, but stay left on the rough path to the north of the road at 1.2 miles and then take a right on the fire road at 1.5 miles. Climb up and keep an eye out to your right—the peak with the water tower on its slope is Mount Chapel, your first summit on this route. At 1.7 miles, head right on Vista del Valle Drive and at 1.9 miles you'll reach a T intersection with Mount Hollywood Drive again. Take a breather here because it's about to get steep. Ignore the use-trails here and instead head south on Mount Hollywood Drive for a very short distance to reach the official fire road ascent toward Mount Chapel to the west. Follow the road to the water tower you spied earlier and look for an established use-trail at 2.3 miles. Climb through the

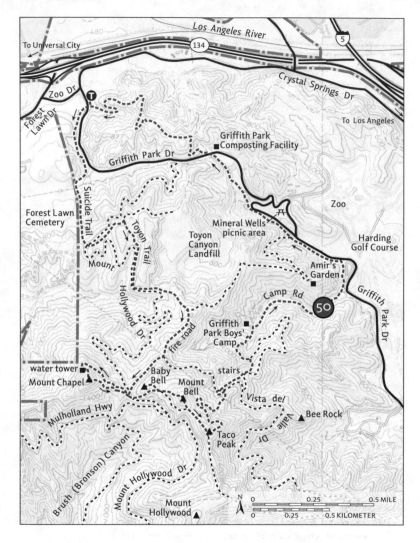

chaparral to the summit of Mount Chapel for stellar views of the park and the distant Verdugos and San Gabriels. In all likelihood, you'll have this perch to yourself.

Look for a steep scramble route on the summit's eastern face and descend another well-worn use-trail back to Mount Hollywood Drive. There are some slippery

A hiker demonstrates an advanced hiking technique known as "the butt-slide."

sections here (and all along the route), so take your time, watch your balance, and remember: there's no shame in a good butt-slide.

Rejoin Mount Hollywood Drive at 2.6 miles and head south for a hot minute before taking a fire road on your left. Continue heading up and just past 2.7 miles, hang a sharp left to make a brush-covered beeline to the summit of "Baby Bell." Backtrack and head southeast, and at about the 2.9-mile mark, look for a very rough use-trail on the left and follow it up (and up and up) to the Mount Bell summit. The trails are very faint here, so when in doubt, just go up!

From the summit, choose a use-trail on the eastern side and carefully descend some steep drop-offs. Briefly rejoin the fire road at 3.1 miles and look for a firebreak on the opposite side. This is the short route to the bump hikers call Taco Peak. A small, octagonal cement structure stands on its summit, where you can have tremendous views in nearly every direction. Head down a steep ridgeline trail on the peak's southeastern face and turn left at the fire road at 3.3 miles. Follow the mercifully wide and flat fire road past the site of the short-lived Griffith Park Tea House and take a sharp right at 3.5 miles to follow the path back down to Vista del Valle Drive at 3.8 miles. Head east and look for a set of concrete stairs on your left. Head down these stairs, pass a water tank, and look for a steep, overgrown path on your left. This turns into a tightly switchbacked single-track that heads into the old Griffith Park Boys' Camp (today an occasional Boy Scout retreat). Take a left at 4 miles and carefully follow the degrading path to the ruins of the camp's old swimming pool at 4.1 miles. Follow the old trail down to Camp Road and follow that east out of the canyon.

At 4.8 miles, take a left on the wide path that runs parallel to Griffith Park Drive and follow it north. Just past 5.2 miles, head through the Mineral Wells picnic area and continue straight, where you'll meet up with Griffith Park Drive again at 5.7 miles, at the Griffith Park Composting Facility. Head up the fire road to the facility's west, take a left at 5.9 miles, and follow this sandy route back down to the trailhead. Whew!

EXTENDING YOUR TRIP

At the 5.2-mile mark of this route (or just near the Mineral Wells picnic area if you feel like parking there instead), consider a short hike up the fire road to Amir's Garden, in my opinion the most beautiful and well-cared-for of Griffith Park's citizen gardens. It's 0.5 mile one way to the shaded, verdant perch above Mineral Wells, and there are hand-cut footpaths that let you wander peacefully through the greenery. This region of the park is cared for completely by tireless volunteers, so please tread lightly and pack out some extra trash if you can.

Opposite: You don't always have to travel far for a decent outdoor experience.

city parks

Although for a major city, Los Angeles has some disappointing rankings in terms of park numbers, accessibility, and budgets (L.A. was tied for 51st in the Trust for Public Land's park rankings of the seventy-five largest American cities in 2015), that's not to say that the city doesn't have some true gems that are worth visiting.

The parks selected for this section have good hiking trails, exercise routes, or educational opportunities. Los Angeles does seem to be finally coming around to the idea that to be a world-class city, you have to have good parks (an idea that was pitched to the city by Griffith J. Griffith in 1896 and again by the sons of Fredrick Law Olmsted in 1930, by the way). Already, new pocket parks are popping up in the city and plans are underway to free the L.A. River from its concrete cage and build a new string of green space through the heart of the city.

I'm hopeful that we'll have many more parks to add to this list in future years.

51 Baldwin Hills Scenic Overlook

RATING/ DIFFICULTY	LOOP	ELEV GAIN/ HIGH POINT	SEASON
**/3	1.3 miles	350 feet/ 427 feet	Year-round

Map: USGS Beverly Hills; **Contact:** Baldwin Hills Scenic Overlook; **Notes:** Open 8:00 AM–sunset daily. Parking fee required for lots; **GPS:** N 34.020506, W 118.382489

If you're looking for a workout or just trying to get some stunning views of the L.A. basin after a winter storm clears the air, join the fitness-minded locals of Culver City on this unassuming staircase trek near Ballona Creek.

GETTING THERE

The trailhead is at the corner of Hetzler Road and Jefferson Boulevard in Culver City and is

A majestic view of downtown from the Baldwin Hills Scenic Overlook

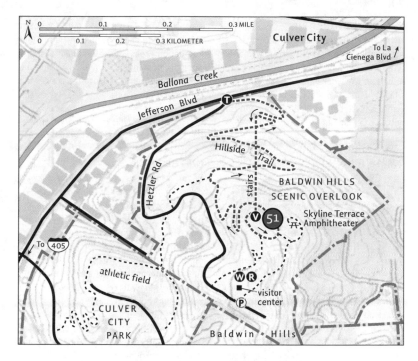

best accessed from La Cienega Boulevard south of Interstate 10. A well-marked off-ramp is accessible from both directions of travel. Follow La Cienega south for 0.9 mile and turn right onto Jefferson Boulevard. Follow it 0.7 mile to the Baldwin Hills Scenic Overlook entrance and park on the street. On weekends and holidays from 8:00 AM to 6:00 PM, a shuttle (25-cent fare) travels to this park from the La Cienega/Jefferson Expo Line stop.

ON THE TRAIL

Beginning from Jefferson Boulevard, follow the Hillside Trail for 0.2 mile, then look south at your challenge—a towering, incredibly steep staircase cut directly into the hillside.

If you have a burning, passionate hatred of switchbacks, this route might make you appreciate them a bit more. Steel yourself and head up the stairs, which gain 277 feet in about 0.15 mile.

The steps are steep and not evenly spaced, so take some rests if you need them and soak in the ever-improving views. Just after 0.3 mile, you'll have made it to the top, where the vistas unfold in nearly every direction. There's a small picnic area to the east and a lovely visitor center to the south (hours seem to vary wildly depending on budgets and available volunteers). If you don't hate your knees, return on the switch-backing Hillside Trail, which crosses the steps a few times on the way down.

EXTENDING YOUR TRIP

Didn't burn enough calories? Head back up for another round! Trail runners will often run these routes like an outdoor track. If you visited on the weekend and took the Metro shuttle, it will also stop at nearby Kenneth Hahn State Recreation Area, where you can hop on the Community Loop Trail (Hike 52).

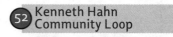

52 Kenneth Hahn Community Loop

RATING/ DIFFICULTY	LOOP	ELEV GAIN/ HIGH POINT	SEASON
***/2	2.6 miles	240 feet/ 519 feet	Year-round

Map: USGS Hollywood; **Contact:** County of Los Angeles Parks and Recreation, Kenneth Hahn State Recreation Area; **Notes:** Park open sunrise–sunset. Dogs allowed on leash. Vehicle entrance fees on weekends and holidays only ($6/vehicle, higher for limos and buses); **GPS:** N 34.006344, W 118.362932

 *If you've ever seen an image of downtown L.A. with snow-capped mountains behind it and wondered, "Where the heck did they take that photo?," the answer is, right here in Kenneth Hahn State Recreation Area—an oasis of parkland amid mid-city sprawl. This relatively easy loop around the park is a lively and lovely hiking experience, especially after a winter storm leaves a dusting on the distant San Gabriels.*

GETTING THERE

Kenneth Hahn State Recreation Area is best accessed from La Cienega Boulevard south of Interstate 10. A well-marked off-ramp is accessible from both directions of travel. Stay on La Cienega south for about 2 miles to the exit for Kenneth Hahn State Recreation Area. Follow the main road into the park, past the ponds and oil wells to the top of a hill. A large parking area is available near Janice's Green Valley. On weekends and holidays from 8:00 AM to 6:00 PM, a shuttle (25-cent fare) travels to this park from the La Cienega/Jefferson Expo Line stop.

ON THE TRAIL

Begin your hike in a counterclockwise direction around Janice's Green Valley—a shockingly large, open, green space for any part of L.A., let alone this one. This bucolic space is actually the site of the former Baldwin Hills Reservoir, which breached in 1963, dumping 292 million gallons of water into the neighborhood below and destroying or damaging nearly three hundred homes. This was a deadly disaster for the city, and KTLA's coverage marked the first time helicopter footage was broadcast on live television. A plaque at 0.3 mile memorializes the deadly deluge. Turn right onto Diane's Trail at 0.6 mile, climbing through some dense groves of prickly pear cactus as views of the Santa Monica Mountains and the rest of the Baldwin Hills open up to the north and west. You will also note significant oil infrastructure; part of the Inglewood Oil Field, this area was first tapped in 1924 for Standard Oil and was a major source of wealth for the still-growing city of Los Angeles. Oil and natural gas extraction continue today.

At 0.8 mile, make a sharp right onto the narrow City View Trail, which loops through some lovely areas shaded by eucalyptus trees before following a ridgeline where you can get those postcard-perfect views of downtown and the San Gabriels (bring your telephoto lens!). At 1.1 miles, the City View

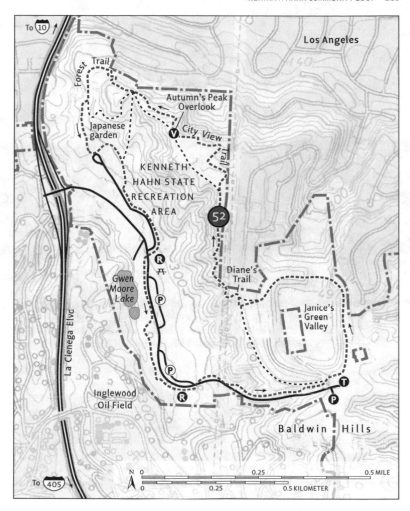

rejoins Diane's Trail near the Autumn's Peak Overlook. Stay on the City View as it makes a quick descent and heads west, opening up the full panorama of the Hollywood Hills all the way out to the Pacific Ocean. Stay to the far right at the five-way junction at 1.2 miles

to continue your descent on the Forest Trail, which visits the park's northern extremities before meandering into a modest Japanese garden at 1.5 miles. From here, stroll through the gardens on the sidewalk. You can take a short side trail at 1.6 miles for a bit more

Looking across the Baldwin Hills to the Santa Monica Mountains

non-sidewalk walking, but it's back on the concrete shortly thereafter.

At 1.9 miles, hop across the street to enjoy the artificial water features at Gwen Moore Lake—a popular stop for waterfowl and for people taking prom and *quinceañera* photos. Stroll through the park area at your leisure and follow the sidewalk back up the hill to the trailhead when you're done.

EXTENDING YOUR TRIP
Want to get some elevation into the day's hiking? If you visit on the weekend and take the Metro shuttle, it will also stop at nearby Baldwin Hills Scenic Overlook, where you can climb up a steep and challenging staircase for even more great views (Hike 51).

53 Elysian Park Loops

RATING/ DIFFICULTY	LOOP	ELEV GAIN/ HIGH POINT	SEASON
**/3	5.2 miles	232 feet/ 768 feet	Year-round

Maps: USGS Hollywood, Los Angeles; **Contact:** City of Los Angeles Department of Recreation and Parks, Elysian Park; **Notes:** Park is unstaffed and unlocked at all hours. Dogs allowed on leash; **GPS:** N 34.086200, W 118.243258

This double loop shows off some of the highlights of the oldest city park in Los Angeles, passing by landmarks little known and seldom visited other than by Echo Park locals (Dodger Stadium is a notable exception, of course). This park has poor signage and is known to harbor an unsavory element at night, but during the day it's a wonderful place to get outside.

GETTING THERE

The trailhead is near the Grace E. Simons Lodge at the intersection of Elysian Park Drive and Stadium Way. From the north, Stadium Way enters Elysian Park from Interstate 5 southbound or Riverside Drive.

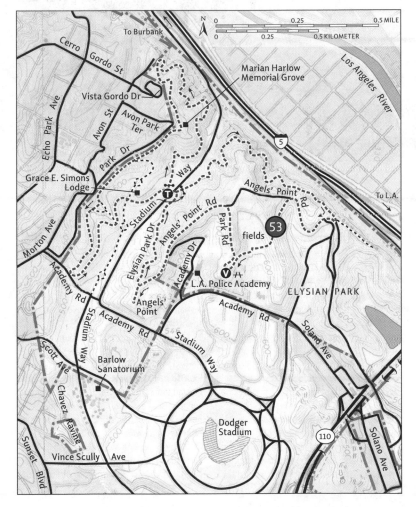

The sculpture at Angel's Point has some of the best views in the city.

From the south, the easiest entry is from the Echo Park Avenue exit off US Highway 101, keeping right at Morton Avenue at 0.8 mile, right at Academy Road after 0.2 mile, and left onto Stadium Way in another 0.2 mile. Park on the street. Metro bus lines 2/302 and 4 stop at Sunset/Portia. Walk 0.2 mile north on Portia and take a right onto Scott Avenue and in 500 feet turn left and walk north along the dirt Elysian Park Drive to start on the southwesternmost corner of this loop.

ON THE TRAIL

Look for a beaten footpath to the east of the Simons Lodge heading toward a white gate. Pass through this gate and the narrow path widens through a dense cover of fragrant eucalyptus. At 0.4 mile, the 5 comes into view—normally not a point of interest on a hike, but on clear winter and spring days you'll have beautiful views toward the Verdugos and San Gabriels from here. At 0.8 mile, ignore the very short use-trail to Vista Gordo Drive and follow a (relatively) steep incline to the Marian Harlow Memorial Grove at 1.1 miles. Continue along the path to the south as views of downtown L.A. peek up from behind the tree cover. At 1.8 miles, the trail meets up with Academy Road. Take a sharp left and follow the paved path back to the trailhead.

Carefully cross Stadium Way—a road clearly built during L.A.'s "Hey, let's put some freeways through our parks" phase—and look for another gate on the north side of Elysian Park Drive at 2.5 miles. This fun and rugged single-track meanders along the northern rim of the park near the 5 again, offering more views of the San Gabriels as it hops ridges and washouts. At 3.4 miles, scramble up the use-trail to Angel's Point Road. Head west on Angel's Point Road and stay to the right to continue on the higher road. At 3.6 miles, leave Angel's Point Road and follow a footpath along a drainage ditch, which abruptly ends at a series of playing fields often used for impromptu soccer matches. Head southwest and follow the ridgeline to a viewpoint and picnic tables at 4 miles, where you'll have stunning views of the Los Angeles skyline. Stunning in a different way is the view of the seemingly never-ending Dodger Stadium parking lot, built during L.A.'s "Hey, let's displace an entire neighborhood and bulldoze a mountain to build a stadium" phase. (Fun fact: The former Palo Verde Elementary School sits beneath the pavement here.)

When you've soaked in the skyline, head north on Park Road and take a left back onto Angel's Point Road. There are no trails heading into the bowl west of the overlook because it's part of the Los Angeles Police Academy. Hike along the road, enjoying the stately palm trees along the way. At 4.7 miles, turn left for a short side trip to Angel's Point, where an oddly modernist sculpture by Echo Park artist Peter Shire stands in tribute to Grace E. Simons and her husband, Frank Glass. Simons founded the Citizens Committee to Save Elysian Park in the 1960s, when the city wanted to build a new convention center in the park. Under her watch, the group fought off oil wells, condominiums, and even an airport to preserve this green space. While the park may be a bit run-down these days, we can thank Simons and the committee that it's still there for us to enjoy, and hope others continue follow in her footsteps to ensure it stays that way.

Return to the road, which now becomes Elysian Park Drive, and follow it down to the trailhead.

54 Ernest E. Debs Regional Park

RATING/ DIFFICULTY	LOOP	ELEV GAIN/ HIGH POINT	SEASON
***/3	5.2 miles	401 feet/ 880 feet	Year-round

Map: USGS Los Angeles; **Contact:** City of Los Angeles Department of Recreation and Parks, Ernest E. Debs Regional Park and the Audubon Center at Debs Park; **Notes:** Debs Park is open 24/7, unstaffed, and ungated, although the parking lot at the Audubon Center closes at night. Audubon Center open Tuesday–Saturday 9:00 AM–5:00 PM. Dogs not allowed on certain trails; **GPS:** N 34.097822, W 118.202111

 A lovely loop through most of this 300-acre park on the Arroyo Seco, this route offers unique views of downtown Los Angeles, a small artificial pond, plenty of uphill for the fitness-minded, picnic areas, and a top-notch Audubon center that will even let you borrow bird-watching kits.

GETTING THERE
From CA-110 northeast of downtown, take the exit for Avenue 52 and head southeast, crossing the Arroyo Seco and making a sharp turn to the west. This becomes Griffin Avenue as the road curves south. At 0.5 mile from the 110, the entrance to the Audubon Center is on the east side of the road. Park in the lot or on the street and walk in via the entrance road. The Metro Gold Line Southwest Museum stop is also just across the arroyo. Walk through Sycamore Grove Park and cross the bridge and you'll be right at the entrance.

ON THE TRAIL

There are no signs at trail junctions here, so study a map carefully…or just be okay with wandering a bit. Head northeast from Griffin Avenue up the western park access road and in about 500 feet leave the pavement and head onto a broad dirt path called the Scrub

Jay Trail. Ignore the old staircase at 0.4 mile and stay to the right to continue your ascent, soaking in views of Pasadena and the San Gabriels to the north. At 0.6 mile, take a left at the three-way junction onto the Walnut Forest Trail and prepare for a bit of incline gain. At 1.1 miles, take a short side trip to the

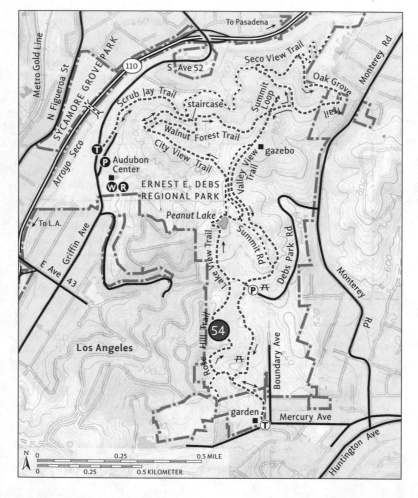

The aptly named City View Trail in Ernest E. Debs Regional Park

left for the Summit Loop—a shaded area with some benches at the highest point on the trail. Backtrack to the Walnut Forest Trail and continue to the east, then keep left at 1.2 miles, where the trail makes a quick descent to meet the Seco View Trail at 1.4 miles. Keep right at this junction and stay right again at 1.6 miles to head onto the Oak Grove Trail—a picturesque single-track trail that's a merciful break from the fire roads. This trail meanders beneath some lovely native oaks and by remnants of the land's ranching past before rejoining the Walnut Forest Trail. Revisit the intersection south of the Summit Loop and head south on the paved road.

Pass a gazebo at about 2.2 miles and just past this, look for a faint use-trail to the left. Hop onto this (the Valley View Trail) to save your boots some pavement pounding; it parallels the paved road but offers a much nicer hiking experience, not to mention views to the east. At 2.6 miles, rejoin the paved road and follow it to a large, popular picnic area. Head south along the paved paths through the first picnic area and you'll spot another, smaller picnic area farther south. Look for a white gate near an old dirt road at the southwest corner of the second picnic area and follow this short path to the park's southern entrance, where a native plant garden welcomes visitors.

Backtrack to the southern picnic area and look left for a small dirt path at 3.5 miles to join the Rose Hill Trail, turning right at 3.6 miles. After you pass a beautiful birdwatching bench at 3.7 miles, the trail skirts the park's western boundary and rejoins the northern picnic area's parking lot. Look for a small staircase at the western end of the lot and climb up to join the Lake View Trail at 4 miles. This steep trail takes you to the shore of Peanut Lake, a firefighting reservoir that doubles as a lovely little pond in the hills. Follow the trail to the Summit Road at 4.3 miles and head north, then turn left onto the City View Trail at 4.4 miles to follow this back to the Scrub Jay Trail, enjoying some really stellar views of the City of Angels along the way.

Opposite: Many hikes in this region offer astounding views of the rugged terrain of Los Angeles County.

verdugo mountains/
san rafael hills

If you like your outdoors undeveloped and uncrowded, the Verdugos and San Rafaels are for you. The relatively small Verdugo Range is a true island-in-the-sky, rising dramatically above the developed communities and providing hikers, cyclists, and equestrians with miles of trails and unpaved fire roads.

Routes here range from leg-busting climbs to gentle ascents, and almost all of them feature some truly unbelievable city views and panoramas of the San Gabriel Mountains along the way. The smaller, lower San Rafael Hills are a bit more developed but offer many outdoor opportunities for nearby residents as well.

55 Vital Link Trail and Verdugo Peak

RATING/ DIFFICULTY	ROUNDTRIP	ELEV GAIN/ HIGH POINT	SEASON
****/4	5.8 miles	1836 feet/ 3126 feet	Nov–Apr

Map: USGS Burbank; **Contact:** City of Burbank, Wildwood Canyon Park; **Notes:** Park open sunrise–sunset. Dogs allowed on leash; **GPS:** N 34.202667, W 118.298628

Want to kick your body into gear real fast? The Vital Link Trail is one of the toughest short hikes in the region—

A tiny sliver of shade in the Verdugos. You will learn to greatly appreciate these little respites.

a no-nonsense, totally shadeless ascent that crawls up a narrow ridgeline to the highest point in the Verdugo Mountains. Start early or late to avoid the midday sun, and soak in some top-notch views for your efforts. And, okay, maybe earn that Double-Double on the drive home.

GETTING THERE

From Interstate 5 in Burbank, take the Burbank Boulevard exit and head east. Take the second right onto Third Street and then the first left onto Harvard Road. Follow this for 1.6 miles to the entrance of Wildwood Canyon Park and park at the large lot just to the north.

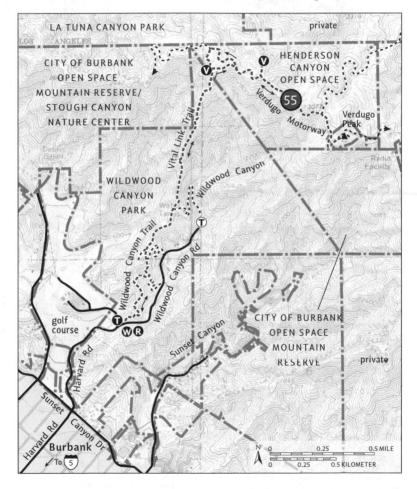

ON THE TRAIL

There are several trailheads along the entrance road to Wildwood Canyon Park, but this one starts at the lowest point, directly adjacent to the park's entrance. If you're in the mood for a lighter amount of punishment, feel free to drive farther into the canyon. I won't judge. Promise.

From the southeast corner of the parking lot, follow the north side of Wildwood Canyon Road. Just past some toilets and a water fountain, look for a picnic bench and trail sign in the shade of some oaks. Enjoy this shade, because it's pretty much the only time you'll get it on this route. Follow the trail to the left as it makes a quick ascent through the sage scrub—about 400 feet of gain in the first 0.4 mile. Ignore all the side trails and continue on the Wildwood Canyon Trail as it climbs and climbs and climbs. By 0.8 mile, you'll pass the last of the alternate access trails and see a sign for the Vital Link Trail.

Where other trail designers may have looked at this narrow ridge and decided to opt for a sensible switchbacking route farther up the canyon, it seems like Team Vital Link just pointed at a ridge and said, "Put it there!" And so, you will find yourself climbing 1066 feet in less than 0.9 mile along a route that could generously be described as "punishing." When you do reach the top at 1.7 miles, the trail apologizes by offering up a comfortable wooden lounge chair for you to catch your breath on and enjoy some spectacular views.

Follow a faint use-trail east along the summit ridge and descend to Verdugo Motorway. At 2 miles, take a quick left to an insanely beautiful lunch spot beneath the shade of an out-of-place but very welcome Scotch pine, then return to the motorway and head east. Stay straight at 2.5 miles and

make the final push up to Verdugo Peak, topped by radio towers. Enjoy the views, and then head back the way you came.

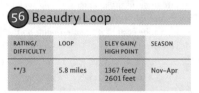

56 Beaudry Loop

RATING/ DIFFICULTY	LOOP	ELEV GAIN/ HIGH POINT	SEASON
**/3	5.8 miles	1367 feet/ 2601 feet	Nov–Apr

Maps: USGS Pasadena, Burbank; **Contact:** City of Glendale Community Services and Parks; **Notes:** Dogs allowed on leash; **GPS:** N 34.193446, W 118.241095

This easily overlooked loop in the southern Verdugos is a wonderful, moderate hike during the cooler months. In winter and spring, clear skies reveal sweeping views of the Los Angeles basin and beautiful chaparral and sage scrub bloom.

GETTING THERE

From CA-2 0.9 mile north of CA-134, exit at Mountain Street and head west. In 0.5 mile turn right onto Verdugo Road, and in 0.2 mile stay left to follow Cañada Boulevard. In 1.8 miles, take a left onto Country Club Drive. Follow this 0.4 mile and turn left onto Beaudry Boulevard. In 0.4 mile, park on the street where it makes a sharp turn northward. The trailhead is on an access road next to a flood control dam and spillway.

ON THE TRAIL

Hike west along a paved access road and pass a gate. The pavement ends in less than 400 feet and becomes a wide dirt fire road. To your right, housing development presses against the Verdugo Mountains. To your left, one of the region's flood control dams stands

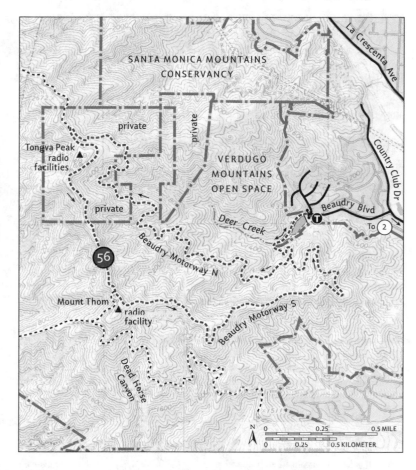

guard—an expensive and extensive conse-quence of building houses in areas that tend to turn into temporary rivers in the rainy seasons. Leave this infrastructure behind and at 0.5 mile, keep right at the junction to take Beaudry Motorway North. Although it doesn't matter which direction you go here, the north path has a bit more shade than the south and isn't quite as steep.

Follow the north motorway as it slowly winds and rises to the northwest, providing some epic views of the San Gabriels and the Crescenta Valley. Not visible to the naked eye is the Sierra Madre Fault Zone, which runs generally along the Front Range of the San Gabriel Mountains here. At 2.6 miles, take a sharp left to head to the south branch of Beaudry Motorway. Here, your views swing

An old street sign near the Beaudry Motorway

from the San Gabriels toward Burbank and—if it's a clear day—Palos Verdes and Catalina Island.

At 2.9 miles, pass a locked, fenced, and gated radio tower complex atop Tongva Peak, and stay left at 3.6 miles to continue on Beaudry Motorway South, where another tower farm lives atop Mount Thom. Descend back to the trailhead on this route, which offers up some very nice views of the downtown core along with huge clusters of lupines in the spring.

TAKE THE HIKE HOME WITH YOU

Do you love the subtle beauty of chaparral? Can't stop touching all the fragrant sages in the scrub? If you want to gain a better appreciation for California's native plants—or even try your hand at growing some of your own—you absolutely must stop by the Theodore Payne Foundation in nearby Sun Valley. The recently renovated and expanded grounds house an extensive nursery of California natives along with offering informative signs and even a short wildflower trail. The staff is knowledgeable and extremely helpful, and the nonprofit foundation holds a variety of classes and volunteer opportunities for every shade of green thumb. The grounds are located at 10459 Tuxford Street in Sun Valley. Call (818) 768-1802 or visit www.theodorepayne.org for more info.

57 La Tuna Canyon Trail

RATING/ DIFFICULTY	ROUNDTRIP	ELEV GAIN/ HIGH POINT	SEASON
****/3	4.2 miles	926 feet/ 2269 feet	Year-round

Map: USGS Burbank; **Contact:** Mountains Recreation and Conservation Authority (MRCA); **Notes:** Park open sunrise–sunset. Dogs allowed on leash; **GPS:** N 34.233228, W 118.311343

  The relatively hidden La Tuna Canyon Trail is a great hike when you're looking for something a little off the beaten path but still wouldn't mind keeping an eye on civilization. There is a surprising variety of scenery packed into this trip—from beautiful examples of sage scrub to deep canyons shaded with native oaks . . . and even some old car parts strewn mysteriously amidst the folds of the earth.

GETTING THERE

The easy-to-miss trailhead is on the southern side of La Tuna Canyon Road in Sun Valley. From Interstate 210, 3.7 miles west of CA-2, take the La Tuna Canyon Road exit and head west for 1.4 miles. Look on the left for a

Some remnants of yesteryear along the La Tuna Canyon Trail

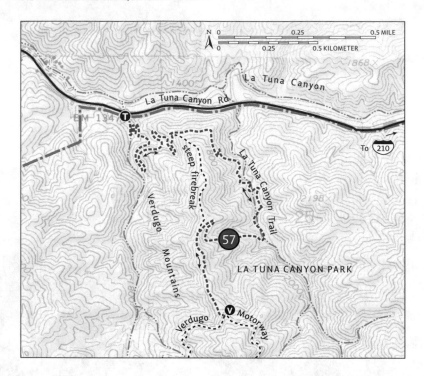

small pullout for parking and a green MRCA sign marking the entrance.

ON THE TRAIL

Almost immediately, the trail drops down from the road grade in La Tuna Canyon into a dense canyon shaded by mature oaks. Keep your eye out for California sagebrush and black sage (and feel free to sniff!) as the trail starts making its way up some tight switchbacks. Others have cut the switchbacks to save time—don't follow in their footsteps. The route doubles back on itself numerous times before reaching a straightaway on a narrow ridge above La Tuna Canyon Road at

0.8 mile. At 0.9 mile, the trail turns south and descends to the floor of a neighboring canyon. Hike past white sage on the southern-facing slopes and cross the streambed at 1.2 and 1.4 miles. This canyon section is full of beautiful oaks and sycamores, which will lose their leaves and provide a bit of California fall foliage in the cooler months.

Here, the trail starts a sizable climb. Keen eyes may be able to spot a rusted vehicle chassis just before the incline kicks in, and just around the corner is the relatively full body of an old truck, abandoned among the California buckwheat. At 1.8 miles, turn left at the firebreak and follow this ridge south

A shaded trail in La Tuna Canyon

to Verdugo Motorway at 2.1 miles, where a welcoming bench provides stellar views of the San Fernando Valley to the west. Return the way you came.

58 Descanso Trail

RATING/ DIFFICULTY	ROUNDTRIP	ELEV GAIN/ HIGH POINT	SEASON
***/3	4.8 miles	574 feet/ 1879 feet	Year-round

Map: USGS Pasadena; **Contact:** City of Glendale Community Services and Parks and City of La Cañada Flintridge; **Notes:** Trails open sunrise–sunset. Dogs allowed on leash; **GPS:** N 34.203996, W 118.211489

A recently constructed route above Descanso Gardens to an old Cold War watchtower, this winding trail through the San Rafael Hills provides tremendous views of the San Gabriel and Verdugo mountains and a good excuse to visit the gardens too.

GETTING THERE

From Interstate 210 east of CA-2, take the exit for Angeles Crest Highway (CA-2) and head south. Turn right onto Foothill Boulevard in 0.2 mile, then turn left onto Verdugo Boulevard in 0.3 mile. In 0.4 mile, turn left onto Descanso Drive and park where the road curves southeast, just to the west of the garden's main entrance.

Switchbacks on the Descanso Motorway

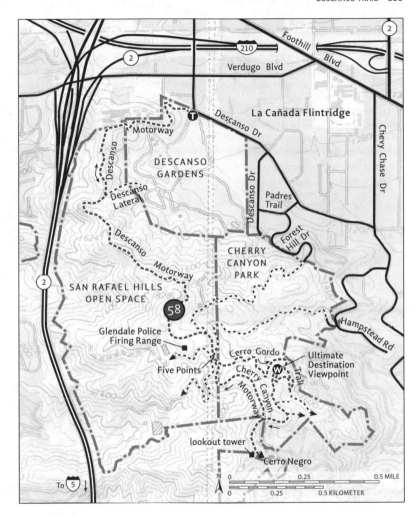

ON THE TRAIL

Hike along a short stretch of the paved Descanso Motorway and cross a drainage ditch. Almost immediately, the trail turns to the right, following the fenced boundary of Descanso Gardens along an incredibly picturesque oak woodland. At 0.1 mile, the trail makes a steep climb up shaded, well-constructed switchbacks and continues a gradual ascent on the park's northwestern border. Enjoy views of the gardens below and stay straight at the junction with

Descanso Lateral at 0.7 mile. Follow the fire road southeast as it climbs along the San Rafael Hills, providing stunning panoramic views of the San Gabriels to the north. Perhaps less inspiring but more audible may be the nearby freeway and Glendale Police Firing Range . . . but if the air is clear, you can at least look past them toward the Verdugos and the northeast side of Griffith Park.

Stay to the right at 1.5 miles and then to the left at the Five Points junction at 1.6 miles to hike on the Cerro Gordo Trail. This single-track winds around the north side of the San Rafaels and provides even more exceptional views of the San Gabriels and a beautiful stretch of sage scrub. At 2.1 miles, make a hard right to hike to the Ultimate Destination Viewpoint at 2.2 miles. The name is a bit of a mystery, as it is neither the highest point nor the turnaround point, but it is a lovely, open picnic area with benches and a water fountain. Continue the upward climb, staying to the right at 2.3 miles and the right at the next junction to follow the broad trail toward the now-visible lookout tower on Cerro Negro. Keep left at the junction with the Cherry Canyon Motorway at 2.5 miles to make the final climb to the tower, a remnant of L.A.'s Cold War civil defense systems. There is a small summit marker just to the east of the fenced-off tower. Enjoy the views and return back to Five Points via the Cherry Canyon Motoroway, continuing back to the trailhead the way you came.

EXTENDING YOUR TRIP

Consider wrapping up your trek with an exceedingly lovely walk through the 150-acre Descanso Gardens just near the trailhead. The grounds have several different traditionaly landscaped gardens as well as a new garden of California native plants, art galleries, and a miniature railroad. The larger and showier Huntington Gardens in San Marino gets more attention, but Descanso has a much more low-key, neighborhoody feel. For more info, call (818) 949-4200 or visit www.descansogardens.org.

Opposite: Geology is always on display in the Antelope Valley.

antelope valley

Who says you need to drive a few hours to get your desert fix? Lying just north of the San Gabriel Mountains, the Antelope Valley is the far western tip of the Mojave Desert and offers unique outdoor experiences that differ from those in the more Mediterranean climate near Los Angeles.

The major player here is the San Andreas Fault, which slices to the northwest, giving the northern San Gabriels their dramatic inclines and tearing up the ground near the geological oddities of Vasquez Rocks and Devils Punchbowl. Joshua trees grow here, and when the region gets decent winter rains, the desert floor absolutely explodes with wildflowers in the spring.

59 Vasquez Rocks

RATING/ DIFFICULTY	LOOP	ELEV GAIN/ HIGH POINT	SEASON
****/3	3.4 miles	312 feet/ 2626 feet	Nov–Apr

Map: USGS Agua Dulce; **Contact:** Vasquez Rocks Natural Area Park; **Notes:** Park open sunrise–sunset. Open to vehicles 8:00 AM–5:00 PM or 7:00 PM depending on the season.

You've probably seen these rocks before.

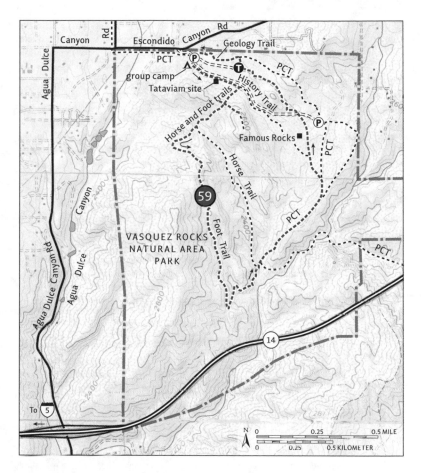

Dogs allowed on leash. Interpretive center open Tuesday–Sunday 8:00 AM to 4:00 PM. Group camping by reservation only; **GPS:** N 34.488044, W 118.318515

Hike through one of the most distinctive and recognizable rock formations in the world. Named for an infamous horse thief and/or Mexican freedom fighter, depending on your perspective, Vasquez Rocks has since been featured in countless films and television shows—most famously, perhaps, in the Star Trek episode "Arena," in which Captain Kirk fights a man in an ill-fitting lizard suit in what may be one of the worst fight scenes in television history.

GETTING THERE

From Interstate 5 just south of Santa Clarita, take the Antelope Valley Freeway (CA-14) toward Palmdale/Lancaster for 14.3 miles. Then take the Agua Dulce Canyon Road exit and head north. After a sharp right turn, the road becomes Escondido Canyon Road. The Vasquez Rocks Natural Area Park entrance is on your right in 0.4 mile. Drive past the ranger station and park at the moderately sized spillover lot near the center of the park for best access to the park's trails.

ON THE TRAIL

At the parking area, check the bulletin board on the east side of the lot for some pamphlets about the park's highlights and some very basic, mildly useful park maps. Head north from the parking area to hop onto the Pacific Crest Trail (PCT) and head west, back toward the park's entrance. In 0.2 mile, you'll meet up with the short Geology Trail, which highlights some of the area's unique earthquake history. Cross the entrance road at 0.3 mile and head south on the History Trail, passing through the group campsite as the massive "Famous Rocks" loom on the horizon. At 0.5 mile, take a very short spur trail to see some *morteros* (mortars embedded in the rocks used to grind acorns) and pictographs left from the region's ancient Tataviam people. At 0.6 mile, take a right onto the Horse and Foot trails to explore the park's western end, which is more rugged and much less trafficked than the area close to the main road.

At 0.7 mile, a short, prominent ridgeline provides brilliant views in both directions. Take the side trips and continue west. The Horse Trail diverges from the Foot Trail at about the mile mark. Follow the Foot Trail, which turns south at 1.2 miles and heads

through some beautiful grassland that's occasionally punctuated by oddly tilted and jagged rocks. This is especially gorgeous in the late winter and early spring, when the landscape is alive and verdant, and it's easy to imagine what it was like when Tiburcio Vasquez was hiding from Anglo posses here (minus the freeway, of course). This extremely pleasant stretch of trail hits an old road grade at 2 miles. Take a sharp left here, ignore the Horse Trail at 2.3 miles, and keep left at the three-way junction just beyond to head north on the PCT. At 2.8 miles, the PCT continues to the right on a faint footpath while an even more faint trail heads to the northeast. Stay to the left here to cross a field and end up at a large parking area right in front of the Famous Rocks—the largest and most impressive rock formations in the park. Scramble around and explore at your leisure, then follow the dirt road back to your car.

60 Antelope Valley California Poppy Reserve

RATING/ DIFFICULTY	LOOP	ELEV GAIN/ HIGH POINT	SEASON
*****/1	3.3 miles	222 feet/ 2934 feet	Mar–May

Maps: USGS Fairmont Butte, Lake Hughes, Del Sur, Little Buttes; **Contact:** Antelope Valley California Poppy Reserve State Natural Reserve; **Notes:** Park open sunrise–sunset. Parking fee required; **GPS:** N 34.731422, W 118.393821

Remember those never-ending poppy fields from The Wizard of Oz? *You can visit their real-life counterparts right here in the Antelope Valley. This otherwise nondescript patch of the western Mojave*

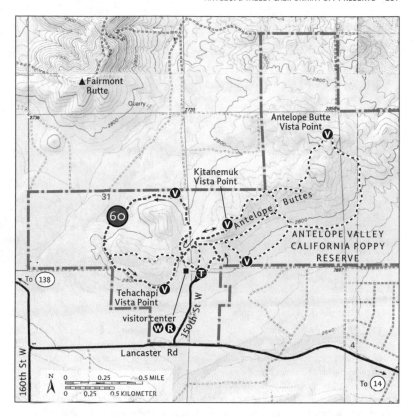

becomes a brilliant carpet of orange when the conditions are right and the state flower makes its annual appearance. Unlike their Ozian counterparts, Eschscholzia californica won't put you to sleep forever—they just make for phenomenal photographs.

GETTING THERE

From Interstate 5 just south of Santa Clarita, take CA-14 toward Palmdale/Lancaster. In 43.5 miles, take exit 44 for Avenue I. Turn left (west) and stay on this road as it changes names a few times, ultimately becoming

Lancaster Road. In 13.7 miles, enter the park by turning right onto 150th Street West. If the regional wildflowers are putting on a show, consider taking the 5 farther north to CA-138 east instead. Follow the 138 east for 14.5 miles, then turn right onto 245th Street Southwest. Follow this street for 11.6 miles as it changes names multiple times and eventually settles on Lancaster Road, then take a left onto 150th Street West. The trailhead is in 0.5 mile. The drive is longer and more remote, but passes through several stunning wildflower fields on the way.

The brilliant orange of California poppies is hard to appreciate in black and white.

ON THE TRAIL

Head to the visitor center first to find out where the best blooms in the park are. Be sure to pick up a brochure, which has a basic trail map as well as a nice guide to the many other native plants that may be putting on a show along with the poppies. There are a total of 7 miles of trails in the park, though you may omit some loops if nothing is blooming in those regions.

This route begins heading east from the visitor center. At 0.3 mile, keep left to close a southern loop. (An alternate, longer loop continues to the east to the Antelope Butte Vista Point and will add about 2.75 miles to the Kitanemuk Vista Point.) At the junction with the trail that heads directly north from the visitor center, head right and climb up to the Kitanemuk Vista Point, where you can soak in views of almost the entire park and

see which regions are worth trekking to. Backtrack to 1.2 miles and turn right (north) to loop around the southernmost of the Antelope Buttes in a figure-eight pattern. Since it's a bit farther away from the parking area, this part of the park tends to be a bit quieter and is a great place to spot some other flowers like red stem filaree, cream cups, Davy gilia, and owl's clover, which provide some nice contrast to the bright orange and yellow of the California poppies. Ignore the cutoff at 2.4 miles to complete the loop.

EXTENDING YOUR TRIP

An entry at a California State Park is good for the entire day at all other state parks charging the same or lower entry rates, so if the blooms are looking good at Saddleback Butte State Park (Hike 61), consider adding that trek to your itinerary!

CHASING FLOWERS

On the East Coast, throngs swamp quaint New England towns for a few weeks in the fall to grab snapshots of multicolored leaves on formerly quiet rolling hills. Here in Southern California, the same thing happens with wildflowers. So many variables can determine whether an annual wildflower show is a bust or a bonanza that, in many cases, it's not worth planning trips until you know for sure what the conditions may be. Thankfully, you don't have to drive all over the state to keep track of what's blooming. Beginning in early March, three websites do a fantastic job of compiling crowdsourced citizen science to predict where and when peak blooms will occur. The Theodore Payne Foundation runs its Wild Flower Hotline from March through May, providing and archiving weekly wildflower updates. See www.theodorepayne.org/education/wildflower-hotline or call (818) 768-3533. What's Blooming (www.smmflowers.org/whatsblooming) focuses on the Santa Monica Mountains and also has tons of resources for those looking to start identifying the blooms they see on the trail. And DesertUSA (www.desertusa.com/wildflo/wildupdates .html), as you'd expect, has a broader scope but covers Southern California as well as nearby desert parks like Anza-Borrego Desert State Park, Joshua Tree National Park, and Death Valley National Park.

61 Saddleback Butte

RATING/ DIFFICULTY	ROUNDTRIP	ELEV GAIN/ HIGH POINT	SEASON
*****/3	4.8 miles	969 feet/ 3649 feet	Jan–May

Map: USGS Hi Vista; **Contact:** Saddleback Butte State Park; **Notes:** Day-use area open sunrise–sunset. Visitor center open weekends 10:00 AM–3:00 PM. Dogs allowed only in picnic area, campground, and on the park road. Camping available first-come, first-served. $6 day-use fee; **GPS:** N 34.689234, W 117.823968

Trek through a beautiful Joshua tree woodland in the Mojave Desert with explosive wildflower displays in the spring and climb to a prominent butte with 360-degree views of the Antelope Valley. This is a must-see during peak bloom and can be combined with the nearby Antelope Valley California Poppy Reserve (Hike 60) if the blooms time out together.

GETTING THERE

From Interstate 5 just south of Santa Clarita, take CA-14 toward Palmdale/Lancaster for 29.5 miles. Take exit 30 toward Pearblossom Highway (CA-138). In 8.4 miles, turn left onto 87th Street East and in 0.6 mile, veer right to continue on 90th Street East. In 4.6 miles, turn right onto East Avenue O, then left onto 150th Street East in 6.1 miles, and right onto East Avenue J in 5.1 miles. In 0.1 mile, the northern entrance to Saddleback Butte State Park will be on your right.

ON THE TRAIL

From the park entrance and fee station, head south on the sidewalk nature trail, gazing at the distant San Gabriels and the closer Joshua trees along the trail. In about

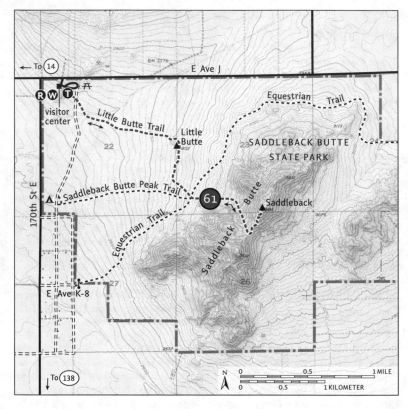

400 feet, look for the Little Butte Trail, which leaves the nature trail heading east through some expansive fields of yellow coreopsis. When those flowers are at their peak, the beige desert floor becomes a brilliant gold that can go on for miles. Careful bloom-spotters will also notice white dune evening primroses and purple Davy gilias spicing up the mix. The trail here meanders through some beautiful (and surprisingly large) groves of Joshua trees—a slightly closer and significantly less crowded option for fans of the fancy yucca than its namesake

national park. Cross the dirt road at 0.1 mile and continue east, the now sandier trail lined with desert dandelions, lupines, and the wonderfully named Fremont's pincushions.

Top the small bump of Little Butte at the 1-mile mark to follow the sometimes faint footpath south and at 1.5 miles join the Saddleback Butte Peak Trail. Ignore the wider Equestrian Trail and continue east.

Here, the trail leaves the wildflower-covered desert floor and climbs through some California sagebrush and Mormon tea on a rockier, somewhat rougher trail

Enjoy Joshua trees and wildflower displays at Saddleback Butte State Park.

than you've been on so far. There are a few places where you'll have to look for cairns and maybe do some light scrambling before a small flat at 2.2 miles provides your first unobstructed views of the San Gabriels to the south. From here, it's another steep, rocky 0.2 mile to the summit, which contains two USGS markers and plenty of amazing boulders to perch on as you drink in the beauty of the panoramic desert in all directions. Retrace your steps to the trailhead.

EXTENDING YOUR TRIP

If the flowers are blooming at the Antelope Valley California Poppy Reserve (Hike 60), I strongly recommend doing both hikes on the same trip. The entrance fee at the poppy reserve is more expensive, but go there first and you won't have to pay a fee at Saddleback Butte. Call ahead to check bloom reports at the poppy reserve by calling (661) 724-1180.

62 Devils Punchbowl

RATING/ DIFFICULTY	LOOP	ELEV GAIN/ HIGH POINT	SEASON
*****/2	1.3 miles	323 feet/ 4745 feet	Year-round

Map: USGS Valyermo; **Contact:** Devils Punchbowl Natural Area and Angeles National Forest/San Gabriel Mountains National Monument, Santa Clara/Mojave

The Devils Punchbowl is an incredible place to explore.

Rivers Ranger District; **Notes:** Devils Punchbowl open sunrise–sunset. Visitor center hours Tuesday–Sunday, 9:00 AM–5:00 PM. Dogs allowed on leash; **GPS:** N 34.413933, W 117.858743

This easy nature trail descends into the shockingly angular oddness of the Devils Punchbowl, a formation just north of the San Gabriel Mountains where it looks like the rocks are exploding out of the ground. A variety of nature center programs make this a great stop for a family hike, and there are longer hike options nearby for those looking for a more strenuous outdoor experience.

GETTING THERE

From Interstate 5 just south of Santa Clarita, take CA-14 toward Palmdale/Lancaster for 29.5 miles. Take exit 30 toward Pearblossom Highway (CA-138). Stay on Pearblossom Highway for 14 miles and take a right onto 131st Street East/Longview Road (County Road N6). Drive south for 2.2 miles and turn left onto Fort Tejon Road. In 0.3 mile, take a right back onto 131st Street East/Longview Road (CR N6). In 2.3 miles, turn left onto Tumbleweed Road (CR N6) and follow the signs to Devils Punchbowl Natural Area, reaching the parking area in 2.6 miles.

ON THE TRAIL

Stop inside the nature center for a free, self-guided tour brochure and map, then head east toward the edge of the Punchbowl formation. For a short detour, take the Piñon Pathway to the north for a 0.2-mile mini-loop that provides an excellent introduction to the different plant communities in this transition zone between the Mojave Desert and the piñon (sometimes Anglicized as "pinyon") pine forest of the nearby San Gabriels. Plants found in the transition zone can also be found in many of the north slopes and at higher elevations of the nearby San Gabriels,

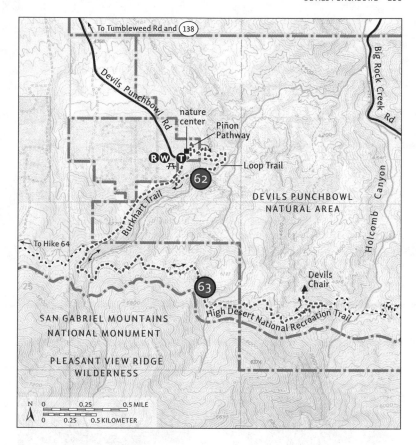

including its namesake piñon pines, mountain mahogany, bigberry manzanita, and basin sagebrush—the high desert cousin of the California sagebrush.

Return to the Loop Trail and continue east along the rim, stopping to enjoy the tilted rock slabs standing in front of the San Gabriel Mountains to the south. Ancient streams and rivers flowing from the north and west deposited these strips of beige about thirteen million years ago, while the

very active faults in the neighborhood lifted the San Gabriel Mountains, exposing the old alluvial deposits and the softer ground to erosion. Along the trail, you'll see countless examples of these geologic forces in action, from huge slabs of parallel rock to perfectly spherical boulders to proto-hoodoos and even a handful of small arches. The trail skims the bottom of the canyon floor at 0.6 mile. If you're feeling adventurous, a number of use-trails depart from the established trail, letting you scramble and explore the bottom of the Punchbowl itself. (Just make sure you remember where you came from—that terrain gets disorienting very quickly!)

If you stick to the Loop Trail, it will hug the edge of the canyon and slowly climb back up to the nature center. At 1.2 miles, keep right at the junction with the Burkhart Trail to return to the nature center through a few established picnic areas.

EXTENDING YOUR TRIP

For a moderate day hike addition to this trip and a different perspective on the Devils Punchbowl, keep left at the Burkhart Trail and head to the Devils Chair (Hike 63). A much tougher trail to Burkhart Saddle (Hike 64) is a full-day option. The nature center also leads San Andreas Fault tours every Sunday at 1:00 PM as well as moonlight hikes and telescope programs through the year.

63 Devils Chair

RATING/ DIFFICULTY	ROUNDTRIP	ELEV GAIN/ HIGH POINT	SEASON
****/3	7.3 miles	581 feet/ 5332 feet	Year-round

Map: USGS Valyermo; **Contact:** Devils Punchbowl Natural Area and Angeles National Forest/San Gabriel Mountains National Monument, Santa Clara/Mojave Rivers Ranger District; **Notes:** Devils Punchbowl open sunrise–sunset. Visitor center hours Tuesday–Sunday, 9:00 AM–5:00 PM. Dogs allowed on leash; **GPS:** N 34.413918, W 117.859167

The scope of the Punchbowl is best appreciated from the Devils Chair.

A moderate trek around one of the most unusual and breathtaking natural landmarks in the region, this route to the precarious perch of the Devils Chair gives you an unparalleled view of what happens to the ground near one of the world's most active seismic zones.

GETTING THERE

From Interstate 5 just south of Santa Clarita, take CA-14 toward Palmdale/Lancaster for 29.5 miles. Take exit 30 toward Pearblossom Highway (CA-138). Continue on the Pearblossom Highway for 14 miles and take a right onto 131st Street East/Longview Road (County Road N6). Drive south for 2.2 miles and turn left onto Fort Tejon Road. In 0.3 mile, take a right back onto 131st Street East/Longview Road (CR N6). In 2.3 miles, turn left onto Tumbleweed Road (CR N6) and follow the signs to Devils Punchbowl Natural Area, reaching the parking area in 2.6 miles.

ON THE TRAIL

From the trailhead near the visitor center, hike south on the Burkhart Trail from the southeastern corner of the parking lot. The majority of the gentle elevation gain on this route is in the first mile. Stay on the main Burkhart Trail, ignoring the old access roads and use-trails that pop up along the way. At the 1-mile mark, leave the Burkhart Trail by heading left toward the Devils Chair and South Fork Camp on the High Desert National Recreation Trail.

Here, the trail becomes a beautiful single-track as it skims the border communities between the high desert below and the subalpine forest above. To your north, the strange, angular rock slabs of the Devils Punchbowl stand as Tim Burton–esque evidence of the lock-and-release movement of the tectonic plates below the ground, while to the south the massive forested peaks of the Pleasant View Ridge stand watch—often dusted with snow even into the warmer months. The trail travels over a few bumps but remains relatively level until just before mile 3, where it descends some tight switchbacks on the western limit of Holcomb Canyon. At 3.5 miles, stay to the left as the trail enters a fenced-in area that protects hikers from falling off the extremely narrow, rocky ledge that makes up the Devils Chair.

Views of the Punchbowl are phenomenal from here, and if you time your trek just right you may be able to catch the low winter sun beaming almost directly through Holcomb Canyon near the end of the day. Hike back the way you came—and keep your fingers crossed that the San Andreas stays put until you can get out of there.

64 Burkhart Saddle

RATING/ DIFFICULTY	ROUNDTRIP	ELEV GAIN/ HIGH POINT	SEASON
****/5	14.1 miles	2344 feet/ 6961 feet	May–Oct

Maps: USGS Valyermo, Juniper Hills; **Contact:** Devils Punchbowl Natural Area and Angeles National Forest/San Gabriel Mountains National Monument, Santa Clara/ Mojave Rivers Ranger District; **Notes:** Devils Punchbowl open sunrise–sunset. Visitor center hours Tuesday–Sunday, 9:00 AM– 5:00 PM. Dogs allowed on leash. Wilderness permit not required unless your group exceeds twenty-five people; **GPS:** N 34.413918, W 117.859167

Burkhart Saddle is a window into the rugged terrain of the high San Gabriels.

  A grueling trek from the floor of the high desert to an impressive gateway into the high San Gabriel Mountains, this full-day adventure is a demanding and rewarding way to spend time in the wilderness. Along the way, you'll hike through several plant communities and soak in views of the broad horizon of the Antelope Valley.

GETTING THERE

From Interstate 5 just south of Santa Clarita, take CA-14 toward Palmdale/Lancaster for 29.5 miles. Take exit 30 toward Pearblossom Highway (CA-138). Continue on the Pearblossom Highway for 14 miles and take a right onto 131st Street East/Longview Road (County Road N6). Drive south for 2.2 miles and turn left onto Fort Tejon Road. In 0.3 mile, take a right back onto 131st Street East/Longview Road (CR N6). In 2.3 miles, turn left onto Tumbleweed Road (CR N6) and follow the signs to Devils Punchbowl Natural Area, reaching the parking area in 2.6 miles.

ON THE TRAIL

From the trailhead near the visitor center, hike south on the Burkhart Trail, ignoring the old access roads and use-trail. At the 1-mile mark, stay to the right to continue on the High Desert National Recreation Trail/Burkhart Trail to Burkhart Saddle. This route

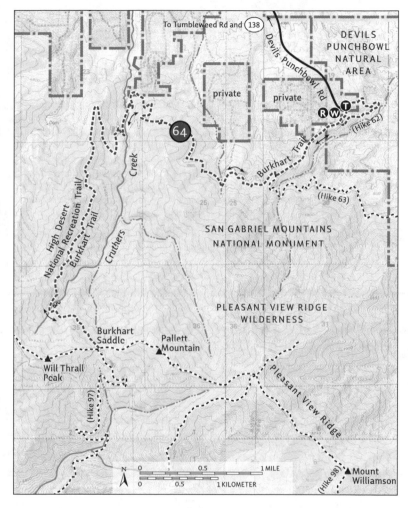

To Tumbleweed Rd and (138)

Devils Punchbowl Rd

DEVILS
PUNCHBOWL
NATURAL
AREA

private

private

R W T

(Hike 62)

64

Burkhart Trail

(Hike 63)

High Desert
National Recreation Trail/
Burkhart Trail

Cruthers

Creek

Dam

SAN GABRIEL MOUNTAINS
NATIONAL MONUMENT

PLEASANT VIEW RIDGE
WILDERNESS

Burkhart
Saddle

Pallett
Mountain

Will Thrall
Peak

(Hike 97)

Pleasant View Ridge

N

0   0.5   1 MILE

0   0.5   1 KILOMETER

(Hike 98) ▲ Mount
Williamson

takes a rather meandering approach to the saddle by following a ridgeline to the west and almost as far north as the trailhead itself. Although it looks like there might have been a closer access point, private land prevents a shorter trek here. At 3.5 miles, the trail passes an old windmill and dips down to cross Cruthers Creek, about 180 feet below the trailhead's elevation.

From here on out, it's all uphill with very few breaks along the way. As you ascend, you'll be traveling through several different plant communities. By the end of this hike, including your drive to the trailhead, you'll have passed through Joshua trees and California junipers, then into piñon pine woodland. Desert chaparral is visible in the Antelope Valley and makes some appearances at higher elevations, while the canyon floors have thirstier plants like cottonwoods and willows in the washes. As you climb up toward the saddle, you'll spot Coulter, Jeffrey, and ponderosa pines.

The trail passes a small spring near 6.6 miles, and you'll reach Burkhart Saddle just past the 7-mile mark. Pleasant View Ridge Wilderness opens up in all directions, and if you still have energy left you can continue up some even more challenging use-trail routes to the nearby peaks. Or just soak in the views, breathe the crisp mountain air, and return the way you came.

EXTENDING YOUR TRIP

To the west of Burkhart Saddle, a faint, extremely steep use-trail climbs up to Will Thrall Peak and is described in Hike 97. You may follow that route or climb an even steeper, less-defined trail to the east up to Pallett Mountain, which follows Pleasant View Ridge to Mount Williamson (Hike 98) and down to Islip Saddle.

Opposite: Reliably flowing Sturtevant Falls is one of the many delights that have lured Angelenos into the San Gabriels since the Great Hiking Era.

san gabriel foothills
and front range

Did you know L.A. has a 970-square-mile mountain range in its backyard with five federally protected wilderness areas and a brand-new 346,000-acre national monument? It's okay—a lot of Angelenos don't know that either, but thankfully the tide is turning.

The San Gabriel Mountains are an absolute treasure to outdoorsy Southern Californians and the foothills and Front Range—generally speaking, the low peaks and hills on the southwestern part of the range from around five thousand to six thousand feet in elevation—have some of the most popular and breathtaking hikes in the Los Angeles region. Due to their proximity to the foothill cities, this part of the range has been more developed than other sections. The human history here is astounding, from the Tongva and Serrano Native Americans to prospectors and pioneers to the famed wilderness resorts of the Great Hiking Era. Peaceful canyons, wild rivers and arroyos, and challenging peaks await hikers of all ability levels here in the gateway to the mountains. Get ready to fall in love.

65 Placerita Canyon

RATING/ DIFFICULTY	LOOP	ELEV GAIN/ HIGH POINT	SEASON
****/4	6.9 miles	1655 feet/ 3183 feet	Year-round

Map: USGS San Fernando; **Contact:** Placerita Canyon State Park and Placerita Canyon Nature Center; **Notes:** Park open sunrise–sunset. Nature center and parking lot open Tuesday–Sunday, 9:00 AM–5:00 PM. Dogs allowed on leash. Group camping by reservation only; **GPS:** N 34.377813, W 118.467873

Climbing up the firebreak at Placerita Canyon

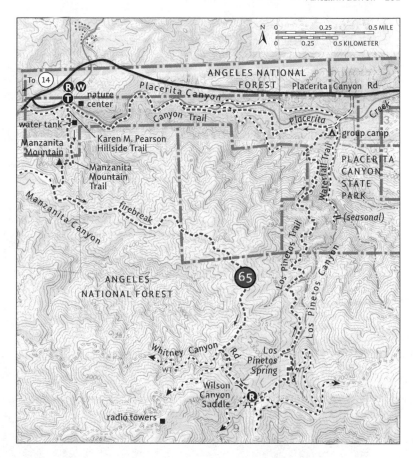

This unique loop is like two hikes in one. The first half is a challenging, shadeless crawl up steep firebreaks with stunning views of the rugged terrain while the second half meanders through the creek-fed riparian woodlands in Los Pinetos Canyon. This trail also features old ranch land, one of the best nature centers in the region, and the site of California's first gold rush.

GETTING THERE

From Interstate 5 just south of Santa Clarita, take CA-14 toward Palmdale/Lancaster for 2.6 miles. Take exit 3 for Placerita Canyon Road. Take a right and stay on Placerita Canyon Road heading east for about 1.5 miles until you see the entrance on your right to Placerita Canyon Natural Area, where you'll find a sizable, partially paved parking lot.

ON THE TRAIL

Consider stopping in at the excellent nature center before you kick off your hike, both to get a little more info on the terrain you'll be hiking through and to pick up a helpful map. There are a *lot* of trails in this park and most of them converge near the trailhead. For this hike, head south from the parking area and cross Placerita Creek to get to the main trailhead. Look for the short but steep incline of the Karen M. Pearson Hillside Trail and at 0.1 mile you'll hit a water tank with some benches nearby. Continue on the Hillside Trail to the Manzanita Mountain Trail. At 0.5 mile, follow an optional use-trail up to the bump of generously named Manzanita Mountain if you're so inclined; otherwise, continue hiking south. The Manzanita Mountain Trail ends at a firebreak at 0.7 mile. Follow this steep, rough route on a series of nearly straight ups and downs over the undulating SoCal terrain. When you see radio towers to the south you're almost done.

At 2.5 miles, stay left at the junction with Whitney Canyon Road, then ignore the spur trails on your right, and at 2.9 miles you'll be greeted by the small picnic area and well-maintained outhouse at Wilson Canyon Saddle. Look for the sign for the Los Pinetos Trail on the north side of the road and get ready for a drastic change in scenery as it makes an immediate descent into a shaded canopy of oaks. At 3.2 miles, pass a spring with a small water tank on the side of the trail and ignore the old ranch roads heading east. Continue north on the trail, ignoring another old road grade heading west at 3.4 miles, and by 5.2 miles you'll be walking through some gorgeous grassy oak woodland near a few group campsites. If it's been a wet year, consider taking the 1.5-mile (roundtrip) side trip on the Waterfall Trail for a view of a small, ephemeral waterfall; otherwise, stay left at the group campsite to head west on the Canyon Trail for a pleasant, mostly shaded trip back to the nature center and trailhead.

THE OAK OF THE GOLDEN DREAM

Many history books will tell you the first gold rush in California was at Sutter's Mill in 1848, but this was neither the first gold strike in California nor the first gold rush. Six years earlier, the Mexican mineralogist Francisco Lopez was napping under an oak tree on his family's rancho when he dreamt he was floating on a pool of gold. When he woke, he pulled some wild onions from the ground, noticed gold flakes on the roots, and confirmed his find. Unlike the '48 strike, this one was kept mostly secret and mostly within Mexico—probably because there wasn't a loudmouthed American newspaperman running through the streets of the largest nearby city yelling, "Gold! Gold! Gold from Placerita Canyon!" like there was in San Francisco. And yet L.A. gets the reputation as the city of shameless self-promoters.

A small rush did draw a few thousand settlers to the area to mine the shiny stuff, though. During the Mexican-American War, the rancho owners destroyed the mine to prevent Americans from cashing in on its riches, but the oak tree where Lopez fatefully plucked some onions from the dirt still stands as the Oak of the Golden Dream, California Historic Landmark No. 168.

EXTENDING YOUR TRIP

Placerita Canyon State Park has several short nature walks and interpretive trails as well as the longer route described here. Consider adding on the short Botany and Nature trails, which head behind the nature center and parking areas to the historic Walker Cabin—a remnant of the area's ranching days—and a trip to the Oak of the Golden Dream.

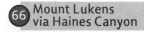

66 Mount Lukens via Haines Canyon

RATING/ DIFFICULTY	LOOP	ELEV GAIN/ HIGH POINT	SEASON
****/4	8.4 miles	2937 feet/ 5066 feet	Year-round

Maps: USGS Sunland, Condor Peak; **Contact:** Angeles National Forest, Los Angeles River Ranger District; **Notes:** Adventure Pass required at trailhead. Dogs allowed on leash, **GPS:** N 34.2596820, W 118.2780830

 This route is a tough, challenging climb to the highest point within Los Angeles city limits. You'll need to pay attention to follow this trail—and you may need to take your time on some sections that are in need of a little TLC, but the views and the sense of accomplishment are worth the effort.

GETTING THERE

From Interstate 210 in Tujunga, take exit 16 for Lowell Avenue and travel north. Continue until the road ends, and turn left onto Day Street. In 0.8 mile turn right onto Haines Canyon Avenue and continue until the end of the road in 0.4 mile. There is a gated parking area (with rough road), or you can park on the street about half a block south of the gate. If you park inside the gate, be sure to display your Adventure Pass.

ON THE TRAIL

Head east on the dirt Haines Canyon Motorway as it passes a small lake behind a flood check dam and continues to climb

Spanish bayonets make a rough section of trail on Mount Lukens a little tougher to navigate.

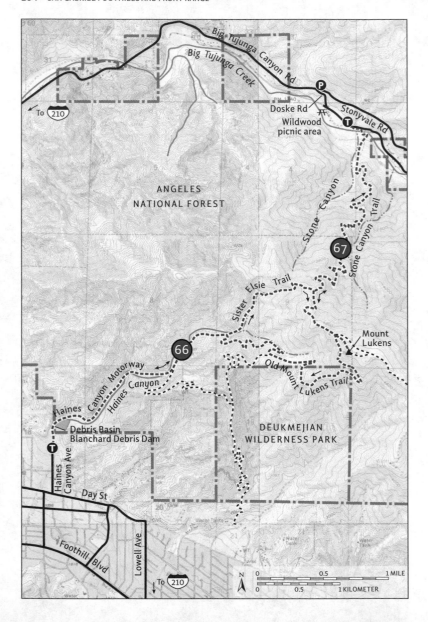

past several smaller dams, built to reduce the intensity of debris flows during heavy rains. Follow this road until the three-way junction at 1.3 miles. The road heads to the south, offering an easy if long (and not terribly interesting) route to the summit. Instead, stay to the left to follow a narrow single-track trail as it climbs through shaded woodlands. Stay quiet and you may hear the sound of Haines Canyon Creek below you. At 1.9 miles, the trail splits at a formerly signed junction. To your right, the Old Mount Lukens Trail will be your return route. To the left, the Sister Elsie Trail offers a tough, overgrown, steep climb to the summit.

The Sister Elsie Trail is a remnant of Mount Lukens's past—the peak used to be called Sister Elsie Peak in honor of a Roman Catholic nun from La Crescenta who tended an orphanage, but in 1918 the name went to Pasadena's Theodore Lukens, a former supervisor of the Angeles National Forest and enthusiastic self-taught botanist who helped found the reforestation nursery at Henninger Flats (Hike 83). At times, the Sister Elsie Trail seems as distant a memory as its namesake—often overgrown and tough to spot as it crawls up the side of the mountain. At 2.8 miles, stay straight at the junction with the Stone Canyon Trail (Hike 67) and head toward the radio towers that mark Lukens's summit, which you'll reach at 3.7 miles.

Backtrack to 3.9 miles and take the Old Mount Lukens Trail south. At 5.5 miles, look for a faint trail on the right-hand side of the fire road. This surprisingly beautiful stretch of trail will return you to the Sister Elsie Trail (and past an old VW Bug that got stranded in the canyon). At the Sister Elsie Trail, turn left to reach Haines Canyon Motorway and the trailhead.

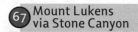

67 Mount Lukens via Stone Canyon

RATING/ DIFFICULTY	ROUNDTRIP	ELEV GAIN/ HIGH POINT	SEASON
****/4	8.6 miles	3266 feet/ 5066 feet	Year-round

Map: USGS Condor Peak; **Contact:** Angeles National Forest, Los Angeles River Ranger District; **Notes:** Adventure Pass required to park at trailhead. Dogs allowed on leash. Weather conditions may make crossing Big Tujunga Creek difficult or impossible; **GPS:** N 34.294104, W 118.239633

  A tough and steep alternate route to the top of the highest point in the city of Los Angeles—this time from the north—this hike is slightly more shaded than the Haines Canyon approach (Hike 66) and the trail is in better shape, but it requires crossing a sizable creek and has more overall elevation gain. In fact, many hikers preparing for even tougher climbs like Mount Whitney will train on this route.

GETTING THERE

From Interstate 210 in Sunland, take exit 11 for Sunland Boulevard and head east on Sunland Boulevard/Foothill Boulevard. In 0.7 mile, turn left onto Oro Vista Avenue. In 0.9 mile this becomes Big Tujunga Canyon Road and in 5.4 miles, look for the signed Wildwood picnic area on your right at Doske Road. Park in the picnic area or on the road if the gate is locked. If you park in the picnic area, display your Adventure Pass.

ON THE TRAIL

One of the toughest parts about this hike is finding the actual trail. Head to the far

Tujunga Canyon as seen from the Stone Canyon Trail

southeastern end of the Wildwood picnic area and walk the banks of Big Tujunga Creek. Your target is the east side of the wide, rocky wash of Stone Canyon across the creek to your south—but there isn't really one easy way to get over there. Depending on the time of year, the creek may be a tiny trickle, a series of meandering ribbons, or a raging torrent. Find the path of least resistance across the water and keep hiking east until you see the established Stone Canyon Trail heading south.

Follow this route as it hugs the east bank of the broad wash. At about 0.8 mile, the trail switchbacks away from the wash and begins its long, relentless climb upward. This area was hit by wildfires in 2002 and 2009, and much of the vegetation still has visible scars, but the chaparral is recovering nicely with chamise, buckwheat, ceanothus, and sagebrush sprawling out in its former territories. At 3.4 miles, stay to the left at the junction with the Sister Elsie Trail and straight at the junction with the fire road at 4.1 miles to hit the radio-towered summit of Mount Lukens. Enjoy the sweeping views of the foothill cities and the San Gabriel Mountains and return the way you came.

68 Trail Canyon Falls

RATING/ DIFFICULTY	ROUNDTRIP	ELEV GAIN/ HIGH POINT	SEASON
****/3	3.6 miles	637 feet/ 2511 feet	Year-round

Map: USGS Sunland; **Contact:** Angeles National Forest, Los Angeles River Ranger District; **Notes:** Adventure Pass required to park at trailhead. Dogs allowed on leash; **GPS:** N 34.308118, W 118.252977

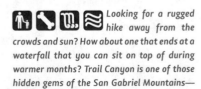 *Looking for a rugged hike away from the crowds and sun? How about one that ends at a waterfall that you can sit on top of during warmer months? Trail Canyon is one of those hidden gems of the San Gabriel Mountains—*

one whose minor inconveniences mean you can feel like you have the entire mountain range to yourself.

GETTING THERE

From Interstate 210 in Sunland, take exit 11 for Sunland Boulevard and head east on Sunland Boulevard/Foothill Boulevard. In 0.7 mile, turn left onto Oro Vista Avenue, which becomes Big Tujunga Canyon Road in 0.9 mile. In about 5.3 miles, turn left onto Trail Canyon Road (dirt) and stay right at the first fork to descend into Trail Canyon. Park at

the gated lot near the Forest Service cabins. The road is rough but passable by two-wheel drive passenger cars.

ON THE TRAIL

Look for the signs pointing to the trail amid the trees at the shaded trailhead and parking area and pass the informational sign and register. The trail in the repetitively named Trail Canyon follows an old access road that's been left to disintegrate into a trail. A sign near the trailhead stating the trail is not maintained will give you a sense of what to

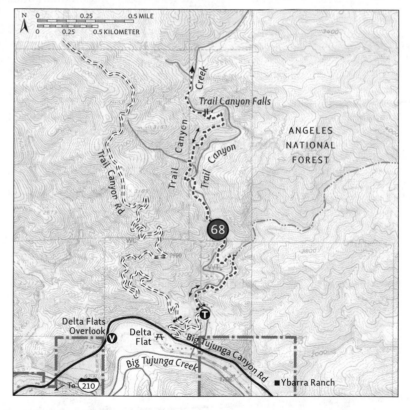

During the warm, dry months, hikers can sit right on the edge of the Trail Canyon Falls.

expect. This route ducks down to the canyon floor and crosses Trail Canyon Creek several times before starting a steep climb up its western slope at 1.1 miles.

The 2009 Station Fire hit this part of the San Gabriels badly, and where there used to be shade making this climb a bit easier, there is now just open, low chaparral. What we lost in shade we've gained in views, though—the perspective on this north–south stretch of the canyon is truly stunning. At 1.6 miles the trail makes a sharp turn to the west, providing your first view of forty-foot Trail Canyon Falls. At 1.7 miles there is a steep, slippery, exposed use-trail you can take to get to the base of the falls, or stay on the main path and you'll reach the top of the falls in no time. Just a short distance upstream is a nice natural swimming hole, too. The trail continues beyond the falls, but it gets much tougher. Save that adventure until trail crews can repair the route to Condor Peak. Hike back the way you came in.

EXTENDING YOUR TRIP

If you're in the mood to continue, the diminutive Lazy Lucas Trail Camp is about a mile farther up the canyon, and the remains of the slightly larger Tom Lucas Trail Camp are 2.3 miles from the waterfall. Both are heavily fire-damaged. This section of trail was overgrown before the Station Fire and is even tougher going these days. A longer route beyond the trail camps to towering Condor Peak has all but vanished in the post-fire undergrowth, meaning it will likely be some time before hikers find themselves atop its rocky summit from this canyon.

69 Fox Mountain

RATING/ DIFFICULTY	ROUNDTRIP	ELEV GAIN/ HIGH POINT	SEASON
****/5	11.3 miles	2998 feet/ 5033 feet	Year-round (best Nov–Apr)

Map: USGS Condor Peak; **Contact:** Angeles National Forest, Los Angeles River Ranger District; **Notes:** Adventure Pass required to park at trailhead. Dogs allowed on leash; **GPS:** N 34.287633, W 118.224890

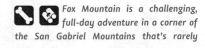 *Fox Mountain is a challenging, full-day adventure in a corner of the San Gabriel Mountains that's rarely*

visited by most hikers. This long but for the most part straightforward route climbs from Big Tujunga Canyon to a prominent peak overlooking some of the most rugged terrain in the San Gabriel Mountains. You may want to pack your trekking poles for the final ascent on this one.

GETTING THERE

From Interstate 210 in Sunland, take exit 11 for Sunland Boulevard and head east on Sunland Boulevard/Foothill Boulevard. In 0.7 mile, turn left onto Oro Vista Avenue. After 0.9 mile, continue on Big Tujunga Canyon Road for 6.7 miles. Park on the side of the

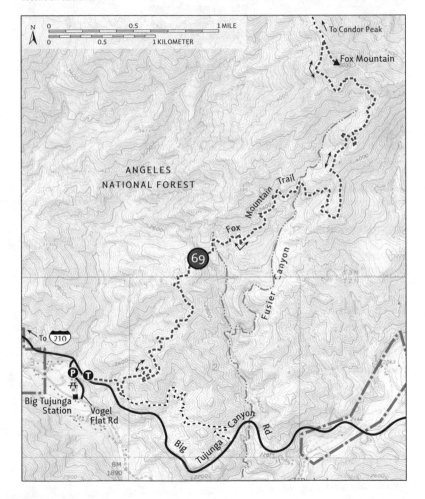

A lush section of the Fox Mountain Trail, near a seasonal arroyo

road just past Vogel Flat Road. The trailhead is on the north side of the road across from a small dirt pullout, but can be very difficult to spot. At mile marker 4.5 on the north side of the road, look for what appears to be a nondescript drainage ditch covered by scrub and chaparral. There will be a small opening in the brush here, and that's your trailhead!

ON THE TRAIL

When you find the opening in the brush it's pretty obvious, but don't feel bad about having to search for it—many a hiker has stumbled around here searching for it longer than they'd like to admit, this author included. The trail parallels Big Tujunga Canyon Road for the first 0.3 mile, then it emerges from the brush at another unmarked junction. While the trail heading east seems more heavily traveled, the actual Fox Mountain Trail takes a sharp left and heads north.

That's the end of this trail's trickery for a while; stay on the single-track trail as it leaves the shade behind. The looming figure of Fox Mountain and the long ridge that connects it to Condor Peak to the northwest are often right ahead of you, but very distant. If you don't want to think about how far you have to go, just enjoy the lonely peaks and canyons on this trail's gentle climb. At 2.9 miles, a pocket of lush greenery (depending on the strength of the rainy season) surrounds a small arroyo. The welcome shade makes this a nice place for a snack, too.

The trail loops around the north end of Fusier Canyon and crosses the south face of Fox Mountain at 5 miles. At 5.5 miles, you'll reach the rocky ridge between Fox and Condor. Look for a steep use-trail to your right and make the final push.

Soak in the spectacular views from this lonely, rocky summit before returning the way you came.

 Switzer Falls

RATING/ DIFFICULTY	ROUNDTRIP	ELEV GAIN/ HIGH POINT	SEASON
****/2	3.6 miles	362 feet/ 3147 feet	Year-round

Maps: USGS Condor Peak, Pasadena; **Contact:** Angeles National Forest, Los Angeles River Ranger District; **Notes:** Adventure Pass to park at trailhead required. Dogs allowed on leash; **GPS:** N 34.266346, W 118.144045

An easy and popular hike to one of the most visited waterfalls in the Los Angeles area, the trail to Switzer Falls also passes an expansive, shaded picnic area and the historic grounds of the first wilderness resort in the San Gabriel Mountains.

GETTING THERE
From Interstate 210 in La Cañada Flintridge, take exit 20 toward the Angeles Crest Highway (CA-2) and follow it for 9.8 miles. Pass the Clear Creek Information Center, then take a right on the Switzer Truck Trail. There is an often-crowded parking lot at the bottom of the canyon near the picnic areas, as well as two overflow lots along the way. Display your Adventure Pass.

ON THE TRAIL
The first section of the hike is on a paved section of the Gabrielino Trail heading southwest along the Arroyo Seco through the usually fairly busy picnic area. There are a few side spurs to the various picnic sites, but as the pavement turns to a dirt road and eventually a single-track trail, you'll leave the barbecues behind and soon be hopping

Bear Canyon is a lovely place to explore.

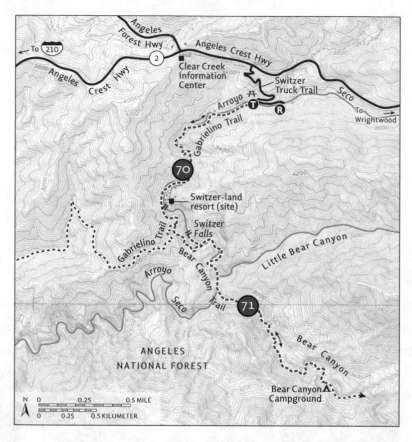

boulders in the creek bed. At 1.1 miles, stay to the right to cross the arroyo again and begin crawling out of the canyon's shade. While climbing, be sure to look across the canyon toward the site of Commodore Perry Switzer's famous "Switzer-land" wilderness resort, founded in 1884. Directly across the canyon from the trail here was a gorgeous stone chapel built in 1924 overlooking a cascade. It's all gone now, but you may be able to spot some of the stone arches on the slopes.

At 1.3 miles, stay left to continue on the Bear Canyon Trail and enjoy some of the most spectacular views of the Arroyo Seco a hiker can see. The scrub and chaparral were hit hard by the Station Fire in 2009 but are bouncing back nicely. At 1.7 miles, the trail switchbacks down to the shaded canyon floor. Keep left here and you'll reach the base of two-tiered Switzer Falls at 1.8 miles. Depending on the water levels, there may be a nice swimming hole just above the falls.

Enjoy a soak or just the cool of the shaded canyon and return the way you came.

EXTENDING YOUR TRIP

Adventurous swimmers can climb above Switzer Falls on use-trails to an even larger swimming hole and—with more effort (and probably more swimming than hiking)—even the base of the larger falls just south of Switzer-land. Do not attempt to climb up that waterfall, though—the rock is extremely loose and many an overeager hiker has had to be rescued or taken out on a stretcher. If the waterfall trip isn't enough mileage for you, consider hiking farther down Bear Canyon to a remote backcountry trail camp (Hike 71).

71 Bear Canyon

RATING/ DIFFICULTY	ROUNDTRIP	ELEV GAIN/ HIGH POINT	SEASON
****/3	6.8 miles	500 feet/ 3147 feet	Year-round

Maps: USGS Condor Peak, Pasadena; **Contact:** Angeles National Forest, Los Angeles River Ranger District; **Notes:** Adventure Pass required. Dogs allowed on leash; **GPS:** N 34.266346, W 118.144045

Love the experience of hiking the Arroyo Seco to Switzer Falls but want a little more solitude and privacy? This route travels deeper along

One of many excellent swimming holes in Bear Canyon (following a good rainy season, of course)

the Arroyo Seco and into Bear Canyon, leaving the crowds at Switzer Falls a distant memory as it passes fish-filled pools and swimming holes. Bring your sleeping bag and boulder hop all the way to the remote Bear Canyon Campground to really get in touch with the Front Range's canyon country.

GETTING THERE
From Interstate 210 in La Cañada Flintridge, take exit 20 toward the Angeles Crest Highway (CA-2) and follow it for 9.8 miles. Pass the Clear Creek Information Center, then take a right on the Switzer Truck Trail. There is an often-crowded parking lot at the bottom of the canyon near the picnic areas, as well as two overflow lots along the way. Display your Adventure Pass.

ON THE TRAIL
Follow the route for Switzer Falls (Hike 70). At 1.3 miles—or after you've visited the falls—continue south along the Arroyo Seco. Although Arroyo Seco means "dry creek" in Spanish, here in its narrow, upper reaches there's almost always water flowing, with sycamores, alders, and live oaks providing shade. The 2009 Station Fire caused a lot of damage in this region, but the relatively ample water supply means it's mending faster than other areas—although the farther down into the canyons you hike, the more often you'll have to duck under or hop over downed trees and other debris.

Pass a series of deep pools that are perfect for swimming (or fishing!) after a good rainy season. At 2.2 miles, keep left to leave the banks of the arroyo and enter Bear Canyon. The trail sticks close to the canyon wall here, but there are plenty of places to stop and enjoy the white noise of the rushing water (keeping in mind that good water

flow is a bit less dependable in this tributary canyon). By 3.4 miles you'll reach the open clearing of Bear Canyon Campground—the perfect place to unroll that sleeping bag for the night or maybe just eat a nice lunch and hike back the way you came in.

72 Dawn Mine Loop

RATING/ DIFFICULTY	LOOP	ELEV GAIN/ HIGH POINT	SEASON
****/5	5.9 miles	1505 feet/ 3602 feet	Year-round

Maps: USGS Pasadena, Mount Wilson; **Contact:** Angeles National Forest, Los Angeles River Ranger District; **Notes:** Adventure Pass required at trailhead. Chaney Trail gate open 6:00 AM–8:00 PM; **GPS:** N 34.214811, W 118.147712

A mostly bushwhacking and boulder-hopping route in Millard Canyon to the site of the Dawn Mine and back out along sections of the historic Mount Lowe Railway, this canyon hike is tougher than its distance would lead you to believe. Budget plenty of extra time for routefinding—and prepare yourself for one of the most epic days you'll have in the San Gabriels.

GETTING THERE
From Interstate 210 in Altadena, take exit 23 for Lincoln Avenue and head north. In just under 2 miles, turn right onto Loma Alta Drive and in 0.6 mile turn left onto Chaney Trail. Head north on Chaney Trail for 1.2 miles and park near the gate. If the trailhead parking is full, you can also park at the Millard Canyon trailhead at the end of Chaney Trail. The Sunset Ridge Trail can be accessed

Old mining equipment rusts near the site of the Dawn Mine.

from the Millard Canyon Campground (0.8 mile one way).

ON THE TRAIL

Hike east on the paved Mount Lowe Road. At 0.1 mile a trail on your left leads down to Millard Canyon Campground. Continue east and at 0.4 mile, look for the signed Sunset Ridge Trail descending from the road on the left near a large toyon shrub. At 0.8 mile, keep left at the junction, crossing a rusted iron bridge and passing an old cabin before reaching the canyon floor at 0.9 mile, staying right to head northeast up the canyon.

Millard Canyon was reopened to hikers in 2015 after the Station Fire but the already rough use-trail was wiped out in places and is badly overgrown in others. It's passable but you will need to keep your eyes peeled for the route, which has a habit of swapping streambed sides and climbing between boulders without warning. Enjoy the thick canopy of oak and alder and—depending on the time of year and annual precipitation levels—the gurgling sound of the brook on the canyon floor. At 1 mile, climb up out of the canyon for a short while, and look for a small concrete check dam at 1.1 miles. Just past this is a junction where Millard Canyon continues to the east, while the Saucer Branch spurs off to the north with a tough, optional side trail that leads to the base of a waterfall. Continue boulder hopping to the east in Millard Canyon, passing a retaining wall at 1.3 miles and keeping your eye open for the mining remnants scattered throughout the canyon—mostly pipes and rusted iron cables.

At 1.6 miles, the canyon makes a sharp turn to the north, where the tree canopy parts enough to let in some sunshine and the creek bed becomes more densely populated

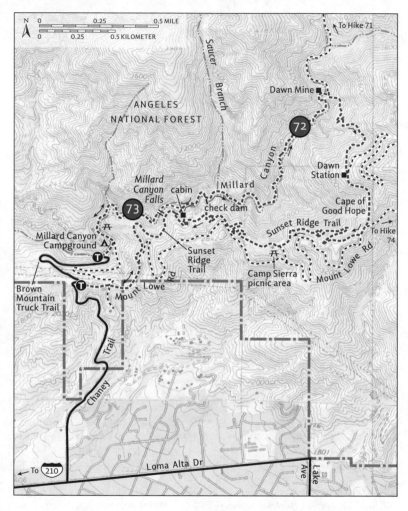

with large boulders and flood debris. There's another climb here, and when the boulders get really thick at 1.7 miles, look for a steep use-trail on the canyon's western wall, which will save you *a lot* of scramble time. Look for cairns and arrows painted on the rocks

to help you, but in some cases you may just have to put your head down and push through the forest's understory (watching out for poison oak, of course). At 2.2 miles, hike beneath an elevated section of the old pipe that's been appearing intermittently throughout the hike, and dip back into the streambed. Look for more mining refuse in the gravel here, and around the bend, you'll spot remnants of one of the mine's mills cemented into the north side of the canyon. Climb up to this artifact and continue a few yards to the west to see the entrance to the mine itself.

NOTE: Do not attempt to enter the Dawn Mine tunnels. Like all abandoned mines, they are extremely dangerous and often littered with deep, unseen shafts and pockets of toxic gases.

When you're ready to leave, look directly across the canyon from the mine to the southeast for a very faint incline. Climb up this route, staying to the left at an unmarked junction at 2.3 miles and then making a sharp right about 90 feet farther along the trail. Heading north here will eventually get you to Tom Sloane Saddle and Bear Canyon (Hike 71), but instead you'll head south along a trail cut to carry ore by mule up to the Mount Lowe Railway. This trail is steep, exposed, eroded, and in need of some love—but the route is clear and the views of Millard Canyon are spectacular. At 3 miles, reach the site of Dawn Station and head south along the old railway, soaking in phenomenal views of the Arroyo Seco and Pasadena area along the way. Pass the Cape of Good Hope at 3.2 miles and the Echo Mountain Trail (to Hike 74) at 3.3 miles. At 3.5 miles, stay right to rejoin the Sunset Ridge Trail. This switchbacking route is exquisitely cared for and especially popular with mountain bikers, not to mention an extremely welcome change of pace from the rougher hiking in Millard Canyon. Keep your ears open while you descend, passing the Camp Sierra picnic area at 4.1 miles. Meet your inbound route at 5.1 miles and follow the path back to the trailhead.

73 Millard Canyon Falls

RATING/ DIFFICULTY	ROUNDTRIP	ELEV GAIN/ HIGH POINT	SEASON
****/2	1.2 miles	268 feet/ 2064 feet	Year-round

Map: USGS Pasadena; **Contact:** Angeles National Forest, Los Angeles River Ranger District; **Notes:** Adventure Pass required to park at trailhead. Chaney Trail gate open 6:00 AM–8:00 PM. Dogs allowed on leash. Campground is first-come, first-served and may be closed due to bear activity; **GPS:** N 34.216256, W 118.146065

 The sound of a bubbling stream is music to the ears of any L.A. hiker sick of hot, dry, endless summers. When that sound is accompanied by an easy, shaded trail that finishes with a beautiful and picturesque waterfall, then you've just found one of the most rewarding treks in the San Gabriel Mountains.

GETTING THERE
From Interstate 210 in Altadena, take exit 23 for Lincoln Avenue and head north. In just under 2 miles, turn right onto Loma Alta Drive and in 0.6 mile turn left onto Chancy Trail. Head north on Chaney Trail for 1.2 miles and take a sharp left onto Brown Mountain Truck Trail. Park at the end of the road and display your Adventure Pass.

ON THE TRAIL
Follow the signs for Millard Canyon Campground, passing a wooden cabin and a junction with the Sunset Ridge Trail at 0.1 mile. Walk through the campground and look for a well-worn trail on the right-hand side of

The water sneaks past a large boulder lodged in Millard Canyon Falls.

the road, just before it crosses the creek and continues toward Brown Mountain.

Follow this trail through the canyon, one of the first to be homesteaded by European settlers. This canyon—like many in the San Gabriels—was heavily damaged by the 2009 Station Fire. While the fire itself didn't leave many scars, the debris pushed down the canyons in the ensuing winter storms definitely did. This trail wasn't reopened until 2015, but other than a few piles of branches and washed-out sections of trail, you could probably hike this entire route and not even notice the signs of the inferno.

Enjoy the shade, the sounds of birdsong, and the pleasant challenge of hopping over the creek until you reach the base of the falls at 0.6 mile. In wet months or after a recent rain, expect a small pool at the bottom of the falls . . . and maybe some soaked boots, too.

EXTENDING YOUR TRIP

For a significantly longer and more difficult trek, follow the Sunset Ridge Trail 0.8 mile to the trailhead for the Dawn Mine Loop (Hike 72). There is also a use-trail that continues past the falls and into Millard Canyon. Look for a steep trail heading up from the east side of the canyon floor about 100 yards from the falls. Proceed on these options only if you have experience routefinding on rough trails—this upper area of the canyon has not yet received nearly as much trail work as the section below Millard Canyon Falls.

 74 Echo Mountain

RATING/ DIFFICULTY	ROUNDTRIP	ELEV GAIN/ HIGH POINT	SEASON
****/3	5.6 miles	1377 feet/ 3210 feet	Year-round

Maps: USGS Pasadena, Mount Wilson; **Contact:** Angeles National Forest, Los Angeles River Ranger District; **Notes:** Dogs allowed on leash; **GPS:** N 34.2040230, W 118.1314620

 Attention, historically minded hikers: Put this trail on the very top of your list. This accessible and moderate day hike is popular with trail runners and fitness buffs too—but the real gems here are the leftover bits and pieces of L.A.'s Great Hiking Era, including old railway

The old funicular bullwheel at Echo Mountain

grades, funicular inclines, and the foundations of what was once a sprawling and famous mountaintop hotel complex.

GETTING THERE

From Interstate 210 in Pasadena, take the Lake Avenue exit and head north into Altadena. At about 3.8 miles, park near the sharp left-hand turn at Loma Alta Drive outside the Cobb Estate. No permits are required.

ON THE TRAIL

Walk through the gates of the Cobb Estate. Follow the pavement 0.2 mile, then keep to the right to stay on the Lower Sam Merrill Trail as it dips down into a canyon with a flood control dam. At 0.4 mile, you begin your climb into the San Gabriel Mountains on a beautiful single-track trail. There are sporadic oaks that provide a bit of shade, but most of this trail is in the full sun. If you want to avoid some solar heat, hit the trailhead

A CITY IN THE SKY

By the time he retired to Pasadena in 1888, Professor Thaddeus S. C. Lowe was famous for his early meteorological theories and his exploits as the US Army's first chief aeronaut of the Union Army Balloon Corps. Eternally restless, even after he retired, Lowe built a gasworks, an ice-making company, and founded two banks ... and that still wasn't enough.

After meeting the engineer David Joseph Macpherson, the two conspired to build railways into the San Gabriels. In 1892 the pair began construction on the world's first electric-powered incline railway from Rubio Canyon to the summit of Echo Mountain. A hotel and pavilion were built first at the bottom of Rubio Canyon in 1893, quickly followed by the Chalet and the Echo Mountain House atop Echo Mountain itself by 1894. Not satisfied, Lowe built a small zoo, and an observatory, and also installed the world's largest searchlight at a complex that came to be known as the White City. More than 30 miles of trails were constructed, along with an extended railway with 127 curves and eighteen bridges from the Echo Mountain House to another hotel called Ye Alpine Tavern, completed in 1895. Unfortunately, fire and windstorms destroyed the Echo Mountain House and the Chalet by 1905, and Lowe lost ownership of his railway to the Pacific Electric system. That sale provided the railway with the cash for numerous improvements and reconstruction as well as a connection to L.A.'s famous Red Cars—indeed, you can still find locals who remember riding the train from Long Beach all the way to Ye Alpine Tavern.

More than three million people rode the trains to these alpine hotels before the tavern burned in 1936. The last train ran in 1937, and by 1939 the system was being dismantled. By the early 1960s, the Forest Service had destroyed what remained of the tavern and the powerhouse on Echo Mountain—but the ruins, stories, and photographs of Echo Mountain continue to inspire dreamers today.

For more info and excellent historical photographs, be sure to visit the Mount Lowe Preservation Society at www.mountlowe.org.

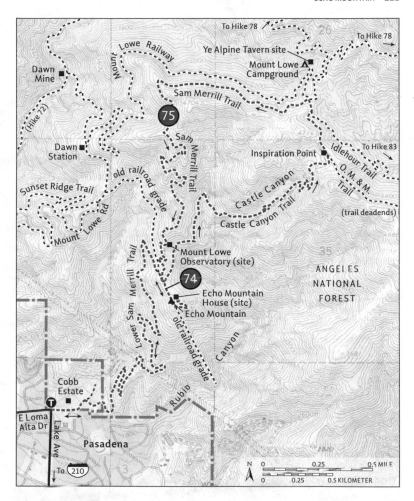

early when at least some of the western-facing lower trail will still be shaded.

The trail here is lined with California sagebrush, black sage, and some pockets of white sage, making this route an especially fragrant ascent (your own bodily contributions grant ascent (your own bodily contributions notwithstanding). As it climbs and switchbacks, the views of Pasadena become more and more spectacular. You'll also be able to see the Verdugos, San Rafael Hills, the backside of Griffith Park, and even farther on clear days.

Just before the 2.5-mile mark, stay right to join the old railroad grade and ignore the trails on your left until you get to Echo Mountain. Although the many buildings that once stood atop this peak have been destroyed by fire, windstorm, deconstruction, and vandalism, a surprising number of artifacts remain. The foundation of the Echo Mountain House hotel is the main attraction, but hikers can also visit the sites of old dance pavilions and zoos, walk past the enormous bullwheel that pulled visitors to the mountaintop along a funicular from Rubio Canyon, and test their lungs and vocal cords on a metal megaphone. There are a number of historical plaques and markers near the top of the mountain that do an excellent job of giving the visitor a taste of Echo Mountain's undeniable magic.

EXTENDING YOUR TRIP

Hikers looking for a longer trip can extend this route to Inspiration Point via Castle Canyon (Hike 75). You can also hike along the old route of the Mount Lowe Railway, but that is a much longer and more circuitous route, which may not be worth the extra time and effort if you're not into history.

75 Inspiration Point

RATING/ DIFFICULTY	LOOP	ELEV GAIN/ HIGH POINT	SEASON
****/4	9.9 miles	2692 feet/ 4531 feet	Year-round

Maps: USGS Pasadena, Mount Wilson;
Contact: Angeles National Forest, Los

Viewing tubes at Inspiration Point

Angeles River Ranger District; **Notes:** Dogs allowed on leash; **GPS:** N 34.2040230, W 118.1314620

◣ ⌂ ❖ *If you want to visit the site of the Echo Mountain House (Hike 74) but want an additional, tougher loop hike with even more history, well, you're my kind of hiker. This trip follows the Castle Canyon and Sam Merrill trails above the White City to the sites of the old Mount Lowe Observatory and a series of lovingly reconstructed viewing tubes at Inspiration Point.*

GETTING THERE
From Interstate 210 in Pasadena, take the Lake Avenue exit and head north into Altadena. At about 3.8 miles, park near the sharp left-hand turn at Loma Alta Drive outside the Cobb Estate. No permits are required.

ON THE TRAIL
Follow the directions for Echo Mountain (Hike 74) and at after visiting the ruins, backtrack to the Castle Canyon Trail at 3 miles. The Castle Canyon Trail is much narrower, more rugged, and significantly less traveled than the route to the ruins, and will be a nice change of pace for hikers looking for more solitude. By 3.7 miles, the trail begins a long, switchbacking climb up Castle Canyon, topping out and joining a wider trail at 4.7 miles that's a remnant of the sprawling railroad system that used to cover these mountains. Inspiration Point is here—a reconstructed shade shelter with viewing tubes looking out to various Los Angeles landmarks and neighborhoods.

Continue north to a major trail junction at 5 miles. The broader old Mount Lowe Railway path continues west to the former site of Ye Alpine Tavern, now called the Mount Lowe Campground. To the east, the wide trail heads toward Mount Lowe itself (Hike 78), while the smaller Idlehour Trail makes a long descent to Henninger Flats (Hike 83). Keep to the far left at the junction to return to the Sam Merrill Trail, which hugs the shaded, northern side of the mountain until 5.8 miles, where it turns south and heads back toward the Echo Mountain House ruins. The foundation of the Mount Lowe Observatory is at 7.2 miles. Close the loop at 7.4 miles and follow the Lower Sam Merrill Trail back to the trailhead.

EXTENDING YOUR TRIP
At Inspiration Point, a path heading southeast follows the old O. M. & M. Railroad (One Man and a Mule) 1.5 miles to a ridge overlooking Eaton Canyon to the east. Visitors on this route rode in an open-air observation cart that was pushed by a mule named Herbert. The walk-in Mount Lowe Campground is just north of the junction at 5 miles on the old Mount Lowe Railroad grade. You can also follow this path all the way back to the Sam Merrill Trail, although hikers not interested in the history will likely find its extended length a bit on the tedious side.

76 San Gabriel Peak and Mount Disappointment

RATING/ DIFFICULTY	ROUNDTRIP	ELEV GAIN/ HIGH POINT	SEASON
****/3	4.3 miles	1275 feet/ 6161 feet	Year-round

Maps: USGS Chilao Flat, Mount Wilson; **Contact:** Angeles National Forest, Los Angeles River Ranger District; **Notes:** Dogs allowed on leash; **GPS:** N 34.254300, W 118.101999

In the winter, San Gabriel Peak can get a few dustings of snow.

This moderate trek hits two peaks and the former home of one of the Los Angeles area's many Nike missile defense sites. Today only foundations remain of the Cold War defense system, but this trail offers great views from the tallest peak in the Front Range, as well as access to a handful of other treks in the area. Despite the mountain's name, you won't be disappointed by this hike. Sorry. I had to.

GETTING THERE

From Interstate 210 in La Cañada Flintridge, take exit 20 toward the Angeles Crest Highway (CA-2) and follow it north for 13.9 miles. Take a right onto Mount Wilson–Red Box Road and in 0.4 mile, look for a nondescript dirt road on the right-hand side. There is a small parking area here, and the trailhead is just to the south.

ON THE TRAIL

Just before the parking area, where the road turns slightly to the north, look for a sometimes tough-to-spot trailhead on the southern side of the road and follow the Bill Reilly Trail as it quickly switchbacks up. In the colder months, this section can get a little icy, so hike cautiously. In 0.2 mile you'll start to get some excellent views east along the West Fork San Gabriel River. At 0.3 mile you'll have your first view of the sharp, small summit of San Gabriel Peak, the tallest in the Front Range of the San Gabriel Mountains. The trail continues climbing the north side of Mount Disappointment through a forested area recovering from recent fire damage.

The trail roughly parallels an old access road through most of this portion but maintains enough distance from it that you may not even notice. Ignore the short spur that hops onto the road at 1.1 miles but take a left onto the road when the trail ends just a few hundred feet later. At 1.4 miles, you'll reach the edge of a ridge between San Gabriel Peak to the east and Mount Disappointment to the west. The latter peak's unusual name comes from the surveyors who initially thought its summit was the tallest in the region but after climbing it discovered that neighboring San Gabriel Peak was 167 feet higher. Head left to tackle taller San Gabriel Peak first, passing the foundations of some

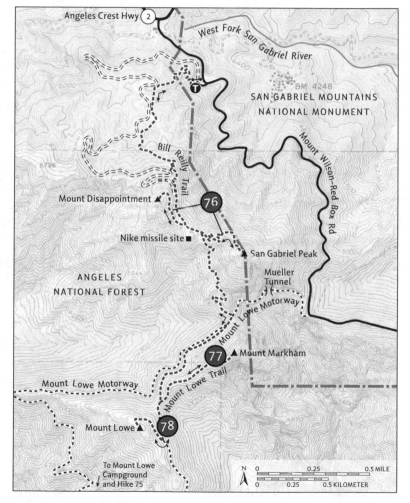

of the old Nike missile control center buildings along the way. A single-track trail drops into a small saddle here. Stay straight to head up a steep and narrow route to the top of San Gabriel Peak, which you'll reach at 1.9 miles.

Enjoy the views and backtrack to the saddle at 2.4 miles, and stay left to continue following the road up to Mount Disappointment, which you'll reach at about 2.7 miles. This peak's summit was flattened in 1955 for a missile launch site, but after ten years the program was abandoned and now it's home to telecommunications equipment. Return the way you came or consider tackling one of the other nearby summits.

EXTENDING YOUR TRIP

There are several additional peaks that can be added onto this trek for a longer day trip, including Mount Markham (Hike 77) and Mount Lowe (Hike 78).

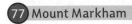
77 Mount Markham

RATING/ DIFFICULTY	ROUNDTRIP	ELEV GAIN/ HIGH POINT	SEASON
****/4	6.3 miles	1027 feet/ 5781 feet	Year-round

Maps: USGS Chilao Flat, Mount Wilson; **Contact:** Angeles National Forest/San Gabriel Mountains National Monument, Los Angeles River Ranger District; **Notes:** Dogs allowed on leash, but may have trouble with some of the scramble sections on Mount Markham; **GPS:** N 34.254300, W 118.101999

An intermediate challenge on a rarely visited, unusually shaped peak, a trip to Mount Markham offers some wonderful views of the nearby Front Range peaks and a few sections of easy scrambling to get your hands nice and dirty.

They don't make trail signs like this anymore!

GETTING THERE

From Interstate 210 in La Cañada Flintridge, take exit 20 toward the Angeles Crest Highway (CA-2) and follow it north for 13.9 miles. Take a right onto Mount Wilson–Red Box Road and in 0.4 mile, look for a nondescript dirt road on the right-hand side. There is a small parking area here, and the trailhead is just to the south.

ON THE TRAIL

Follow the route described in Hike 76 to the junction between San Gabriel Peak and Mount Disappointment at approximately 1.5 miles. Instead of ascending to San Gabriel Peak, stay to the right to descend a narrow trail on the southwestern slope of the mountain. By 1.7 miles, Mount Markham comes into view and appears to be a double-summited bump, although the shape will seem to change depending on what angle you're viewing it from. From the southeast, it appears broad and flat-topped, not unlike Mount Disappointment behind you, while from the northeast it looks pointed. To its immediate right is the taller summit of Mount Lowe.

Continue your switchbacking descent and reach a four-way junction at 2.1 miles. To the east, Mount Lowe Motorway heads to Mount Wilson–Red Box Road via the Mueller Tunnel (this stretch of trail seems to be fairly prone to landslides) while to the west, the motorway takes the long way around Mount Lowe to the Mount Lowe Campground at the site of Ye Alpine Tavern (see sidebar "A City in the Sky"). Cross the motorway and look for a single-track that parallels the road heading west but climbs above it. At the small saddle at 2.7 miles, look for a faint use-trail heading to the northeast while the Mount Lowe Trail continues straight. Turn left to head up this rough, shadeless climb through crumbling rock and sharp Spanish bayonets. By 3 miles, the ridge begins to narrow considerably, and you may need to use your hands and feet to continue climbing upward. It's nothing like the difficulty of Strawberry Peak (Hike 80), but it is significantly tougher than the trail you've been on so far.

At 3.1 miles, there's a concrete marker that seems like it's the summit, but the actual summit lies about another tenth of a mile to the northeast. Enjoy the views of the surrounding peaks and return the way you came. Some use-trail descents may be visible from the summit of Mount Markham, but these routes are extremely difficult and may require technical rock climbing skills on this region's notoriously crumbly rock.

EXTENDING YOUR TRIP

If you still have gas in your tank, consider making the trip up to Mount Lowe (Hike 78) as well. It's a different feel than Markham and easy hiking once you get back to the Mount Lowe Trail.

78 Mount Lowe

RATING/ DIFFICULTY	ROUNDTRIP	ELEV GAIN/ HIGH POINT	SEASON
***/3	6.1 miles	1027 feet/ 5781 feet	Year-round

Maps: USGS Chilao Flat, Mount Wilson; **Contact:** Angeles National Forest/San Gabriel Mountains National Monument, Los Angeles River Ranger District; **Notes:** Dogs allowed on leash; **GPS:** N 34.254300, W 118.101999

 *If you've hit San Gabriel Peak, Mount Disappointment, and Mount Markham but still want to*

The summit of Mount Lowe still has a few relics from the past.

spend more time on the trail, this route to Mount Lowe is worth the extra time and effort. The nearly 360-degree views from the summit of Mount Lowe give you an excellent lay of the land of this region of the San Gabriel Mountains, along with some brilliant views of the Los Angeles basin on clear days. Just remember: it's uphill both ways!

GETTING THERE

From Interstate 210 in La Cañada Flintridge, take exit 20 toward the Angeles Crest Highway (CA-2) and follow it north for 13.9 miles. Take a right onto Mount Wilson–Red Box Road and in 0.4 mile, look for a nondescript dirt road on the right-hand side. There is a small parking area here, and the trailhead is just to the south.

ON THE TRAIL

Follow the route described in Hike 77 to the saddle at 2.7 miles. Continue on the broader Mount Lowe Trail as it makes some long switchbacks up the north face of Mount

Lowe, and at 2.9 miles look to your right for a steep, narrow trail that leads directly to the summit. Named for Professor Lowe of Echo Mountain fame, this summit features the remnants of Lowe's insanely ambitious and sprawling empire of San Gabriel amusements. Visitors to Ye Alpine Tavern (see sidebar "A City in the Sky") about 2.5 miles away would trek up to this summit on foot or horseback, where they could use the still-standing viewing tubes to identify neighboring peaks. On your way up, you may pass some strange metal signs that seem to be embedded in tree trunks; these are signs installed by Professor Lowe's workmen, and you can find historic photos of many of them from more than a hundred years ago. The seemingly never-satisfied professor had plans to extend his famous railway to the summit of this peak, where he wanted to build another hotel *and* an aerial tram to San Gabriel Peak (where, you will not be surprised to learn, he also wanted to build another observatory).

None of those plans came to fruition, but the mostly bare summit of Mount Lowe does offer some spectacular views of the region, especially on clear winter and spring days. Standing atop this peak, it's not difficult to imagine what drove people like Lowe to create these impossible-sounding palaces in the mountains.

79 Josephine Peak

RATING/ DIFFICULTY	ROUNDTRIP	ELEV GAIN/ HIGH POINT	SEASON
***/3	8 miles	1898 feet/ 5558 feet	Year-round

Map: USGS Condor Peak; **Contact:** Angeles National Forest/San Gabriel Mountains National Monument, Los Angeles River Ranger District; **Notes:** Adventure Pass required to park at trailhead. Dogs allowed on leash; **GPS:** N 34.271052, W 118.153714

A relatively mild fire road ascent of one of the most prominent peaks in the Front Range, the hike to Josephine Peak is a great introduction to moderate trails in the San Gabriels and has some exemplary views. Look out over nearby peaks and downtown Los Angeles (on clear days) for a comprehensive view of the size of the Station Fire burn area.

GETTING THERE

From Interstate 210 in La Cañada Flintridge, take exit 20 toward the Angeles Crest Highway (CA-2) and follow it north for about 9.3 miles to the Clear Creek Information Center at the intersection of the Angeles Crest Highway and Angeles Forest Highway. You can turn left onto the Angeles Forest Highway to reach a very small parking area right before the trail (don't block the gate!) but it's often easier to park in the pullout on the north side of CA-2 just across from the Clear Creek Information Center.

Strawberry Peak and Mount Lawlor as seen from the summit of Josephine Peak

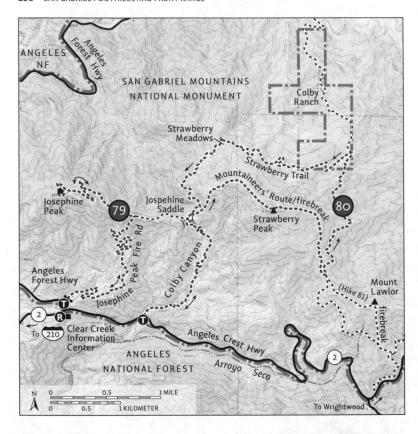

ON THE TRAIL

This is a pretty easy trail to follow—you basically just walk past the gate on the Josephine Peak Fire Road . . . and then you stay on it. Easy peasy. While the trail itself isn't the most exciting or difficult—it's broad, gently sloping fire road almost all the way to the top—there are some interesting things to watch for along the way. Near the bottom, note the singed pine trees. Nearly torched in the Station Fire, these resilient conifers are sprouting again.

By 1.2 miles, the views start to open up a bit. The distinctive granite face of Strawberry Peak looms to the northeast while to the south, the north faces of the Front Range peaks keep sprawling civilization at bay. At 2.4 miles, stay to the left at the junction with the ridgeline trail to Josephine Saddle and Strawberry Peak. Looking north from here, you'll get a sense of the scope of the Station Fire burn area.

Continue west on the fire road as it slowly winds its way along the north side of

L.A.'S INFERNO

On August 26, 2009, an arsonist ignited a small brush fire in dense, dry shrubs in the San Gabriel Mountains. At first it appeared firefighters had the blaze under control, but when the fire jumped into steep, inaccessible canyons and communication confusion diverted airborne tankers, it quickly spiraled into an inferno. The Station Fire would eventually become the largest wildfire in modern Los Angeles County history, charring 160,557 acres before it was finally contained on October 16. It destroyed 209 buildings, killed two firefighters, and the smoke could be seen from the Sierra Nevada.

The effects of the Station Fire will be long felt for Los Angeles outdoor enthusiasts. The entire Angeles National Forest was closed for the rest of the year and even in 2016 large sections remain off-limits to hikers. Areas that have been opened have seen trails lost to erosion and chaparral regrowth. Although Forest Service and volunteer crews are hard at work repairing trails, restoring signs and structures, and replanting burned areas, it will be awhile before the San Gabriels fully recover.

Josephine Peak to the summit. This section tends to be shaded more often than not, which can dramatically cool temperatures in the winter months. Keep your eye out for poodle-dog bush along the side of the trail. The road ends at 3.7 miles and a short use-trail climbs another 0.3 mile past the radio equipment to the small, rocky summit, which provides very nice 360-degree views. Return the way you came.

80 Strawberry Peak

RATING/ DIFFICULTY	LOOP	ELEV GAIN/ HIGH POINT	SEASON
★★★★/5	10.8 miles	2731 feet/ 6167 feet	Year-round

Map: USGS Chilao Flat; **Contact:** Angeles National Forest/San Gabriel Mountains National Monument, Los Angeles River Ranger District; **Notes:** Dogs allowed on leash but not recommended on the Mountaineers' Route; **GPS:** N 34.269549, W 118.140730

This route to Strawberry Peak is one of the steepest, most exciting treks in the Front Range—a heart-pounding journey that includes some class 3 scrambling on the exposed face of the peak. Those who conquer the Mountaineers' Route will earn some serious bragging rights in addition to spectacular views and a sense of accomplishment . . . just don't try this one if you're even mildly afraid of heights.

GETTING THERE

From Interstate 210 in La Cañada Flintridge, take exit 20 toward the Angeles Crest Highway (CA-2) and follow it north for 10.1 miles. There are two small dirt lots on the north side of the road at Colby Canyon, just past the turnoff for the Switzer picnic area and trail.

ON THE TRAIL

Head into Colby Canyon from the trailhead. There's a creek bed at the bottom of the canyon that's dry most of the year, but still has enough water to make poison oak

The distinctive slope of Strawberry Peak is one of the most recognizable in the San Gabriels.

happy. This trail was damaged in the Station Fire and although much work has been done to restore it, sharp Spanish bayonets and the occasional poodle-dog bush have recolonized in the undergrowth here—so definitely watch where you're hiking. The trail climbs up the eastern side of Colby Canyon, swapping to the west at 0.7 mile. From here, it's steep switchbacks up to the small flat of Josephine Saddle at 2 miles. Now comes the fun part.

Look for a faint use-trail that climbs up the ridge to the east, above the more established Strawberry Trail. Walk northeast until it looks like the trail ends at a rock wall at 2.2 miles. This is the first of the scrambling sections on the Mountaineers' Route, and definitely the easier of the two. The igneous rock here is more solid than most of what you'll find in the San Gabriels and its fins provide plenty of hand- and footholds. Previous climbers have left some cairns and paint streaks to provide hints (though many have faded since the fire), so just take your time.

Top this climb, then continue along the ridgeline as it bends to the southeast, hopping over boulder piles before stopping at the seemingly sheer rock wall that is Strawberry Peak's western flank at 2.9 miles. This scramble is tougher than the first—more exposed and requiring complicated movements—but if you have experience using your hands and feet on the trail and keep calm, you should be okay. Few summits inspire such a combined sense of accomplishment and thoughts of "What the heck did I just do?!" as Strawberry Peak, so enjoy it when you reach it at 3.1 miles.

If you climbed to the top and thought, "I'd now like to do that backwards without really being able to see where my feet are going," then by all means, head back the way you came. Otherwise, follow the firebreak east, dodging more Spanish bayonets until it meets the Strawberry Trail at 4.1 miles. Take a sharp left to head north and keep left again at 5.8 miles to loop around the north side of Strawberry Peak. The scenery really picks up near Strawberry Meadows at 7.5 miles—a flat, boulder-strewn clearing that's a perfect place for a snack. This trail continues to Josephine Saddle at 8.8 miles, where you can return to the trailhead the way you came in.

81 Mount Lawlor

RATING/ DIFFICULTY	LOOP	ELEV GAIN/ HIGH POINT	SEASON
***/4	4.2 miles	1270 feet/ 5957 feet	Year-round

Map: USGS Chilao Flat; **Contact:** Angeles National Forest/San Gabriel Mountains National Monument, Los Angeles River Ranger District; **Notes:** Adventure Pass required to park at trailhead. Dogs allowed on leash but not recommended on firebreak; **GPS:** N 34.258352, W 118.105088

Mount Lawlor is often overshadowed by its showier neighbor, Strawberry Peak, but this path less traveled has its own charms and challenges that make it a worthwhile destination. The trail begins innocuously enough from Red Box, but the climb to its peak is a serious leg buster and should not be underestimated. The views of the interior San Gabriels are worth the trip, and a tough and rugged descent down a firebreak offers a final challenge for those willing to dodge spiny Spanish bayonets.

GETTING THERE
From Interstate 210 in La Cañada Flintridge, take exit 20 toward the Angeles Crest Highway (CA-2) and follow it north for 13.9 miles east to Red Box Gap. Park at the Red Box lot at the corner of the Angeles Crest Highway and Mount Wilson–Red Box Road.

Spanish bayonets

ON THE TRAIL

Carefully cross the Angeles Crest Highway and look for the Strawberry Trail trailhead just to the east of the parking area. The trail parallels the Angeles Crest Highway for the first 0.8 mile before turning away from the buzz of cars and motorcycles and toward the deceptively unassuming profile of Mount Lawlor. Keep left at a junction here to continue on the trail. At the 1-mile mark, note a firebreak that comes barreling down the south slope of Lawlor and meets with the trail; should you choose the challenge of the descent described here, this is where you'll return to maintained trail.

Continue west on the Strawberry Trail, hopping over one of the farthest-reaching branches of the Arroyo Seco at 1.2 miles and hitting a major trail junction at 2.2 miles. To the west, a firebreak travels up to the summit of Strawberry Peak. Straight ahead, the trail continues to Colby Ranch and Strawberry

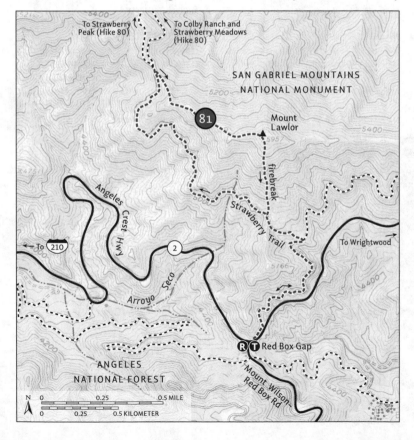

Meadows. You'll take a hard right here and set out on the no-nonsense firebreak climb toward the summit of Mount Lawlor. This steep, rocky climb will get you to the summit at 2.8 miles. After you enjoy the views, look for the continuation of the firebreak to the south and just head down.

Note the emphasis on "down" here, because it's almost a straight-down shot back to the trail on loose ground dotted with Spanish bayonets, which will poke holes in both your clothes and your skin. The descent is not technical, although previous travelers have placed a few cables in the ground to help you along the sketchier sections. When you reach the Strawberry Trail, turn left and retrace your steps to the trailhead.

82 Eaton Canyon

RATING/ DIFFICULTY	ROUNDTRIP	ELEV GAIN/ HIGH POINT	SEASON
****/2	3.8 miles	592 feet/ 1585 feet	Year-round

Map: USGS Mount Wilson; **Contact:** Eaton Canyon Nature Center; **Notes:** Park open sunrise–sunset. Eaton Canyon Nature Center open 9:00 AM–5:00 PM daily. Dogs allowed on leash. Check for docent-led programs and guided hikes; **GPS:** N 34.176281, W 118.098441

Forty-foot-high Eaton Canyon Falls is one of the most beautiful and accessible waterfalls in the San Gabriel Mountains, which means it can also be one of the most crowded. Get here early in the day or during the week to enjoy this highlight of the Front Range and walk in the footsteps of one of the world's most famous naturalists.

GETTING THERE
From Interstate 210 westbound in Altadena, take exit 29A for Sierra Madre Boulevard and Altadena Drive. At the end of the ramp, stay straight for one block and turn right on Altadena Drive. From the eastbound 210, take exit 28 for Altadena Drive and turn left to head north on Altadena Drive. At 1.7 miles you can turn right on Veranada Avenue to park inside the Eaton Canyon Natural Area Park for a fee or use free street parking on Altadena Drive and walk into the center on its trails. This trailhead is also accessible from Metro bus 32, which stops at Altadena Drive/New York Drive. This bus line departs from the Gold Line's Sierra Madre Villa.

ON THE TRAIL
Head north from the nature center and hike through the boulders strewn in every direction amid the large basin of Eaton Wash. These rocks are the former pieces of the San Gabriels looming in front of you, brought down to your feet via various canyons and washes in landslides, earthquakes, and floods over thousands of years. In the spring, this area is absolutely covered in wildflowers and makes for a beautiful sight. At 0.5 mile, keep left at the junction with the equestrian trail and hike along the east side of the wash, keeping left again at the Walnut Canyon Trail just a bit farther north. As you approach the San Gabriel Mountains, the trail enters the narrowing mouth of Eaton Canyon and crosses beneath the Mount Wilson Toll Road at 1.3 miles.

Follow the trail as it skips across the Eaton Wash multiple times, and delight in the sound of rushing water, the cooler temperatures, and the lush greenery. At about 1.8 miles, the canyon makes a sharp turn to the west and the cascading waterfall is just beyond. In

Eaton Canyon Falls is one of the most popular hiking destinations in the Front Range.

1877, another traveler came here and walked this same exact route, describing Eaton Falls as "the Yosemite of the San Gabriel . . . a charming little thing, with a low sweet voice, singing like a bird." This visitor was John Muir, and because he was John Muir, he and his beard spent the next few days climbing from here all the way to Mount Lowe and Mount Wilson and back with no trails, no $170 hiking boots, and no ultralight backpack with high-protein snacks or built-in hydration reservoirs. If you're not John Muir, just enjoy the waterfall and return the way you came, and maybe visit the excellent nature center to learn a bit more about the region's plants and animals.

83 Henninger Flats

RATING/ DIFFICULTY	ROUNDTRIP	ELEV GAIN/ HIGH POINT	SEASON
****/3	6 miles	1546 feet/ 2525 feet	Year-round

Map: USGS Mount Wilson; **Contact:** County of Los Angeles Fire Department Forestry Division; **Notes:** Dogs allowed on leash. Henninger Flats Visitor Information Center is staffed 24 hours a day. Campers need a campground and campfire permit from the visitor center; **GPS:** N 34.176281, W 118.098441

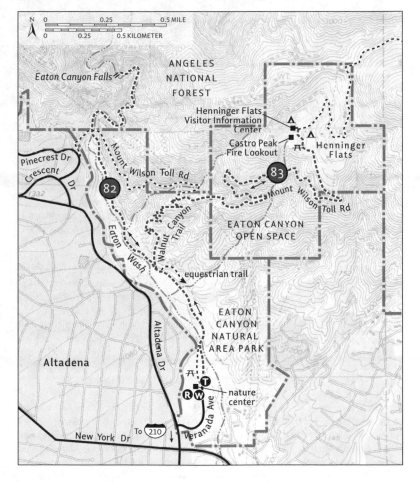

This tough climb winds through a boulder-strewn creek bed and a narrow canyon before making a challenging ascent along a historic toll road. Your rewards for making the climb are stunning panoramic views of the L.A. basin, a peaceful, shaded campground with unique views of the city, and a charming visitor center at Henninger Flats. This is a great weekend getaway and perfect spot for a trail run.

GETTING THERE

From Interstate 210 westbound in Altadena, take exit 29A for Sierra Madre Boulevard and Altadena Drive. At the end of the ramp, stay straight for one block and turn right on

The historic Castro Peak Fire Lookout is a long-term visitor from the Santa Monica Mountains.

Altadena Drive. From the eastbound 210, take exit 28 for Altadena Drive and turn left to head north on Altadena Drive. At 1.7 miles you can turn right on Veranada Avenue to park inside the Eaton Canyon Natural Area Park for a fee or use free street parking on Altadena Drive and walk into the center on its trails. This trailhead is also accessible from Metro bus 32, which stops at Altadena Drive/New York Drive. This bus departs from the Gold Line's Sierra Madre Villa.

ON THE TRAIL

Head north from the Eaton Canyon Nature Center, hiking through beautiful sage scrub in the rough boundaries of the Eaton Canyon Wash. At 0.5 mile, keep left at the junction with the equestrian trail and hike along the east side of the wash to just past 0.6 mile, then take a right into Walnut Canyon. This steep, narrow, switchbacking trail elevates you above the canyon walls, giving you your first glimpses of the urban basin around you. At 1.2 miles, take a right onto the old Mount Wilson Toll Road, built in 1891 with the initial purpose of installing state-of-the-art telescopes at Mount Wilson and the eventual,

more profitable purpose of charging visitors a toll to travel into the mountains.

Follow in the footsteps of these travelers, making use of the benches along the way to catch your breath and soak in ever-increasingly cinematic views. At 2.8 miles, pass the sign for Henninger Flats and stroll through the shaded picnic and campground areas to the Henninger Flats Visitor Information Center. L.A. County Fire Department staff will happily share the region's colorful mountain getaway turned orchard turned toll road rest stop turned experimental tree nursery history with you and let you browse the collection of artifacts on display. At one point, this was the largest nursery of forest trees in the world—back when the Forest Service was trying to figure out what sorts of nonnative trees it could grow in the San Gabriels for dependable lumber. (Spoiler: The answer was "None, really".)

Just outside the center, be sure to stop by the relocated Castro Peak Fire Lookout tower, which sat atop the Santa Monica Mountains from 1925 to 1971 (near Hike 9). Have your lunch in a spectacular picnic area, set up camp, or return the way you came.

84 Mount Wilson via Devore Campground

RATING/ DIFFICULTY	LOOP	ELEV GAIN/ HIGH POINT	SEASON
***/4	10.5 miles	2824 feet/ 5675 feet	Year-round

Map: USGS Mount Wilson; **Contact:** Angeles National Forest/San Gabriel Mountains National Monument, Los Angeles River Ranger District; **Notes:** Adventure Pass required at trailhead. Dogs allowed on leash. Camping at West Fork and Devore campgrounds is first-come, first-served. Mount Wilson's Cosmic Cafe is open weekends, Apr–Nov; **GPS:** N 34.223589, W 118.062557

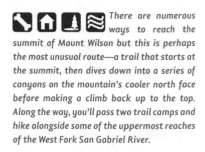 There are numerous ways to reach the summit of Mount Wilson but this is perhaps the most unusual route—a trail that starts at the summit, then dives down into a series of canyons on the mountain's cooler north face before making a climb back up to the top. Along the way, you'll pass two trail camps and hike alongside some of the uppermost reaches of the West Fork San Gabriel River.

GETTING THERE

From Interstate 210 in La Cañada Flintridge, take exit 20 toward the Angeles Crest Highway (CA-2) and follow it north for 13.9 miles, then take a right onto Mount Wilson–Red Box Road. Continue for 4.2 miles, then bear

The West Fork San Gabriel River is popular with hikers, campers, and anglers alike.

right at the roundabout onto Mount Wilson Circle Road. After 0.4 mile, bear right at the gate onto Mount Wilson–Red Box Road again. Continue approximately 0.2 mile to a parking area. There is a sign that prevents vehicular traffic beyond this point. Park here and display your Adventure Pass.

ON THE TRAIL

Begin walking west on Mount Wilson Road and keep right to continue counterclockwise on the Mount Wilson Circle Road. At 0.4 mile, look for the Kenyon Devore Trail on your right (sometimes called the Rattlesnake Trail) and leave the pavement for the trail.

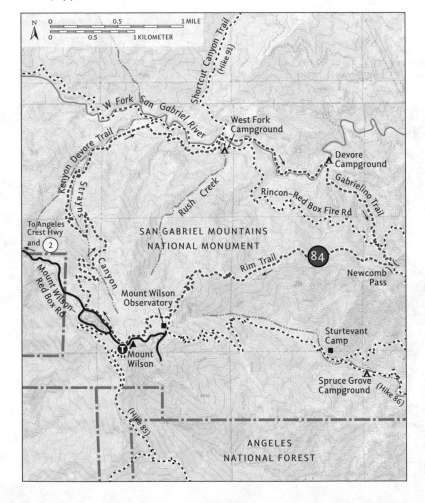

A FIRST LOOK AT THE UNIVERSE

Since its founding in 1904, the Mount Wilson Observatory has played an important role in the development of astrophysics and our understanding of the universe. Built in 1905, the Snow solar telescope was the world's first permanently mounted solar telescope; the 60-inch Hale telescope was the world's largest when it was built in 1908; and the 100-inch Hooker telescope was the largest aperture telescope in the world from 1917 until 1949. Because of its position above the inversion layer that usually sits on top of the Los Angeles basin, the Mount Wilson Observatory has some of the steadiest air in North America, and for a time this was the world's preeminent astronomy center. Some of the biggest names in science worked here, and—among other accomplishments—they were the first to detect magnetic fields outside of Earth, discovered that the sun reverses its polarity on a regular schedule, proved that our Milky Way is just one of many galaxies, discovered that our universe is expanding, and found some of the first evidence for dark matter. Today, the facilities are still used for research but are also important places for public outreach. Numerous educational programs and tours are offered, and groups can even reserve observation time with the 60- and 100-inch telescopes. For more information, to book tours or observation times, and to see a live Towercam view (spectacular during the winter!), head to www.mtwilson.edu.

This trail descends into Strayns Canyon, shaded by both its northern exposure and the tree cover (where it hasn't been singed by fire). The trail passes a brick building and hops the seasonal creek in Strayns Canyon at 1.4 miles and again at 2.1 miles, by which point the creek bed has become quite a bit wider and rockier. At 2.5 miles the trail enters a gulch, and it crosses the creek again at 2.9 miles just above a small but deep pool. At 3.6 miles, stay to the right to head toward West Fork Campground, which you'll reach at 4.6 miles after trekking through some shadeless, low chaparral. The first Forest Service cabin in California was built here in 1900, although only the foundation remains.

The Shortcut Canyon Trail heads north from here and the Rincon–Red Box Fire Road leaves the camp from the southeast, but for more quality time with the West Fork San Gabriel River, follow a trail east along its banks. This trail boulder hops along the riverside until it reaches the even more secluded Devore Campground at 5.7 miles. From here, an old anglers' trail follows the San Gabriel River all the way to Cogswell Reservoir, but it's an unmaintained route that becomes fairly tough to spot for most hikers after the first mile. Instead, continue south on the Gabrielino Trail as it climbs back up Mount Wilson. Cross the Rincon–Red Box Fire Road at 6.7 miles and reach Newcomb Pass at 7 miles—a fine rest stop just before the last push to Mount Wilson's summit.

It's a fairly straightforward trip up the Rim Trail from here—just mind some eroded, steep, and exposed sections as you continue the climb. At 9.8 miles, you'll reach the easternmost observatory. Feel free to explore the grounds before following the Rim Trail back to the trailhead.

85 Mount Wilson from Chantry Flat

RATING/ DIFFICULTY	LOOP	ELEV GAIN/ HIGH POINT	SEASON
****/5	12.8 miles	3545 feet/ 5712 feet	Year-round

Map: USGS Mount Wilson; **Contact:** Angeles National Forest/San Gabriel National Monument, Los Angeles River Ranger District; **Notes:** Adventure Pass required to park at trailhead. Dogs allowed on leash. Hoegee's Trail Camp is first-come, first-served; **GPS:** N 34.196054, W 118.023249

Ralph Waldo Emerson once said that life is a journey, not a destination, and the same could be said for this route to Mount Wilson. The summit isn't the highlight here; instead, it's the grueling climb up sunblasted firebreaks, the incredible mountain and city views, the contrast of the shaded descent, and—if you time it right—the killer barbecue from the Adams' Pack Station at the end. Give yourself extra time on this, and don't do it on a hot summer day.

GETTING THERE

From Interstate 210 in Arcadia, take exit 32 for Santa Anita Avenue. Head north on Santa Anita Avenue and continue on Chantry Flat Road to its end at 4.9 miles. Parking is notoriously difficult here, especially on weekends. Be extra attentive to parking restriction signage and be patient. The Adams' Pack Station has overflow parking, but you'll have to pay an additional fee—even if you've already purchased an Adventure Pass.

One of the observatories on Mount Wilson

ON THE TRAIL

At the end of the cul-de-sac at Chantry Flat, follow the signs toward the Winter Creek Trail and hike on the broad fire road heading west. This road slowly climbs above Chantry Flat, passing the Upper Winter Creek Trail on your right at 0.3 mile (you'll exit from here on your way out). Stay on the fire road until

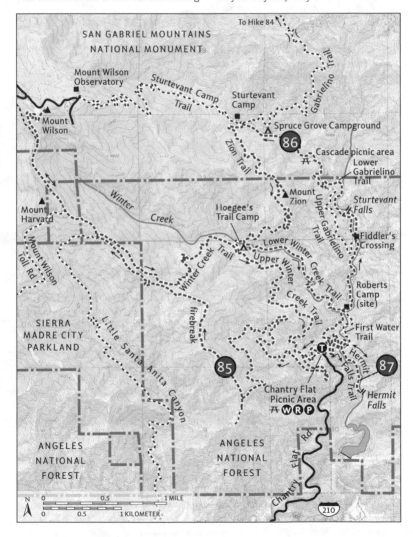

you reach 3.4 miles at a point where the road seems to end on the side of the mountain. This is where the trail gets interesting.

On the north side of the road, look for a faint path that leaves the road and doubles back toward the mountains on a sharp switchback. Here, the trail follows a rugged, roller-coaster firebreak over three bumps on thin ridges between Little Santa Anita Canyon to the west and Santa Anita Canyon to the east. In front of you, Mount Wilson and the San Gabriel Mountains loom larger with every step, while behind you, the views of the foothill cities and urban sprawl become more and more expansive. This is a tough stretch of trail—brutal in the summer sun—but it's also a lot of fun. The firebreak meets up with the Winter Creek Trail and Mount Wilson Toll Road at 5.6 miles near some much-needed shade and a memorial bench. Continue the climb upward and stay right at the junction with the Mount Wilson Toll Road at 6 miles.

You'll reach the summit of Mount Wilson at 7.2 miles, where you'll be greeted by pavement and radio towers. Meander around the observatory grounds (and check out the Cosmic Cafe if you're visiting on a weekend between April and November), then backtrack to the junction with the Winter Creek Trail at 8.8 miles. Keep left here to follow the steep, switchbacking Winter Creek Trail into the welcome shade of Santa Anita Canyon. At 10.5 miles, stay to the right to follow the Upper Winter Creek Trail for 2.3 miles back to Chantry Flat.

EXTENDING YOUR TRIP

Hoegee's Trail Camp is a great place to set up a tent and take your time exploring this majestic canyon. The campground is just beyond the junction at the 10.5-mile mark to the left, about 2.5 miles from the trailhead. From here, you can follow the full Santa Anita Canyon loop (Hike 86) or break that into smaller trips as you see fit.

86 Santa Anita Canyon

RATING/ DIFFICULTY	LOOP	ELEV GAIN/ HIGH POINT	SEASON
*****/3	8.7 miles	1660 feet/ 3575 feet	Year-round

Map: USGS Mount Wilson; **Contact:** Angeles National Forest/San Gabriel Mountains National Monument, Los Angeles River Ranger District; **Notes:** Adventure Pass required to park at trailhead. Dogs allowed on leash. Hoegee's and Spruce Grove campgrounds are first-come, first-served. If you're just headed to Sturtevant Falls, this is a kid-friendly hike; **GPS:** N 34.196054, W 118.023249

Hands down one of the must-do hikes in the Los Angeles area, Santa Anita Canyon is steeped in equal amounts of fascinating human history and spellbinding natural beauty. This "highlight reel" of the region passes one of the few active pack mule stations left in the country, dozens of historic private cabins, one of L.A.'s most beautiful year-round waterfalls, the last remaining wilderness resort from the region's Great Hiking Era, and the oldest existing Forest Service structure still in its original location.

GETTING THERE

From Interstate 210 in Arcadia, take exit 32 for Santa Anita Avenue. Head north on Santa Anita Avenue and continue on Chantry Flat Road to its end at 4.9 miles.

Parking is notoriously difficult here, especially on weekends. Be extra attentive to parking signage and be patient. The Adams' Pack Station has overflow parking, but you'll have to pay an additional fee—even if you've already purchased an Adventure Pass.

ON THE TRAIL

From the east end of the parking area, follow the paved road down from Chantry Flat into Santa Anita Canyon. At 0.2 mile, stay left at the junction with the Hermit Falls Trail. If you're really anxious about getting off the pavement and onto dirt, you can follow that trail to the canyon floor as well (Hike 87); otherwise, the pavement ends before

a wooden bridge at 0.7 mile at the site of Roberts Camp. Built in 1912, this wilderness resort grew to become one of the largest in the San Gabriel Mountains, with a restaurant, store, dance hall, room for 180 guests, a branch of the L.A. County Library, and even a US post office.

Keep straight at the junction to continue in the main branch of Santa Anita Canyon. The dozens of cabins you see along the way are from L.A.'s Great Hiking Era, which occurred near the turn of the century. Many are remnants of wilderness resorts and lodges that have long since vanished, but their current occupants pour their hearts and souls into these buildings to keep them in good

This cabin, build by Louis Newcomb in 1903, is the oldest US Forest Service structure in its original location.

shape—even with the ever-present threat of fire and flood. While they are beautiful and inviting, remember that these are private property—and require an enormous amount of upkeep. Please only get close to them if one of their owners invites you.

At 1.5 miles, take a right at the junction near a cabin called "Fiddler's Crossing" and hop across the creek. You'll reach the bottom of fifty-foot-tall Sturtevant Falls at 1.7 miles, which flows year round and is often a perfect spot to cool off in the hot months. Backtrack to Fiddler's Crossing and the junction with the Upper and Lower Gabrielino trails. Hop onto the Lower Gabrielino, which climbs the edge of Santa Anita Canyon and skirts the very edge of Sturtevant Falls at 2.3 miles.

While the area around the falls can get crowded—especially on hot weekends—the trail above the falls is significantly more serene. The usual sycamore, alder, and oak provide ample shade here, and the only sounds you'll hear are those of rushing water and wind through the leaves above you. The Upper and Lower Gabrielino trails meet at 2.8 miles. Keep right to head toward Spruce Grove Campground, passing the Cascade picnic area at 3.3 miles and reaching the hike-in campground at 3.9 miles. The Gabrielino Trail continues north toward Newcomb Pass (Hike 84) at 4.1 miles; stay left here to skirt the edge of historic Sturtevant Camp, staying on the south side of the creek across from the campground and keeping your eye out for the Zion Trail.

The Upper Zion leaves the creeks you've been enjoying—although thankfully the shade remains mostly intact—and climbs up the north side of Mount Zion. At 5.2 miles there is a short spur to the summit of Mount Zion, where you can enjoy an excellent view of Santa Anita Canyon. Continue the descent

down the switchbacking, more exposed southern section of the Zion Trail and at 6.7 miles, join the Lower Winter Creek Trail and pass through Hoegee's Trail Camp—the site of yet another former wilderness resort that now serves as an excellent hike-in campground. The Lower Winter Creek Trail returns you to the shaded creekside hiking that makes this canyon so wonderful, before it ends at Roberts Camp at 8.1 miles. Return to the trailhead the way you came in, remembering that this route ends with a rather unpleasant, steep climb up that paved road.

EXTENDING YOUR TRIP

If a staff member is working at Sturtevant Camp, feel free to say hello and ask to see some of the historic buildings (and ride on the famous Big Swing). Built in 1897, this is the only surviving wilderness resort from the Great Hiking Era, and currently offers lodging and scheduled events. It is also home to the oldest existing Forest Service structure still in its original location—a cabin hand-built by Louis Newcomb, one of the San Gabriel Mountains' first rangers. Head to www.sturtevantcamp.com for more info and reservations.

87 Hermit Falls

RATING/ DIFFICULTY	ROUNDTRIP	ELEV GAIN/ HIGH POINT	SEASON
****/2	2.6 miles	675 feet/ 2207 feet	Year-round

Map: USGS Mount Wilson; **Contact:** Angeles National Forest/San Gabriel Mountains National Monument, Los Angeles River Ranger District; **Notes:** Adventure Pass required to park at trailhead. Dogs allowed on leash but not recommended if you're headed to the bottom of Hermit Falls; **GPS:** N 34.196054, W 118.023249

 *This smaller, more rugged, and slightly more remote waterfall is a bit off the beaten path for those tired of the crowds at Sturtevant Falls. Although somewhat less crowded, Hermit Falls is still a popular day hike with those looking to cool off in the mist or jump into the pools at the base of the falls.*

GETTING THERE

From Interstate 210 in Arcadia, take exit 32 for Santa Anita Avenue. Head north on Santa Anita Avenue and continue on Chantry Flat Road to its end at 4.9 miles. Parking is notoriously difficult here, especially on weekends. Be extra attentive to parking signage and be patient. The Adams' Pack Station has overflow parking, but you'll have to pay an additional fee—even if you've already purchased an Adventure Pass.

ON THE TRAIL

Follow the paved path east of Chantry Flat to 0.2 mile, where you'll keep right to start on the Hermit Falls Trail. This stretch of trail has extensive views down the canyon as it switchbacks through a lush landscape of oaks, black sage, and California sagebrush. Along the cooler, shadier stretches, you may even see swaths of ferns hugging the canyon walls—a sight you probably wouldn't expect in Southern California.

As you near the bottom of Santa Anita Canyon, the tree canopy thickens, making you feel a hundred miles away from the city you drove in from. Just past 0.7 mile, keep right at the junction with the First Water Trail and boulder hop to the east side of the creek

The shaded Hermit Falls Trail surprises hikers with its lush trailside ferns.

to continue south on the Hermit Falls Trail. Along the way, you'll pass a few of the region's ubiquitous flood control dams and remnants of the First Water Camp, a wilderness resort that operated from 1919 until the floods of 1938 washed most of it downstream.

At 1.3 miles, the trail hugs a narrow ledge on the canyon's west side and approaches the top of Hermit Falls—likely audible before it's visible. If you plan on swimming or jumping, please be aware of water levels—both for the speed of the current and the amount of water to cushion your landing at the bottom. While most jumpers enjoy this thrill without incident, average annual rescues here are starting to get into the double digits, and a few have not made it out of the canyon alive. The trail ends at the top of the falls, where there is usually a distressing amount of graffiti. Use-trails and scramble routes provide paths to the bottom for those too wary to jump but who still want to explore. When you're done, return the way you came in.

EXTENDING YOUR TRIP

Following the First Water Trail north after you visit the falls will get you to Roberts Camp, where you can visit any of the highlights of Santa Anita Canyon (Hike 86) that you still have energy for.

88 Jones Peak

RATING/ DIFFICULTY	ROUNDTRIP	ELEV GAIN/ HIGH POINT	SEASON
****/4	6.4 miles	2240 feet/ 3375 feet	Year-round

Map: USGS Mount Wilson; **Contact:** City of Sierra Madre; **Notes:** Bailey Canyon Wilderness Park open dawn–dusk. Dogs allowed on leash only. No overnight parking allowed; **GPS:** N 34.170856, W 118.061131

A thick marine layer of clouds hides the sprawl below Jones Peak.

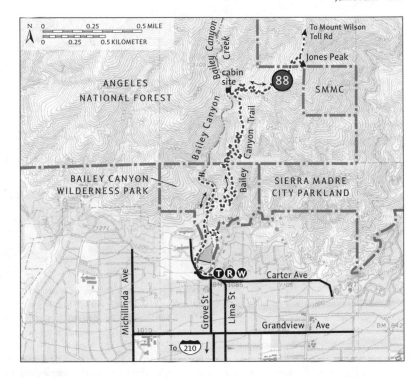

 This heart-pounding climb to one of the most prominent lower peaks in the Front Range provides a nice workout, fantastic views, and plenty of fragrant sage scrub along the way. Optional side trips to an ephemeral waterfall and a densely populated oak grove round out the hiking experience.

GETTING THERE

From Interstate 210 in East Pasadena, take the Rosemead Boulevard North/Michillinda Avenue exit and go north on Michillinda Avenue. Follow Michillinda for 1.3 miles, then take a right onto Grandview Avenue. In 0.4 mile, turn left on Grove Street, which ends at the entrance to Bailey Canyon Wilderness Park where there is a parking lot. The trailhead is at the far western side of the lot.

ON THE TRAIL

Follow the Bailey Canyon Trail west through a few open picnic areas. Pass through a turnstile in the chain link fence and follow the paved road around the edge of a flood control dam. The pavement ends at 0.3 mile and you're immediately plunged into some exemplary SoCal vegetation—prickly pears line the canyon wall to your west, while the Bailey Canyon Creek bed is flanked by live oaks stretching above you to provide shade. You soon reach a junction with a bridge leading to the right. Crossing this bridge will take you to a short nature trail through a beautiful oak grove—it's a lovely addition either before your climb or at the end of the hike. For now, stay to the left to continue on the Bailey Canyon Trail.

At 0.5 mile, stay to the left for a quick trip up Bailey Canyon, which narrows, cools, and becomes dense with foliage. Although this stretch is only a quarter mile, it's surprisingly rugged and may take you longer than you'd expect. You'll reach the bottom of an ephemeral waterfall at 0.7 mile, flowing during the wet season and for a few days after a big rainstorm. There is an unmaintained trail above these falls that eventually meets the main trail near the cabin site, but that route requires technical climbing gear.

Backtrack to the last junction and turn left to start the climb to Jones Peak. Unlike the trail you were just hiking, this route is clear, very well maintained, and mostly exposed to the sun—meaning it can get brutally hot in the summer months. It's a relatively no-nonsense climb from here on out. On clear days, you'll have phenomenal views of the foothill cities below you as you climb, and in the winter and spring the plentiful black sage and California sagebrush that line this route will keep your nose happy.

At 2.5 miles, enjoy a brief, shaded respite near the foundation of an old cabin perched on a ridge with views that would fetch many millions of dollars today. Past this, the trail switchbacks up a branch of Bailey Canyon, twisting and turning through manzanita and ceanothus. At 3.4 miles, pass under a small tree at a saddle just north of Jones Peak and overlooking Little Santa Anita Canyon to the east. A firebreak route heads north toward the Mount Wilson Toll Road, but you'll scramble up the north side of Jones Peak to

its small, exposed summit. From here, enjoy your top-of-the-world views and return the way you came.

89 Monrovia Canyon Falls

RATING/ DIFFICULTY	ROUNDTRIP	ELEV GAIN/ HIGH POINT	SEASON
*****/2	2.6 miles	586 feet/ 1730 feet	Year-round

Map: USGS Azusa; **Contact:** Monrovia Canyon Park; **Notes:** Park open 7:00 AM–5:00 PM on weekends, 8:00 AM–5:00 PM on weekdays. Closed Tuesdays. Dogs allowed on leash. Parking fee required—higher on weekends and holidays; **GPS:** N 34.172726, W 117.991550

Monrovia Canyon Park is one of the true gems of the San Gabriel Mountains. This route heads to the park's year-round thirty-foot waterfall, tucked in the back of Monrovia Canyon amid an impressive canopy of twisted, old-growth oak trees. This is a wonderfully peaceful and serene getaway from city life and is a perfect hiking spot for families.

GETTING THERE

From Interstate 210 eastbound in Arcadia, take exit 32 for Santa Anita Avenue. Travel north on Santa Anita and take a right onto Foothill Boulevard in 0.2 mile. In 2 miles, turn left onto Canyon Boulevard. From the 210 westbound in Duarte, take exit 35A for Mountain Avenue in Duarte. Head north on Mountain Avenue for 1.1 miles, then turn left onto Foothill Boulevard. In 0.7 mile, take a right onto Canyon Boulevard. Once you're heading north on Canyon Boulevard, in 0.7

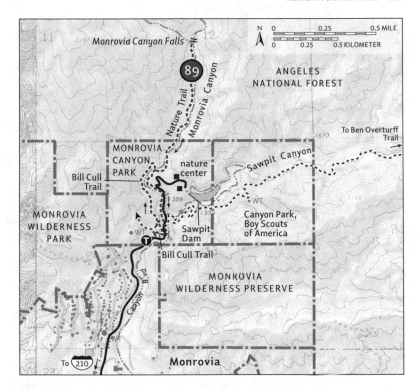

Monrovia Canyon Falls

89

ANGELES
NATIONAL FOREST

To Ben Overturff
Trail

MONROVIA
CANYON
PARK

nature
center

Bill Cull
Trail

Sawpit Canyon

MONROVIA
WILDERNESS
PARK

Sawpit
Dam

Canyon Park,
Boy Scouts
of America

Bill Cull Trail

MONROVIA
WILDERNESS PRESERVE

To 210

Monrovia

mile, take a right to continue on Canyon Boulevard. Take the second right to stay on Canyon Boulevard and travel 0.5 mile to Monrovia Canyon Park's parking lot.

ON THE TRAIL

Hike past the entrance kiosk and look for the signed trailhead for the Bill Cull Trail on your left. Begin your climb in the oak-dappled sunlight and keep right at 0.2 mile as the looming form of the Sawpit Canyon Dam emerges to the northeast. This monstrous 147-foot-tall structure was built in 1927 but shortly after it was completed, engineers discovered the dam's foundation was too weak to hold the water it was planned to contain. It was never filled to capacity and in 2000, a notch was cut into the dam to create a free-flowing, artificial waterfall.

The trail meanders north in a slow but steady climb, almost entirely in shade. At 0.6 mile, a few babbling brooks and streams make their way into the picture inside what feels like an enormous amphitheater of native oaks—it really is a stunning sight. Keep left here to join the Nature Trail heading north toward the waterfall, and at 1.3 miles, hop over a few boulders to reach

Monrovia Canyon's oak trees form an inspiring outdoor cathedral.

the base of Monrovia Canyon Falls—a far nicer sight than the artificial falls cut into that dam.

Backtrack along the Nature Trail to the junction with the Bill Cull Trail, and this time keep left to continue south along the Nature Trail. Beneath the lovely oak canopy, be sure to note the unique ceramic plate signposts along the trail, which correspond to an information sheet you can pick up at the entry station. Here, the trail parallels the paved road that heads to the nature center. Go straight when the road makes a sharp curve east to continue through some of the most beautiful riparian groves anywhere in the San Gabriel Mountains. Keep straight again at 2.5 miles at the junction with the road heading east toward the Ben Overturff Trail and return to the trailhead.

EXTENDING YOUR TRIP

Spur trails and paved roads connect this route with the nature center. More ambitious hikers can walk along the private dirt road past the Sawpit Dam and a Boy Scout camp to the Ben Overturff Trail to the east, which visits the site of the Deer Park wilderness resort (active 1911–1945). This route may occasionally be closed to the public when the nearby police firing range is in use.

90 Fish Canyon Falls

RATING/ DIFFICULTY	ROUNDTRIP	ELEV GAIN/ HIGH POINT	SEASON
****/3	4.8 miles	836 feet/ 1398 feet	Year-round

Map: USGS Azusa; **Contact:** Angeles National Forest/San Gabriel Mountains National Monument, Los Angeles River Ranger District and Vulcan Materials Company Azusa Rock Quarry; **Notes:** Access gates open 7:00 AM–7:00 PM Apr–Sept, 7:00 AM–5:00 PM Oct–Mar. Dogs allowed on leash and on weekends only. Trail may be closed temporarily for safety or maintenance reasons; **GPS:** N 34 09.399, W 117 55.443

 *A quick trip to one of the loveliest waterfalls in the San Gabriels, this moderate trek on a recently restored trail takes you through a working rock quarry and into a beautiful riparian canyon before ending at a three-tiered, eighty-foot-tall waterfall. You'll pass the ruins of long-gone cabins along the way and more than earn a dip in one of the canyon's swimming holes.*

GETTING THERE

From Interstate 210 or the northern terminus of Interstate 605 in Duarte, take the Mount Olive exit. Take a right onto Huntington Drive and in 0.6 mile, take a left onto Encanto Parkway (take note, the street sign is obscured). In 1.2 miles, the road becomes Fish Canyon Road, and in another 0.5 mile it ends at the Vulcan Materials plant. You will see a sign directing you to pass through the center gate to reach the large parking area at the trailhead. In 2016, the City of Duarte began

funding a free shuttle from the Duarte/City of Hope Gold Line stop to the Fish Canyon trailhead. The shuttle runs from 7 AM to 6 PM. At the time of this writing, a year-round schedule had not been solidified, so check with the City of Duarte for more information at www.accessduarte.com.

ON THE TRAIL

In 2014, after years of restricting access to the canyon's mouth, Vulcan opened a new trailhead here, replacing a bypass route described by other hikers as "torturous" and "absurd." Now you can start at the parking area on the 0.7-mile Access Trail, which passes through both an active quarry operation and a riparian canyon being restored by the company. Interpretive signs point out native flora and fauna along the way, highlighting the canyon's slow but steady transition from a natural resource to be exploited to a natural resource to be enjoyed for its own sake. At 0.7 mile, the trail passes through a gate and crosses a bridge into the canyon proper. Consider the bridge your looking-glass gateway—as soon as you cross it, the world of heavy industry is quickly replaced with a beautiful wilderness canyon, lined with white and black sage, California sagebrush, ceanothus, buckwheat, and more riparian trees and shrubs along the creek bank. And yes, that includes poison oak, so watch which plants you're touching.

At the 0.8-mile mark, stay right at the junction with the old bypass route and continue north into the canyon, passing extensive colonies of prickly pear and some surprisingly large agave along the way. The trail stays away from the creek bed for most of the journey, but you'll hop across the

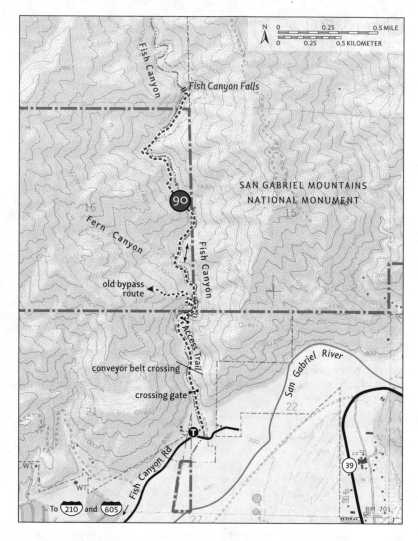

intermittent stream in Fern Canyon at 1.1 miles and pass the few remaining foundations of old twentieth-century getaway cabins at 1.4 miles.

The trail meanders through some shady groves and down one very unusual "spiral staircase"–styled section of trail before hopping the creek again at the 2-mile mark.

Fish Canyon Falls has delighted hikers in the San Gabriels for generations.

From here, the trail takes you on a quick scramble up a steep granite wall before dropping you off at the base of Fish Canyon Falls at 2.4 miles. In the dry months the falls may not be much to look at, but in winter and spring the water forms a beautiful wading pool that serves as your day's reward. Hike back the way you came.

Opposite: The rugged, pine-covered terrain of the Central San Gabriels is a surprisingly stark departure from the landscape of lower elevations.

central san gabriel mountains

Generally speaking, the Central San Gabriels are a bit taller, a bit more rugged, and farther east than their Front Range brethren. The higher elevations here mean the chaparral and sage scrub of the lower peaks give way to oak and pine woodlands that have a drastically different feel than those pointy plants of the low slopes, and the peaks are likely to see snowpack during the winter months.

Hikes here include epic full-day treks to remote peaks in one of the first wilderness areas in the country; routes that wander through ancient, windswept pines clinging to barren summit ridges; moderate hikes that reach gently flowing waterfalls above picturesque foothill towns; and an absolute must-do trek along the banks of the often-underestimated San Gabriel River.

91 Shortcut Canyon

RATING/ DIFFICULTY	ROUNDTRIP	ELEV GAIN/ HIGH POINT	SEASON
****/4	7 miles	1612 feet/ 4758 feet	Year-round (best Nov–Apr)

Maps: USGS Chilao Flat, Mount Wilson; **Contact:** Angeles National Forest/San Gabriel Mountains National Monument, Los Angeles River Ranger District; **Notes:** Adventure Pass

With good winter precipitation, Shortcut Canyon Creek fills up nicely.

required at trailhead. Dogs allowed on leash. West Fork Campground is first-come, first-served; **GPS:** N 34.273332, W 118.032677

🦴🏠🌲〰️ *Before the Angeles Crest Highway was finished, Shortcut Canyon was one of the major thoroughfares for hikers, trappers, and explorers looking to trek deeper into the San Gabriel Mountains. Today, there's a good chance you'll have the trail to yourself.*

GETTING THERE

From Interstate 210 in La Cañada Flintridge, take exit 20 toward the Angeles Crest Highway (CA-2) and follow it for 18.9 miles east. Look for signs marking the Shortcut picnic area and nearby trails (though they may be difficult to spot from the road) and park in the pullout on the north side of the highway. The trailhead is on the south side of the highway. Display your Adventure Pass.

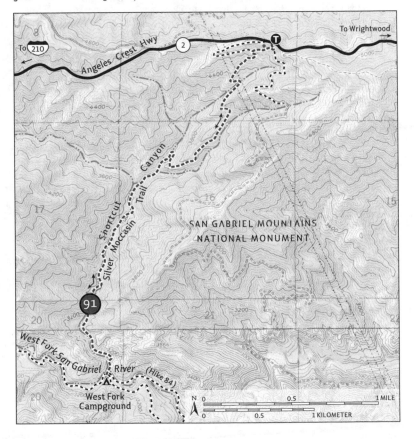

ON THE TRAIL

Before you decide to trek down into Shortcut Canyon, know that this route was especially hard-hit by the Station Fire and is a bit of a work in progress. Crews are working to restore the trail from fire damage, but hiking may still be tough going in spots. If you have your heart set on a babbling brook, wait until after a few good rainstorms to let the rivers and streams really come to life before hiking this route.

Look for a series of switchbacks that descend from the paved road to a fire road running parallel to the highway. Head west along the fire road for a short distance and turn left onto the trail at about 0.2 mile. From here, the trail makes a quick descent into Shortcut Canyon. You'll hop across the bottom of the canyon at 0.7 mile and continue your descent on its eastern flank, rejoining the canyon floor at 1.7 miles.

If the area has had a good, wet winter, this is where the trail really becomes worth the effort of getting here—even if you've had to duck under toppled tree trunks or dodge patches of poison oak. Water pours into pools and cascades down the rocky canyon, requiring several dozen crossings (depending on the water level), ranging from easy boulder hops to full-on fords. If we've had a decent amount of winter rains, be sure to wear either waterproof boots or quick-dry shoes with grippy soles to make your life easier.

The trail continues this way until the 3.4-mile mark, where you'll meet the larger flow of the West Fork San Gabriel River. Look for a good crossing to reach West Fork Campground, where you can enjoy a few minutes or a night before you head back the way you came.

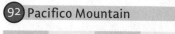

92 Pacifico Mountain

RATING/ DIFFICULTY	LOOP	ELEV GAIN/ HIGH POINT	SEASON
***/5	11.7 miles	2188 feet/ 7124 feet	May–Nov

Map: USGS Pacifico Mountain; **Contact:** Angeles National Forest/San Gabriel Mountains National Monument, Santa Clara/Mojave Rivers Ranger District; **Notes:** Adventure Pass required at trailhead. Dogs allowed on leash. Mount Pacifico Campground is a hike-in campground open May–Nov; **GPS:** N 34.3915860, W 118.0810380

 Seven-thousand-foot Pacifico Mountain is the westernmost high peak in the San Gabriel Mountains and one of the most prominent in the entire range. The views from its summit are some of the best possible, sweeping across the Antelope Valley and over vast swaths of the deep interior of the San Gabriels. Although damage from the Station Fire is noticeable here, it remains a challenging and worthwhile trek.

GETTING THERE

From Interstate 5 just south of Santa Clarita, take the Antelope Valley Freeway (CA-14) toward Palmdale/Lancaster for 25.2 miles. Take exit 26 for Santiago Road and turn right (south). In 0.7 mile, keep right to turn onto Soledad Canyon Road. Stay on Soledad Canyon Road for 0.4 mile, then turn left onto Aliso Canyon Road. In 7.3 miles, turn right onto the Angeles Forest Highway (County Road N3). In 2.7 miles, park at the Mill Creek Summit picnic area and display your Adventure Pass. Note that the Angeles Forest Highway may be seasonally closed for the winter.

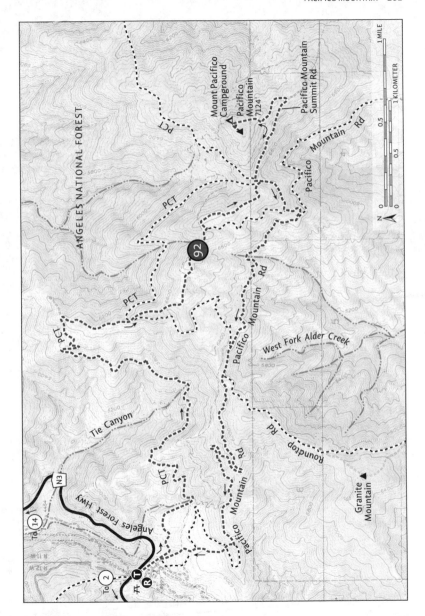

Snow near the summit of Pacifico Mountain

ON THE TRAIL
Head southeast toward the Mount Pacifico Campground on the Pacific Crest Trail (PCT), keeping left at 0.2 mile to continue east on the PCT instead of climbing up the mountainside. This section of trail hugs the north side of Pacifico and makes a very gradual ascent. The trail makes a sharp turn to the north at 2 miles before reaching a flat area at 3.4 miles and turning south. Keep heading south here as the PCT follows one of the region's many old fire roads and at 3.8 miles, you'll reach a junction with some old fire roads. This area can get confusing depending on the age of your map, as the PCT has been rerouted several times here over the years. For this route, head straight, leaving the PCT and ignoring another old fire road to the right to ascend the broad northwest summit ridge. If you don't want the steeper climb, the PCT rejoins this route at a major trail junction to the southwest of Pacifico Mountain's summit. The fire road to your right at 3.8 miles will eventually get you to Pacifico

Mountain Road as well, but it's in very rough shape and it's incredibly easy to lose.

From the junction at 3.8 miles, follow the middle trail as it heads southeast and then makes a sharp turn southward on a slight decline at 4.8 miles, joining Pacifico Mountain Summit Road at 5.3 miles. Head east from here and keep left at 5.9 miles to make the final push to the boulder-strewn, exposed summit of Pacifico Mountain at 6.4 miles.

Backtrack to reach the junction with your approach trail at 7.6 miles. Keep left to continue heading southwest on Pacifico Mountain Summit Road toward Pacifico Mountain Road, which offers an easier descent and new views looking south into the interior of the San Gabriels and the Station Fire burn zone. Keep left at a faint use-trail at 7.9 miles and then turn right onto Pacifico Mountain Road at 8.1 miles. Stay on this road past the next two junctions. At the 11-mile mark, you can either follow Pacifico Mountain Road on a gentle descent back to the Mill Creek area or, for this route, take the hikers' bypass directly down the slope to cut off some unnecessary distance. At the junction with PCT, stay left to return to the trailhead.

93 Mount Hillyer

RATING/ DIFFICULTY	LOOP	ELEV GAIN/ HIGH POINT	SEASON
***/3	5.7 miles	958 feet/ 6215 feet	Year-round

Map: USGS Chilao Flat; **Contact:** Angeles National Forest/San Gabriel Mountains National Monument, Los Angeles River Ranger District; **Notes:** Adventure Pass required at trailhead. Visitor center open weekends. Dogs allowed on leash. Campgrounds and roads may be closed during the winter or during predicted inclement weather; **GPS:** N 34.331039, W 118.011957

This moderate loop along parts of the Silver Moccasin Trail meanders through the boulder-strewn landscape that served as a hideout for horse thieves and early rangers alike. Although the somewhat disputed summit isn't much to write home about, the hike itself is in a lovely region of the San Gabriels with some fine views of nearby prominent peaks.

GETTING THERE

From Interstate 210 in La Cañada Flintridge, take exit 20 toward the Angeles Crest Highway (CA-2) and follow it for 26.2 miles to the turnoff for the Chilao Visitor Center (open weekends). Turn left and continue on this road 0.6 mile, past a few government shelters and the visitor center. The Silver Moccasin Trail crosses the road at a marked sign. There's a small parking area next to the intersection. Display your Adventure Pass.

The rugged terrain near Mount Hillyer was popular with horse thieves and bandits.

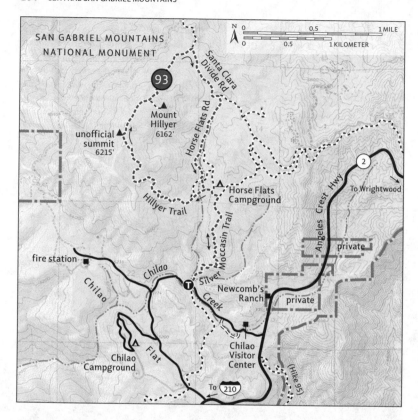

ON THE TRAIL

Head onto the Silver Moccasin Trail from the north side of the road, crossing under some telephone wires and hiking on the sandy floor of a confluence of washes. The sand slowly reveals a rocky, uneven trail as it winds through chamise and at 1.1 miles, turn left onto the Hillyer Trail. Keep left again as the trail hugs the outskirts of Horse Flats Campground and follow the trail west, climbing up through the incense cedars and Jeffrey pines as the low, rocky peaks roll out in all directions. As you keep climbing

upward through a series of large boulders many consider the highlight of this route, keep an eye out on the trail for mountain bikers as well as boulderers lugging their crash pads into the forest—the trail is a popular area for both.

And now, a bit of a topographical controversy: Most maps mark Mount Hillyer's summit as a 6162-foot, moderately prominent bump shortly to the east of the main trail at 2.7 miles. However, most hikers consider a 6215-foot bump at the 2.4-mile mark to be the true summit. (Mount Williamson to the east—Hike 98—suffers from a similar summit identity crisis.) The trail continues to the northeast from the unofficial summit, with views of Roundtop, Granite Mountain, and Pacifico Mountain across the North Fork Alder Creek. If you want to hit the officially mapped summit, head east along the flat at 2.7 miles to the rocky bump at 6162 feet; otherwise, continue on the Hillyer Trail and take a right onto Santa Clara Divide Road at 3.3 miles and another right onto Horse Flats Road at 3.8 miles. Close the loop at 4.6 miles and continue back the way you came in.

94 Vetter Mountain

RATING/ DIFFICULTY	LOOP	ELEV GAIN/ HIGH POINT	SEASON
****/2	3.9 miles	531 feet/ 5909 feet	Year-round

Map: USGS Chilao Flat; **Contact:** Angeles National Forest/San Gabriel Mountains National Monument, Los Angeles River Ranger District; **Notes:** Adventure Pass required to park at trailhead. Dogs allowed on leash; **GPS:** N 34.298069, W 118.005968

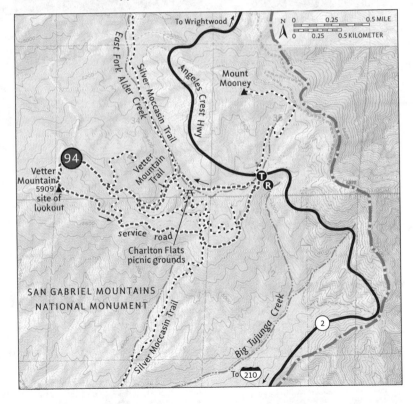

The "Phantom Sea" of the marine layer usually breaks near Vetter Mountain.

🚶‍👦 🦴 🏠 ⚘ **This easy loop takes the hiker through a section of the San Gabriels in recovery. The Station Fire blazed through here in 2009, devastating the tall pines, peaceful picnic area, and fire lookout tower. Volunteer and Forest Service crews are restoring the region's trails and structures, and although the forest will take years to recover, the views from the summit of Vetter are still worth the trip.**

GETTING THERE

From Interstate 210 in La Cañada Flintridge, take exit 20 toward the Angeles Crest Highway (CA-2) and follow it for 23 miles. Park outside the Charlton Flats picnic grounds and display your Adventure Pass.

ON THE TRAIL

Head toward the Vetter Mountain Lookout on the service road, then keep right at 0.1 mile to descend toward the Charlton Flats picnic grounds. The trail follows the East Fork Alder Creek here, and in the winter and spring you may be following a lovely stream through what was once an equally lovely grove of pines. At 0.7 mile, cross the creek bed and head west on the Vetter Mountain Trail, staying to the right at the junction with the long-distance Silver Moccasin Trail just beyond. This section of trail meanders on the north slope of Vetter Mountain and—once the forest recovers a bit—provides a nice contrast in San Gabriel plant communities. This area is in the montane forest community, where canyon oaks and Jeffrey pines reign supreme alongside bigcone Douglas-fir and incense cedar. Beware of large patches of poodle-dog bush here; it should become less prevalent as the landscape recovers.

At 1.7 miles the trail turns south and climbs up the mountain's back. Once you reach the summit ridge, the San Gabriel chaparral community dominates Vetter's sunnier southern slope. Here you'll see the prickly yuccas, dense chamise, ceanothus, and sages that are visible along most of the southern slopes in the Front Range. At 1.9 miles, you'll reach the site of the historic Vetter Mountain Lookout, a low wooden tower built in 1937. The tower remained active through 1981, and a citizen volunteer group restored it to operational service in 1998. Since the Station Fire, those same volunteers have pledged to rebuild a tower matching the original 1937 design, pouring a concrete foundation in 2014 and beginning to work on the surrounding structure.

Whether or not the tower is there when you visit, you'll be able to enjoy some wonderful views of the backside of Mount Wilson to the south, Strawberry Peak and Mount Lawlor to the west, Pacifico Mountain to the north, and the bump of nearby Mount Mooney to the northeast. When you're done, hike back to the trailhead along the service road, crossing the Silver Moccasin Trail again at 3.2 miles.

95 Devils Canyon

RATING/ DIFFICULTY	ROUNDTRIP	ELEV GAIN/ HIGH POINT	SEASON
****/3	5.8 miles	1370 feet/ 5309 feet	Year-round

Map: USGS Waterman Mountain; **Contact:** Angeles National Forest/San Gabriel Mountains National Monument, San Gabriel River Ranger District; **Notes:** Adventure Pass required to park at trailhead. Dogs allowed on leash. No wilderness permit required unless your group exceeds twenty-five people; **GPS:** N 34.323697, W 118.003140

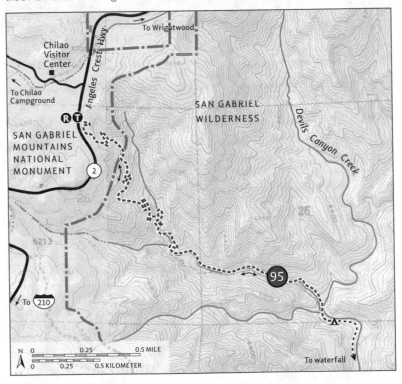

The San Gabriel Wilderness offers peaceful solitude on many of its trails.

This quiet hike will take you from expansive views of the San Gabriel Wilderness down to a narrow canyon floor, where you'll boulder hop and bushwhack your way to a backcountry campsite beside Devils Canyon Creek.

GETTING THERE

From Interstate 210 in La Cañada Flintridge, take exit 20 toward the Angeles Crest Highway (CA-2) and follow it for 25.7 miles. The trailhead will be on your left, just past one of two entrances to Chilao Campground. Display your Adventure Pass.

ON THE TRAIL

Carefully cross the Angeles Crest Highway and head into the well-signed San Gabriel Wilderness. As you'll be starting at the highest elevation and making your way down to the canyon's floor, be sure to leave some energy in the reserves for the climb out. The trail wastes no time in presenting some incredible, sweeping views of Devils Canyon,

with the prominent camel-backed ridge of Twin Peaks to your east. Descend beneath the shade of towering bigcone Douglas-firs, treading carefully on the narrow trail's several washed-out areas. At 1.5 miles, the trail hops into one of the northern tributaries of Devils Canyon. The dense shrubs and trees should clue you in that an ephemeral stream lives at the bottom of this canyon, but unless it's fueled by recent rain or snowmelt it may be dry. This region is especially photogenic in the fall and early winter when the sycamore leaves make their slow transition from green to gold.

The trail continues to the southeast, hopping in and out of the creek bed and enthusiastically switching sides. The path is faint but well-traveled, and if you pay attention to your surroundings you shouldn't have any trouble sticking to it. At 2.6 miles, the trail gets a bit more overgrown, but at 2.8 miles it reaches a wider canyon where Devils Canyon Creek flows year-round. Continue south another 0.1 mile to a broad flat on the creek's west bank that serves as a backcountry campsite.

EXTENDING YOUR TRIP

The most prominent waterfall in Devils Canyon is 2 miles farther down the canyon from the campground. The trail is extremely faint and may require bushwhacking and scrambling in spots. Further progress down the canyon requires technical gear and climbing experience. If you want to see some stars, consider camping at the walk-in backcountry site (no campfires) or staying near the trailhead at Chilao Campground. Chilao is open seasonally and is first-come, first-served.

96 Cooper Canyon Falls

RATING/ DIFFICULTY	ROUNDTRIP	ELEV GAIN/ HIGH POINT	SEASON
****/3	3.1 miles	665 feet/ 6338 feet	May–Nov

Maps: USGS Waterman Mountain, Juniper Hills; **Contact:** Angeles National Forest/ San Gabriel Mountains National Monument, Santa Clara/Mojave Rivers Ranger District; **Notes:** Adventure Pass required to park at trailhead. Dogs allowed on leash. Buckhorn Campground is first-come, first-served and is closed during the winter months; **GPS:** N 34.347485, W 117.911106

The Burkhart Trail is shaded by enormous pine trees.

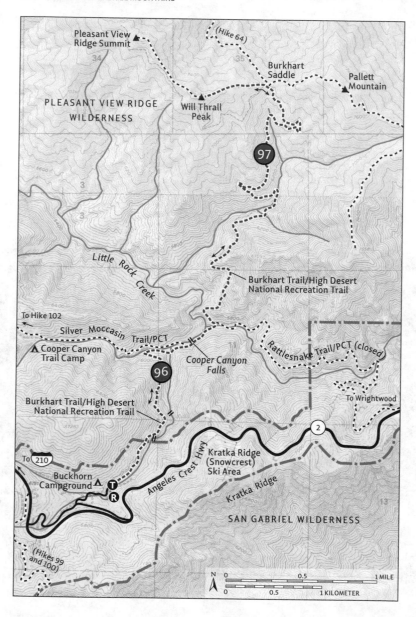

Pleasant View
Ridge Summit

(Hike 64)

Burkhart
Saddle

Pallett
Mountain

34

35

PLEASANT VIEW RIDGE
WILDERNESS

Will Thrall
Peak

97

3

3

Little Rock Creek

Burkhart Trail/High Desert
National Recreation Trail

To Hike 102

Silver Moccasin Trail/PCT

Cooper Canyon
Trail Camp

Rattlesnake Trail/PCT (closed)

96

Cooper Canyon
Falls

To Wrightwood

Burkhart Trail/High Desert
National Recreation Trail

2

To 210

Kratka Ridge
(Snowcrest)
Ski Area

Buckhorn
Campground

T

R

Angeles Crest Hwy

Kratka Ridge

SAN GABRIEL WILDERNESS

(Hikes 99
and 100)

N   0   0.5   1 MILE

0   0.5   1 KILOMETER

Suitable for almost all hikers, this mild journey makes a gentle descent along a branch of Little Rock Creek to a secluded cascade within a stone's throw of one of the San Gabriel Mountains' most beautiful campgrounds. This hike is an exemplary introduction to the San Gabriel high country, where towering Douglas-fir and Jeffrey pines reach into clear blue skies and flood the air with fresh, invigorating scents—a perfect way to escape a warm day in the lower urbanized elevations.

GETTING THERE

From Interstate 210 in La Cañada Flintridge, take exit 20 toward the Angeles Crest Highway (CA-2) and follow it for 33.9 miles. Shortly after you pass the Mount Waterman Ski Area, turn left to enter the Buckhorn Campground. Drive through the campground, following the signs for the Burkhart Trail, and park in the day-use lot. Display your Adventure Pass. If the campground is closed, you'll have to park on the Angeles Crest Highway and hike in.

ON THE TRAIL

From Buckhorn Campground, hike on the Burkhart Trail/High Desert National Recreation Trail into the Pleasant View Ridge Wilderness. Enjoy the cooler, high-elevation air as you meander through giant boulders and even larger pine trees and register the faint white noise of hidden waterfalls in the canyon to the east.

Initially, you may only be able to hear the sound of rushing water in the canyon directly below the trail, but at 1.1 miles the trail makes a sharp switchback descent, hopping over a southern fork of the creek at 1.3 miles in Cooper Canyon. Stay to the right at the junction with the Silver Moccasin Trail/Pacific Crest Trail (PCT) at 1.4 miles and keep your eyes peeled: at just past the 1.5-mile mark, the trail makes another descent while the creek is visible just to your left. If there's a good flow of water, you'll also be able to hear the sound of Cooper Canyon Falls from here. Look for a well-worn series of use-trails descending to the bottom of the canyon on the west, and carefully make your way down. It's a rough, mostly unmaintained route but it should be easy enough for most hikers who aren't afraid to take it slowly and get their hands (and pants) a little dirty. Near the bottom, a series of ropes have been tied around tree trunks and boulders to provide a bit of guidance, but they are more of an aid than a necessity

At the bottom of the short scramble, you'll end up in a beautiful alcove that feels like a natural amphitheater—mossy, cascading Cooper Canyon Falls is to your left, framed by the canyon walls and highlighted by a natural reflecting pool at its base. There are plenty of places to unpack a picnic lunch or just sit and enjoy the sound of falling water and calling birds. When your natural batteries have been recharged, climb your way up and head out the way you came in.

97 Will Thrall Peak via Buckhorn

RATING/ DIFFICULTY	ROUNDTRIP	ELEV GAIN/ HIGH POINT	SEASON
*****/5	11.2 miles	2203 feet/ 7845 feet	May–Nov

Maps: USGS Waterman Mountain, Juniper Hills; **Contact:** Angeles National Forest/ San Gabriel Mountains National Monument, Santa Clara/Mojave Rivers Ranger District;

The Burkhart/High Desert National Recreation Trail crosses Little Rock Creek in a shaded glen.

Notes: Adventure Pass required to park at trailhead. Dogs allowed on leash. Buckhorn Campground is first-come, first-served and is closed during the winter months; **GPS:** N 34.347485, W 117.911106

 *The full-day trek to Will Thrall Peak is one of the toughest, most adventurous, remote, and sublimely rewarding hikes in the high San Gabriels. This absolutely epic day hike offers stunning scenery and profound solitude in equal doses for experienced hikers with high endurance. Be warned that the elevation gain here is misleading—you'll be making that gain both on your way to and from the peak.*

GETTING THERE

From Interstate 210 in La Cañada Flintridge, take exit 20 toward the Angeles Crest Highway (CA-2) and follow it for 33.9 miles. Shortly after you pass the Mount Waterman Ski Area, turn left to enter the Buckhorn Campground. Drive through the campground, following the signs for the Burkhart

Trail, and park in the day-use lot. Display your Adventure Pass. If the campground is closed, you'll have to park on the Angeles Crest Highway and hike in.

ON THE TRAIL

Follow the route for Cooper Canyon Falls (Hike 96). Once you reach the falls, continue past the scramble and hop across another branch of the Little Rock Creek at 1.7 miles. Just beyond this, continue straight at the junction with the Rattlesnake Trail, a branch of the Pacific Crest Trail (PCT) that has been closed since 2005 to protect the endangered mountain yellow-legged frog. The trail rises up and over a crest around the 1.9-mile mark, providing some tremendous views of the Pleasant View Ridge Wilderness in nearly every direction.

There's a long stretch of slow incline now, regaining everything you've lost while descending from the trailhead and then some. The trail here is now mostly on sunny, south-facing slopes below six thousand feet, which means some of the chaparral plant community will begin to make appearances again, providing a nice contrast to the cover of higher-elevation pines you began your hike beneath. Look for Spanish bayonets, toyon, manzanita, and scrub oaks as you continue your long journey north. The trail makes another quick descent to a canyon floor at 3.3 miles and it's all uphill from here, so get ready.

Past this, the trail makes a long switchback up the southeastern face of Will Thrall Peak and then starts a no-nonsense assault heading north. You won't be able to make out the summit from here but you will have some astounding views of the peaks behind you, including Waterman Mountain, Kratka Ridge, Mount Akawie, and Winston Peak. You'll also be able to make out large sections of the Burkhart Trail itself, which means you'll get to have one of those "Whoa, look how far I've hiked!" moments, too.

You'll reach Burkhart Saddle at 5 miles, although it may feel like longer than that when you're hiking. From here, look for a faint use-trail that climbs pretty much straight up the side of the mountain to the west, threading a path between boulders and tree trunks with tight switchbacks on loose, steep dirt. Even if you don't usually hike with trekking poles, you may want to pack them for this exceedingly steep and exposed incline. Although tough, this is also one of the most beautiful and picturesque sections of trail in the entire San Gabriel range—to the north, the flat Antelope Valley stretches out to the horizon, pockmarked with the remnants of old volcanoes and the visible scars of the San Andreas Fault. To the south, an undulating terrain of mountains covered in towering evergreens that mercifully have been spared from recent wildfires. Enjoy these panoramic views as you hike along the summit ridge, and at 5.6 miles you'll reach a small memorial plaque to an influential but sadly little-known writer who was an early advocate for these mountains. Rest up and return the way you came in, remembering that you've also got some elevation gain on the way out!

EXTENDING YOUR TRIP

A faint trail continues northwest from Will Thrall Peak along the Pleasant View Ridge, offering clearer views of the Antelope Valley. Another steep and rough-use trail heads east from Burkhart Saddle to Pallet Mountain, if your legs haven't received enough punishment yet.

98 Mount Williamson

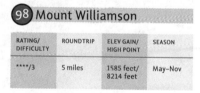

RATING/ DIFFICULTY	ROUNDTRIP	ELEV GAIN/ HIGH POINT	SEASON
****/3	5 miles	1585 feet/ 8214 feet	May–Nov

Map: USGS Crystal Lake; **Contact:** Angeles National Forest/San Gabriel Mountains National Monument, Santa Clara/Mojave Rivers Ranger District; **Notes:** Adventure Pass required at trailhead. Dogs allowed on leash. No wilderness permits required unless traveling with more than twenty-five people; **GPS:** N 34.356975, W 117.850657

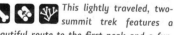 *This lightly traveled, two-summit trek features a beautiful route to the first peak and a fun, rustic trail to the second. Along the way you'll have probably the best views you'll ever get of San Gabriel Canyon, as well as a good perspective on the San Andreas Fault and the chance to extend your hike along a rugged summit ridge.*

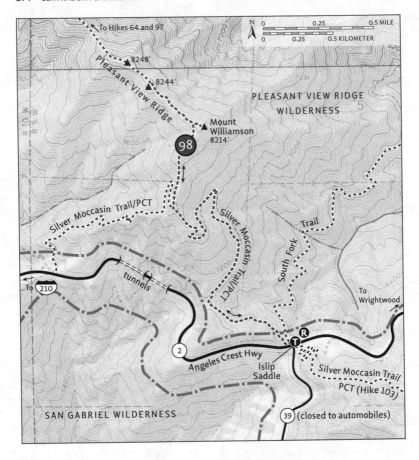

GETTING THERE

From Interstate 210 in La Cañada Flintridge, take exit 20 toward the Angeles Crest Highway (CA-2) and follow it for approximately 40 miles to Islip Saddle (just past the locked junction with CA-39). There is a moderately sized parking area on the north side of the Angeles Crest Highway. Display your Adventure Pass. The trail begins at the northwest corner of the lot.

ON THE TRAIL

Hop onto the Silver Moccasin Trail/Pacific Crest Trail (PCT) and start your climb, ignoring the South Fork Trail branching off to your right. The dry Antelope Valley peers out between tall, forested peaks to the north as you hike beneath the shade of majestic pines and through dense stands of rabbitbrush. To the south, you'll have clear views of Mount Islip and San Gabriel Canyon while

Twin Peaks and Waterman Mountain from Mount Williamson

to the east you can follow the long ridge from Mount Hawkins and Throop Peak to prominent Baden-Powell.

It's a smooth, steady climb to 1.7 miles. Here, the Silver Moccasin Trail/PCT marches west but you'll follow a faint trail along a ridge to the north, climbing and scrambling up the west flank of Mount Williamson to the 2.1-mile mark. Take a right here for a short trip to the official summit. I say official here because while this has the USGS marker, there is a slightly higher point on the mountain just to the northwest. The Sierra Club's Hundred Peaks section maintains a summit register that's moved back and forth between the points—oddly, giving no consideration to another, slightly higher bump along Pleasant View Ridge. I'm sure you could start a really fun comment war about this on Facebook with other topo map enthusiasts if you were bored and stuck in an office one day.

The trip to the second peak is much more rugged and fun than the more established trail you've been on, so give it a go! Follow the well-defined, bumpy trail northwest to the higher summit at 2.5 miles for better views of the San Andreas Fault Zone and deserts to the north. Keen eyes will be able to spot the remains of a C-119 that crashed on nearby Pallett Mountain, as well. Return the way you came.

EXTENDING YOUR TRIP

A rough and rugged use-trail continues to the northwest from the second summit and will eventually top out on Pallett Mountain before reaching Burkhart Saddle between Pallet and Will Thrall Peak (Hike 97). Long-distance hikers can continue on to Devils Punchbowl (Hike 62). Those more interested in staying on established trails can simply hop across the Angeles Crest Highway at the trailhead to add Mount Islip to their day's hike (Hike 103).

99 Waterman Mountain

RATING/ DIFFICULTY	LOOP	ELEV GAIN/ HIGH POINT	SEASON
***/3	6.5 miles	1228 feet/ 8038 feet	May–Nov

Map: USGS Waterman Mountain; **Contact:** Angeles National Forest/San Gabriel Mountains National Monument, Santa Clara/Mojave Rivers Ranger District; **Notes:** Adventure Pass required to park at trailhead. Dogs allowed on leash; **GPS:** N 34.347001, W 117.921412

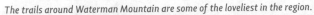 *The Waterman Mountain loop takes you through a historic ski resort and along the edge of the San Gabriel Wilderness. Although the views from the actual summit are blocked a bit by trees, the trail itself is a wonderful experience in the high San Gabriels with plentiful pine trees and nice views south toward Twin Peaks and Bear Creek Canyon.*

GETTING THERE
From Interstate 210 in La Cañada Flintridge, take exit 20 toward the Angeles Crest Highway (CA-2) and follow it for 33.5 miles. Park at one of the pullouts on the highway and display your Adventure Pass. The trail begins on the west side of the road near an old sign marking the San Gabriel Wilderness.

ON THE TRAIL
This route wanders through the historic Mount Waterman Ski Area—the first ski resort in the San Gabriels—and crosses many access roads and ski runs. One such junction happens right near the trailhead: continuing straight on the very steep, unmarked path will save you a bit of distance but will likely also take too much energy right at the start of your hike. Stay left and follow the marked trail, which parallels the Angeles Crest and passes an old horse trough. At 0.3 mile, keep right at the junction with the broader access road. Stay to the right again at the 1-mile mark and straight at 1.7 miles.

The trails around Waterman Mountain are some of the loveliest in the region.

Here, the trail enters an area crisscrossed with ski runs and access roads. Just to the west of the ski lifts, a well-traveled path emerges and climbs to the southwest. By 2.7 miles, the road becomes a single-track trail and, thankfully, also much easier to follow. A short distance later, the trail reaches the summit ridge and turns east, roughly following the boundary of the San Gabriel Wilderness. At 2.9 miles, you'll see a sign that reads "Waterman Summit," which is an odd choice of words considering this sign is not at the summit of Waterman Mountain, nor is there an established trail to the actual

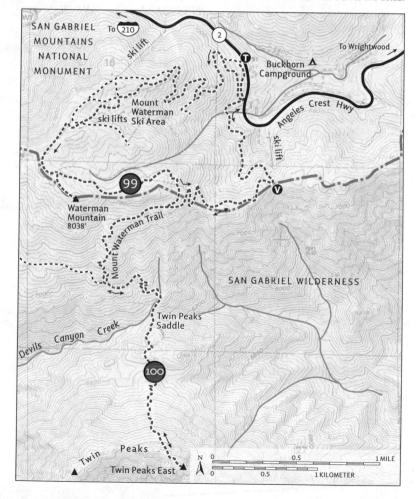

summit. Fortunately, the routefinding here is relatively easy—just head south to the edge of the ridge, then follow it to a bump to the southeast at about 3.1 miles. The rocky summit doesn't offer much in the way of views, but it does have some fun, easy scrambling opportunities. If you decide to skip the actual summit, don't worry, there are better views just down the trail.

You can either return the way you came or make a loop on a more interesting stretch of trail by heading east once you return to the main trail. You'll be on the north side of the mountain until the trail turns south, meeting a trail to Twin Peaks (Hike 100) at 4.3 miles. Stay left to continue your descent to the east. The trail here flirts with the steep northern edge of Bear Creek Canyon, and when you can find views through the breaks in the canopy of conifers, they're pretty stellar.

Make a sharp left turn at one of these viewpoints at 5.4 miles and follow this trail to close the loop at 6.2 miles. Stay straight at the crossing with the fire road and follow the trail back to your car.

100 Twin Peaks

RATING/ DIFFICULTY	ROUNDTRIP	ELEV GAIN/ HIGH POINT	SEASON
*****/5	9.7 miles	1213 feet/ 7761 feet	May–Nov

Map: USGS Waterman Mountain; **Contact:** Angeles National Forest/San Gabriel Mountains National Monument, San Gabriel River Ranger District; **Notes:** Adventure Pass required to park at trailhead. Dogs are allowed on leash on this trail, but due to the difficulty of the climb to Twin Peaks, I wouldn't recommend this for most canines; **GPS:** N 34.347001, W 117.921412

 Most hikers acknowledge the trek to Twin Peaks as one of the toughest and most remote in the San Gabriels. Those who bag this summit will not only get some serious bragging rights, they'll also enjoy incredible peace and quiet on a rarely traveled trail and the company of some of the most enormous conifers in the entire mountain range.

GETTING THERE
From Interstate 210 in La Cañada Flintridge, take exit 20 toward the Angeles Crest Highway (CA-2) and follow it for 33.5 miles. Park at one of the pullouts on the highway and display your Adventure Pass. The trail begins on the west side of the road near an old sign marking the San Gabriel Wilderness.

ON THE TRAIL
I hope you're ready for a big day. This trek begins with a sizable climb up and over the eastern flank of Waterman Mountain, then drops below the trailhead to a saddle between Waterman and Twin Peaks. After that, the maintained trail ends and it's "find your way up" along an incredibly steep use-trail—one that's often difficult to even locate—to Twin Peaks. Once you reach the top, you'll have uphill on the way back out, too—making this one of those up then down then up then down then up then down again hikes you've read so much about.

Just past the trailhead, keep left to stay on the trail as it parallels the Angeles Crest Highway. Cross the fire road at 0.3 mile and hop an intermittent creek at 0.4 mile. From here, the trail begins its first climb, meandering past some seasonal springs and remnants of an old ski lift to the east. The trail provides beautiful views to the east beneath the shade of huge ponderosa

Odds are, you'll have the trail to Twin Peaks all to yourself.

and Jeffrey pines. At 1.1 miles you'll reach a steep drop-off with picture-perfect views of the San Gabriel Wilderness to the south. The trail heads west from here, roughly following this ridge before making a few wide switchbacks. Stay straight on the Mount Waterman Trail at 2.1 miles as it descends along the southern slope of its namesake peak through a mixed forest of majestic conifers and singed, recovering scrub oaks.

At the 3-mile mark, keep to the left to head toward Twin Peaks Saddle. (Yes, I know the sign says the trail dead-ends. Trust me.) After a few tight switchbacks and a quick hop across the easternmost branch of Devils Canyon Creek, the trail settles into Twin Peaks Saddle—a broad saddle between Waterman and Twin Peaks. This is a great place for you to steel yourself for the intense climb you're about to undertake. When you're ready, look for a faint trail heading south and follow it through some fields littered with enormous boulders and more towering trees. By mile 4, you'll be at the base of Twin Peaks and from here it's a tough, nontechnical scramble to the top on loose, slippery ground. The trail is faint and easy to lose, so keep your eyes peeled for previous hikers' bootprints and the occasional ribbon tied to a tree branch. Generally, the route heads south until 4.5 miles, where it curves to the southeast to make a beeline toward the narrow, rocky summit of Twin Peaks East at 4.8 miles. Although the summit is fairly forested, you'll have some insanely memorable views from here, one of the most remote peaks in the San Gabriel Mountains. Go ahead and let out a celebratory howl before you head back—you've earned it.

EXTENDING YOUR TRIP

If you're a summit junkie, you can continue along the long, broad ridge west to Twin Peaks West. This summit is larger, lower, and more forested. Experienced climbers can continue along the ridge east of Twin Peaks East to a prominent formation known to locals as Triplet Rocks. This route is completely unmaintained and requires advanced scrambling and climbing techniques as well as extensive bushwhacking. Hikers who attempt this time-consuming and exhausting route often have to begin before sunrise—even if they're camping nearby.

101 Kratka Ridge

RATING/ DIFFICULTY	ROUNDTRIP	ELEV GAIN/ HIGH POINT	SEASON
****/3	1.5 miles	640 feet/ 7515 feet	May–Nov

Map: USGS Waterman Mountain; **Contact:** Angeles National Forest/San Gabriel Mountains National Monument, Santa Clara/Mojave Rivers Ranger District; **Notes:** Adventure Pass required at trailhead. Dogs allowed on leash, but trail may be too rough for some; **GPS:** N 34.350180, W 117.892331

  What this little-known trail lacks in distance it more than makes up for in scenery and uniqueness. This route climbs up past the Vista picnic area to a stunning view into Bear Creek Canyon and the San Gabriel Wilderness, then treks up a rough ridgeline and old ski runs to the former Kratka Ridge Ski Area, where a lone, wooden, single-seat chairlift stands sentinel, awaiting new snow and perhaps a new life.

GETTING THERE

From Interstate 210 in La Cañada Flintridge, take exit 20 toward the Angeles Crest Highway (CA-2) and follow it 36.2 miles, past the Buckhorn Campground. Park at the Vista picnic area on the south side of the road and display your Adventure Pass. Note that some online directions may tell you to keep driving past the trailhead, even with correct GPS input.

ON THE TRAIL

Head south from the tiny Vista picnic area's parking lot, following an established trail that makes a short climb up the forested ridge to its south. In just under 300 feet,

The historic wooden chairlift at Kratka Ridge

you'll reach a break in the pine cover that provides an incredible look south into Bear Creek Canyon and the greater San Gabriel Wilderness. Head west, generally following the ridgeline boundary of the wilderness area, then turn slightly to the northwest to follow a faint trail to the 0.3-mile mark. Here, the trail turns to the southwest and climbs

THE NON-ABOMINABLE SNOW PLANT

When you're hiking in this area of the San Gabriel Mountains in the spring, keep your eye out for strange clumps of red flowers that seem to burst from the ground or from snow cover underneath the pine trees. This is the snow plant (*Sarcodes sanguinea*), which grows in the thick pine-needle litter at elevations between four thousand and eight thousand feet and often blooms just as the winter snow begins to melt. The snow plant lacks chlorophyll and instead draws nutrients by tapping into the vast network of fungal roots (mychorrhizae) that conifers and many other plants use to soak up food and minerals from the environment. While the snow plant is a parasite, it also provides pollen and nectar to birds and bees long before most other flowers are blooming, playing an important role on the forest floor, where not much else can grow.

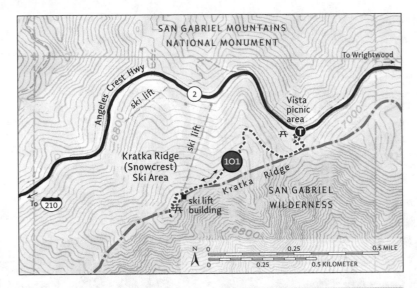

up a series of steep use-trails. The ground here is often soft and loose, so take your time and tread carefully.

By 0.4 mile you'll be on the vague remnants of an old access road, meaning the incline mellows out a bit. The trail passes along (and underneath) the slowly deteriorating structures of the Kratka Ridge Ski Area (sometimes also known as Snowcrest), where scores of Angelenos made fond skiing memories during its active years from the 1950s through 2001. In many places, buildings and skiing artifacts are still in decent shape; when you're visiting, please be respectful and leave everything just as you found it. In 2006, the owners of nearby Mount Waterman resort also acquired this area, although the property remains unused as of 2016.

Walk up behind the old ski lift or past the picnic area, enjoy the views from the ridge, and return the way you came.

102 Winston Ridge and Winston Peak

RATING/ DIFFICULTY	LOOP	ELEV GAIN/ HIGH POINT	SEASON
****/3	4.3	866 feet/ 7502 feet	May–Oct

Maps: USGS Waterman Mountain, Juniper Hills; **Contact:** Angeles National Forest/ San Gabriel Mountains National Monument, Santa Clara/Mojave Rivers Ranger District; **Notes:** Adventure Pass required to park at trailhead. Dogs allowed on leash; **GPS:** N 34.351359, W 117.934299

This short trail has long been a quick favorite for those in the know. It packs a bit of off-trail exploration, a leg-busting slope climb, and fantastic views of Pleasant View Ridge and Little Rock Creek Canyon into its diminutive distance, giving it a lot more character than you'd expect. Combine this short hike with other nearby trails for a full day outside.

GETTING THERE

From Interstate 210 in La Cañada Flintridge, take exit 20 toward Angeles Crest Highway (CA-2) and follow it 32.7 miles to Cloudburst Summit. Park in a pullout along the highway, and display your Adventure Pass.

ON THE TRAIL

From Cloudburst Summit, hike north on an old access road grade. This wide path slopes gently downward from the trailhead through fragrant Jeffrey pines, offering occasional views of Mount Akawie to the southeast and Waterman Mountain to the south. The road roughly parallels the Pacific Crest Trail (PCT) in the canyon below. The PCT crosses the road grade at 0.8 mile. Keep left here to

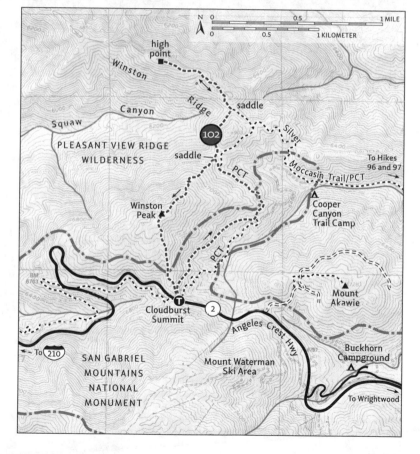

Hikers on the Pacific Crest Trail head toward Winston Ridge.

join the trail and follow the PCT to a small saddle at 1.4 miles. Here, the PCT dives east toward Cooper Canyon Trail Camp, but you'll leave the established route at this point.

Directly behind you lies Winston Peak, while ahead of you is an unnamed bump that stands between you and the high point of Winston Ridge—named in memory of a Pasadena businessman whose body was found on these frozen slopes after an ill-fated hunting expedition in 1893. Unmaintained routes loop around both sides of the bump, but the route to the left is in better shape and offers up some nice views of Squaw Canyon to the west along the way. The two trails join each other at another saddle at 1.7 miles. Look for another faint footpath to the left, which will take you to the high point of Winston Ridge at 2.3 miles. Look for a prominent group of boulders at the summit, which has a nice, panoramic angle on Pleasant View Ridge to the north and a clear view of Winston Peak, almost directly to the south across Squaw Canyon.

Backtrack to the saddle at 3.2 miles; now is when the trail gets tough. The faint use-trail to the summit basically goes straight up the side of Winston Peak at about a 20 percent grade. It's a challenging section due to its steepness, required routefinding, and altitude, but take your time, keep your eyes peeled, and make sure to take breaks to catch your breath in the thin air. You'll reach the rocky summit at 3.8 miles. Look for a well-worn path heading southwest from here, which follows a steep descent back to Cloudburst Summit.

103 Mount Islip

RATING/ DIFFICULTY	ROUNDTRIP	ELEV GAIN/ HIGH POINT	SEASON
****/4	6.9 miles	1616 feet/ 8250 feet	May–Nov

Map: USGS Crystal Lake; **Contact:** Angeles National Forest/San Gabriel Mountains National Monument, Santa Clara/Mojave

Rivers Ranger District; **Notes:** Adventure Pass required to park at trailhead. Dogs allowed on leash. Little Jimmy Campground is first-come, first-served; **GPS:** N 34.357019, W 117.850543

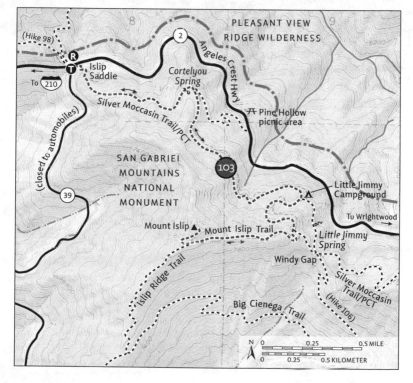

This popular hike along a stretch of the Pacific Crest and Silver Moccasin trails takes you through a picturesque campground and up to the ruins of a historic fire lookout. Although damage from the 2002 Curve Fire is still visible, there is still plenty of shade along the route, making this a good option on a warm summer day.

GETTING THERE

From Interstate 210 in La Cañada Flintridge, take exit 20 toward the Angeles Crest Highway (CA-2) and follow it for 39.6 miles to Islip Saddle (just past the locked junction with CA-39). There is a moderately sized lot on the north side of the highway, and the trailhead is just across from the parking lot's entrance, on the southern side of the Angeles Crest Highway. Display your Adventure Pass.

ON THE TRAIL

The trail begins climbing up steep switchbacks through some rabbitbrush and

Ruins atop Mount Islip

manzanita before ducking into the welcome shade of tall pines that cover the northern slope of Mount Islip. At the 1-mile mark, stay to the right at the junction with the old access road to stay on the Silver Moccasin Trail/Pacific Crest Trail (PCT). The trail remains relatively level and shaded before reaching the Little Jimmy Campground at 2.1 miles. This campground and its nearby spring are named in honor of Jimmy Swinnerton, a Hearst newspaper cartoonist who hiked to this camp all the way from Coldbrook Camp at the base of Smith Mountain in 1909. He stayed the summer, painting and drawing his famous character "Little Jimmy" for passersby.

At the campground—popular with Boy Scouts hiking the Silver Moccasin Trail—keep to the right and look for the Mount Islip Trail, which climbs above the campground to the west. Keep to the right again at 2.5 miles at a connector trail to Windy Gap and continue heading west. The effects of the Curve Fire are most visible here, where charred trees still line the trail. Keep to the right at the junction with the Islip Ridge Trail and you'll reach the bare, prominent summit at 3.4 miles. The ruins of an old stone cabin stand watch here, they are part of an extensive network of fire lookouts that dotted the San Gabriels before smog made it inefficient to staff them all. Thankfully, the air today is much clearer—and getting better every year—so enjoy the wonderful views from the summit and return the way you came.

104 Throop Peak

RATING/ DIFFICULTY	ROUNDTRIP	ELEV GAIN/ HIGH POINT	SEASON
****/2	4.4 miles	1249 feet/ 9142 feet	May–Nov

Map: USGS Crystal Lake; **Contact:** Angeles National Forest/San Gabriel Mountains National Monument, Santa Clara/Mojave Rivers Ranger District; **Notes:** Dogs allowed on leash; **GPS:** N 34.367655, W 117.801028

 This shaded, gradual ascent to prominent Throop Peak (pronounced "troop") is a fine, relatively easy adventure in the high San Gabriels. You'll hike through stretches of white fir, sugar pine, and vanilla-scented Jeffrey pines on the edge of the Sheep Mountain Wilderness.

GETTING THERE

From Interstate 210 in La Cañada Flintridge, take exit 20 toward the Angeles Crest Highway (CA-2) and follow it for 45.5 miles to Dawson Saddle. From Wrightwood, travel west on the Angeles Crest for about 14.2 miles. Pass a small parking area to park in the larger lot on the north side of the highway. You'll find the trailhead just across from the eastern end of the larger parking area, where the highway makes a southward turn. Note that this is east of the smaller, steeper use-trail that switchbacks up across from the shack in the smaller parking area (although both routes do meet up).

ON THE TRAIL

The Dawson Saddle Trail begins on a series of tight switchbacks that climb steeply from the roadside, but the trail mellows considerably once it turns south and makes a steady

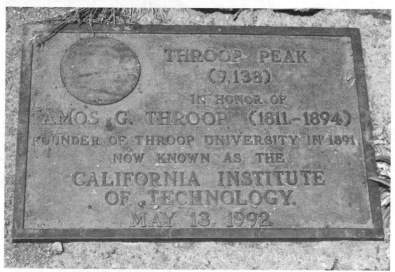

A memorial plaque at the Throop Peak summit

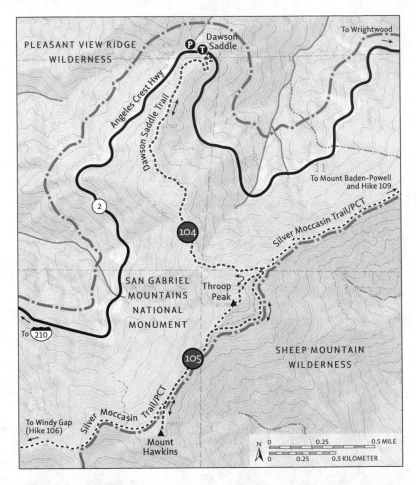

ascent on a forested ridge by 0.4 mile. Enjoy the views north toward the Antelope Valley and the clearly visible oddness of Devils Punchbowl as you make your way south, ignoring the use-trail that makes an unnecessary ridge climb at 0.9 mile. Ignore another use-trail at 1.4 miles and follow the trail as it bends to the east at 1.6 miles.

At 1.9 miles, you'll meet the Silver Moccasin Trail/Pacific Crest Trail (PCT), which heads east toward Mount Burnham and towering Mount Baden-Powell and south toward Mount Hawkins, but you'll make a hard right turn and look for a faint use-trail cutting southwest through the brush. It looks like it's making a beeline for the summit . . . and that's because it is. This stretch is much steeper and more rugged than the trail you've been on so far, but you'll reach the summit and its memorial plaque to Amos Throop at 2.2 miles. Throop founded Pasadena's influential Throop University in 1891, but don't worry if you haven't heard of it—it changed its name to the California Institute of Technology in 1920.

Throop's summit offers fantastic views—you'll be able to see clearly into the rugged Sheep Mountain Wilderness to the east, including the tallest point in the San Gabriel Mountains at Mount San Antonio. You'll enjoy plotting out future peak-bagging adventures and return the way you came.

EXTENDING YOUR TRIP
There are a number of nearby peaks to extend your time on Throop. The trip south to Mount Hawkins (Hike 105) provides more great views into the Sheep Mountain Wilderness. A popular, lengthy route follows the PCT east to Mount Baden-Powell, avoiding the notorious switchbacks on the more traditional ascent from Vincent Gap (Hike 109).

105 Mount Hawkins

RATING/ DIFFICULTY	ROUNDTRIP	ELEV GAIN/ HIGH POINT	SEASON
****/3	6 miles	1029 feet/ 8925 feet	May–Nov

Map: USGS Crystal Lake; **Contact:** Angeles National Forest/San Gabriel Mountains National Monument, Santa Clara/Mojave Rivers Ranger District; **Notes:** Dogs allowed on leash; **GPS:** N 34.367655, W 117.801028

More than a decade later, the effects of the 2002 Curve Fire are still visible.

This extension of the route to Throop Peak is a fine trail in its own right, offering fantastic views of the Sheep Mountain Wilderness and the best view of the Hawkins Ridge to the southwest.

GETTING THERE

From Interstate 210 in La Cañada Flintridge, take exit 20 toward the Angeles Crest Highway (CA-2) and follow it for 45.5 miles to Dawson Saddle. From Wrightwood, travel west on the Angeles Crest for about 14.2 miles. Pass a small parking area to park in the larger lot on the north side of the highway. You'll find the trailhead just across from the eastern end of the larger parking area, where the highway makes a southward turn. Note that this is east of the smaller, steeper use-trail that switchbacks up across from the shack in the smaller parking area (although both routes do meet up).

ON THE TRAIL

Follow the route described in Hike 104. At the junction with the Silver Moccasin Trail/Pacific Crest Trail (PCT) at 1.9 miles, you have the option to summit Throop Peak and descend the mountain's southwest slope along a steep but well-defined use-trail. To follow the route described here, turn right to take the PCT toward Windy Gap. Follow the PCT as it turns west and at 2.9 miles, stay to the left on the unnamed trail while the PCT descends to the right. This short spur trail takes you to the small, rocky summit of Mount Hawkins at 3 miles.

To the southeast, the long line of Copter Ridge divides the spectacular canyons formed by the Iron and South forks of the San Gabriel River, while to the slight west lies the undulating shape of Hawkins

Ridge, where peak-baggers can stand atop South Mount Hawkins, as well as the unofficial bumps of Middle Hawkins and Sadie Hawkins. All three peaks—along with the one you are currently standing on—were named after Nellie Hawkins, a beloved waitress who worked at the now long-gone Squirrel Inn on the San Gabriel River from 1901 to 1906. She must have been quite a remarkable gal.

Retrace your steps to return to the trailhead.

106 South Mount Hawkins from Crystal Lake

RATING/ DIFFICULTY	LOOP	ELEV GAIN/ HIGH POINT	SEASON
*****/4	11.6 miles	2721 feet/ 8373 feet	May–Nov

Map: USGS Crystal Lake; **Contact:** Angeles National Forest/San Gabriel Mountains National Monument, San Gabriel River Ranger District; **Notes:** Adventure Pass required to park at trailhead. Dogs allowed on leash. Campsites available at Crystal Lake (see Appendix I), first-come, first-served. Rates and water availability change seasonally. The hike-in Little Jimmy Campground is also accessible from this route; **GPS:** N 34.326933, W 117.832160

   A spectacular full-day loop above the Yerba Santa Amphitheater and Crystal Lake Recreation Area, this hike climbs up to the Pacific Crest Trail (PCT) and returns along the Hawkins Ridge, providing fantastic views of both the North Fork of San Gabriel Canyon and deeper into the interior San Gabriels. You'll also visit the site of a historic fire lookout and

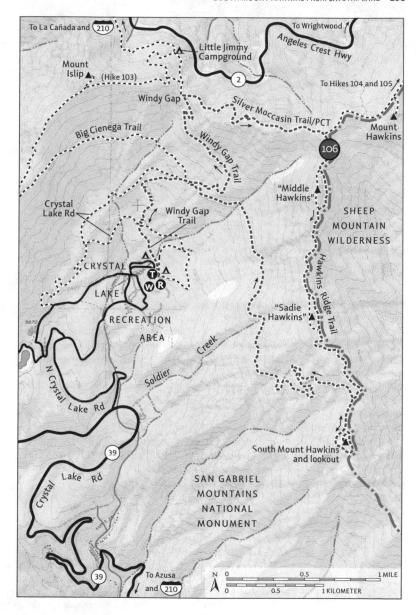

The trails above Crystal Lake provide rugged terrain, amazing views, and very few crowds.

get the chance for some good eats at Crystal Lake on your way home.

GETTING THERE

From Interstate 210 in Azusa, take exit 40 for Azusa Avenue (CA-39) and head north for 24.1 miles on San Gabriel Canyon Road, which eventually becomes Crystal Lake Road. Turn right on North Crystal Lake Road and continue for 2.4 miles. Pass the cafe and campsites and park where the street ends at a sizable parking lot. Display your Adventure Pass. Note that CA-39 reaches the Angeles Crest Highway on most maps, but it is not open to vehicular traffic at that end.

ON THE TRAIL

Begin hiking north on the Windy Gap Trail, which meanders through some of the Crystal Lake Campground sites on a well-groomed path. Shade is sporadic here—the tall pines that once dominated the landscape have been hard hit in recent years by drought, bark beetles, and fire—but it's still a lovely start to your day. You'll cross

the now-dirt Crystal Lake Road at 0.4 mile. At 1.1 miles the trail crosses the road again at a slight diagonal. Look for the sign for the Big Cienega Trail and keep to the right to continue climbing up on the Windy Gap Trail.

Climb through manzanita and scree slopes on a recently repaired trail, taking in the ever-widening views south as you rise. You'll reach Windy Gap at 2.5 miles. Heading left here would take you to Little Jimmy Campground and Mount Islip (Hike 103), but you'll stay to the right to join the Silver Moccasin Trail/PCT heading east. The trail here hugs the north side of the ridge, so while you'll lose views of San Gabriel Canyon for a bit, you'll also have a great view of the San Gabriels to the north.

At 3.5 miles, the trail mercifully begins to level out and descend. At 3.9 miles, turn right to depart the PCT and head south on the Hawkins Ridge Trail, a supremely peaceful and pleasant stretch of hiking that makes a gentle, winding descent while providing some of the most incredible views in the entire San Gabriel Mountains. To the east, you'll see the towering summits of Baden-Powell and the Mount Baldy area. To the south and west, the ridgelines of the Transverse Ranges line up in stunning formation—especially beautiful in the pinkish-purple light of the late afternoon. A use-trail makes a direct route along the spine of the ridge, topping out on the unofficially named Middle and Sadie Hawkins bumps, but stay on the more established Hawkins Ridge Trail to dodge the unnecessary elevation gain and reach a fire road at 6.1 miles. Keep left to head south on the road for one final push to the South Mount Hawkins summit and ruins of the historic fire lookout at 6.7 miles. The all-wooden fire lookout stood watch here from 1935 until 2002, when it fell victim to the 20,857-acre Curve Fire. Thankfully, the views are still phenomenal. Return to Windy Gap Trail via the fire road, closing the loop at 10.5 miles.

EXTENDING YOUR TRIP

This route takes you within striking distance of both Mount Islip (Hike 103) and Mount Hawkins (Hike 105) via the Silver Moccasin Trail/PCT. In addition, the Crystal Lake Recreation Area is worth your exploration time.

107 Lewis Falls

RATING/ DIFFICULTY	ROUNDTRIP	ELEV GAIN/ HIGH POINT	SEASON
****/2	1 mile	422 feet/ 4287 feet	Year-round

Map: USGS Crystal Lake; **Contact:** Angeles National Forest/San Gabriel Mountains National Monument, San Gabriel River Ranger District; **Notes:** Dogs allowed on leash. Crossings and trail may be dangerous during the rainy season; **GPS:** N 34.301273, W 117.838221

The tumbling waters of Soldier Creek provide welcome accompaniment on this short hike.

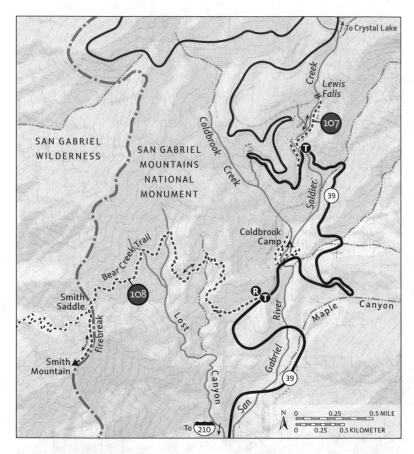

This trek along the dependably flowing Soldier Creek is definitely a worthwhile stop. Follow an unmaintained trail through a former wilderness resort into a narrow, densely forested canyon, then boulder hop and bushwhack your way to the base of a secluded fifty-foot waterfall that—often—you'll have all to yourself.

GETTING THERE

From Interstate 210 in Azusa, take exit 40 for Azusa Avenue (CA-39) and travel north for 20.3 miles. Continue past the turnoff to East Fork Road and note when you pass Coldbrook Camp. In 2.5 miles, reach the unmarked crossing of Soldier Creek and park at the unmarked trailhead on the north side of the road (look for the year-round flowing stream and a "No Fires" sign). If you find yourself driving past Falling Springs Resort, you've gone too far.

ON THE TRAIL

Step off the road and you're instantly transported to an incredibly picturesque canyon, lined by oaks and firs with a gently bubbling stream cascading alongside the footpath. USGS maps label this area as La Cienega and Falling Springs—two names for the same wilderness resort and cabin community that held on until the 2002 Curve Fire. Today, only a few stubborn cabins and memories remain.

Stay on the trail as it passes through a surprising variety of terrain, from gargantuan boulders to ivy-blanketed trees and the ruins of old cabins, while Soldier Creek flows to the west. At 0.4 mile, the trail appears to end near a wooden fence at the bank of the creek. Follow the fence along the ridge and look for a well-worn footpath down into the creek bed itself. From here on out, you're making your own way along the canyon floor, ducking under trees, hopping along boulders, and dodging the waters of the creek itself. It's nothing too difficult, but it is something to be prepared for. Expect this last 0.1 mile to take about as long as the first 0.4 mile, and keep your eye out for poison oak and stinging nettle.

Every branch to the face or boot-slip off a wet boulder will be well worth it, though, when you reach the base of Lewis Falls—an incredibly peaceful glen and for my money, one of the nicest hiking destinations in the entire Los Angeles area. You can't follow this trail farther without technical climbing gear, so return the way you came in.

108 Smith Mountain

RATING/ DIFFICULTY	ROUNDTRIP	ELEV GAIN/ HIGH POINT	SEASON
****/4	6.8 miles	1843 feet/ 5111 feet	Year-round

Map: USGS Crystal Lake; **Contact:** Angeles National Forest/San Gabriel Mountains National Monument, San Gabriel River Ranger District; **Notes:** Adventure Pass required at trailhead. Dogs allowed on leash, but trail is rough and shadeless and may not be appropriate for all dogs. This trail is usually accessible year-round but due to its total lack of shade is best hiked in the spring, when the hills are green and wildflowers are popping; **GPS:** N 34.287350, W 117.842607

This route is all fun and games on the relatively mild, recently reconstructed Bear Creek Trail until Smith Saddle, where a steep, class 2 scramble rises 850 feet in a half mile. Those willing to get their hands dirty on the way up are rewarded with stunning 360-degree views of the North Fork San Gabriel River and the deep backcountry of the San Gabriel Wilderness.

GETTING THERE

From Interstate 210 in Azusa, take exit 40 for Azusa Avenue (CA-39) and travel north for 18.1 miles. Park at the large trailhead at the Bear Creek Trail and display your Adventure Pass. If you've hit Coldbrook Camp, head back 0.25 mile.

ON THE TRAIL

The Bear Creek Trail begins just north of an outhouse and large sign for the San Gabriel Wilderness and quickly rises above

The final push to the summit of Smith Mountain is a challenge, but the views are worth it.

the road, backtracking to the southwest a bit before turning into the upper reaches of Lost Canyon. Just before the 0.9-mile mark, the elevation gain levels out and becomes almost unnoticeable until you reach Smith Saddle. Gazing southwest, you'll see the north flank of Smith Mountain and the firebreak that climbs to the summit. From here, it doesn't look too bad. Remember that thought.

At 2.9 miles, you'll reach Smith Saddle, where the Bear Creek Trail heads right and drops into the rugged upper reaches of Bear Creek Canyon. The firebreak to your left (south), which now probably feels a bit steeper than it did when you saw it earlier, is how you're getting to the summit.

Most scramblers rate this climb a class 2 route, meaning you'll have to exercise a bit of caution and use your hands once in a while, but it's not as tough or dangerous as class 3 routes like the Mountaineers' Route on Strawberry Peak (Hike 80). Still, the slope is steep, the ground is loose, and the drop-offs are exposed, so just stick to the established use-trail and take your time. Oh, and also be sure to take in the ever-improving views along the way. Pass a false summit at 3.3 miles and continue to the real deal at 3.4 miles. This treeless, prominent summit provides incredible panoramas of the surrounding terrain. Soak in all the mountain goodness you can and return the way you came, taking extra precautions on that steep descent down the firebreak.

EXTENDING YOUR TRIP

There are some fine trail camps in the San Gabriel Wilderness accessible via the Bear Creek Trail (free wilderness permits required for overnights). This route can also be done as long day hike with a car shuttle from the West Fork trailhead farther down CA-39.

109 Mount Baden-Powell

RATING/ DIFFICULTY	ROUNDTRIP	ELEV GAIN/ HIGH POINT	SEASON
*****/4	8 miles	2818 feet/ 9406 feet	May–Nov

Map: USGS Crystal Lake; **Contact:** Angeles National Forest/San Gabriel Mountains National Monument, Santa Clara/Mojave Rivers Ranger District; **Notes:** Adventure Pass required to park at trailhead. Dogs allowed on leash. Angeles Crest Highway is often closed in the high country during the winter months and after landslides. Check with Caltrans (see Appendix I) for current conditions before you start the drive to the trailhead; **GPS:** N 34.3733760, W 117.7521970

 *Mount Baden-Powell is the second-highest mountain (and fifth-tallest peak) in the San*

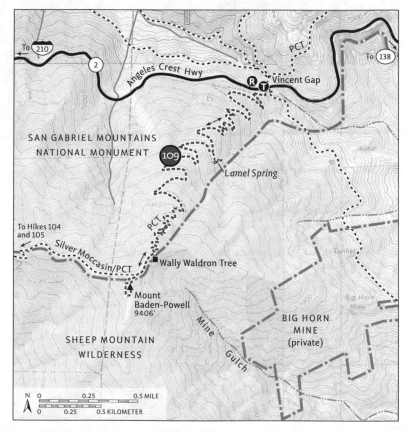

Ancient limber pines on Mount Baden-Powell are some of the oldest living trees in the San Gabriels.

Gabriels, and is named after the founder of the Scouting movement. The tough, steep climb to its summit is a rite of passage for Scouts and hikers of all stripes (and patches and sashes). This popular route from Vincent Gap is a challenging, but nontechnical, high-altitude hike, and it passes by an impressive collection of ancient limber pines.

GETTING THERE

From Interstate 210 in La Cañada Flintridge, take exit 20 toward the Angeles Crest Highway (CA-2) and follow it for 50.3 miles to Vincent Gap. There is a moderately sized parking lot there with a vault toilet and access to several trails. Park here and display your Adventure Pass. Alternatively, you can also reach this trailhead from Interstate 15. From the 15 at Cajon Pass, take exit 131

for CA-138 toward Palmdale and travel 8.6 miles to the junction with the Angeles Crest Highway. Heading west from there, Vincent Gap is just under 14 miles. The trail begins at the west end of the trailhead parking area.

ON THE TRAIL

From the parking area, head south on the Silver Moccasin/Pacific Crest Trail (PCT). The trail begins by climbing up the northern slope of the mountain on a seemingly never-ending series of switchbacks. This region is under the shade of a thick forest of evergreens, including ponderosa and lodgepole pines as well as fragrant incense cedars, so you'll definitely want to breathe in this fresh mountain air on your way up. If we've had a wet winter, snow also tends to linger here late into the spring and even early summer.

At 1.7 miles, pass a short spur trail to Lamel Spring—probably more useful to the PCT thru-hikers than you responsible day hiker types who've brought enough water. After 3 miles on the trail you'll be up above 8500 feet, where the trees begin to thin and those that are left take on more gnarled forms than those at lower elevations. At 3.5 miles, a very short, unmarked use-trail will lead you through a small grove of ancient limber pines where you'll find the gnarled Wally Waldron Tree, which is believed to be the oldest living tree in the San Gabriel Mountains. At 3.7 miles the trail heads across a narrow ridge toward Mount Baden-Powell's summit, providing some heart-pounding views down in either direction. Stay to the left at 3.9 miles to leave the PCT and top out near the concrete monument to Lord Robert Baden-Powell at the mountain's summit. Poke around the small summit plateau to enjoy the stunning, panoramic views and return the way you came.

110 The Bridge to Nowhere

RATING/ DIFFICULTY	ROUNDTRIP	ELEV GAIN/ HIGH POINT	SEASON
*****/5	10.1 miles	809 feet/ 2810 feet	Year-round

Maps: USGS Glendora, Crystal Lake, Mount San Antonio; **Contact:** Angeles National Forest/San Gabriel Mountains National Monument, San Gabriel River Ranger District; **Notes:** Adventure Pass required to park at trailhead. A free wilderness permit is required to hike in the Sheep Mountain Wilderness and can be obtained at a Forest Service ranger station or visitor center or self-issued at the trailhead. Dogs allowed on leash but not recommended during warmer

months—many have had to be carried out after burning their paws and becoming dehydrated. Bungee jumping is available at the Bridge to Nowhere and is operated by Bungee America (see Appendix I); **GPS:** N 34.237050, W 117.765071

🏠 🌊 *Few day hikes are as steeped in history and adventure as this epic, exhausting route along the East Fork San Gabriel River. Hiking through the rugged Sheep Mountain Wilderness, you'll pass the ruins of old mining camps, wade through icy rivers, hike on a long-abandoned roadway, and cross a 120-foot-high concrete arch bridge that stands as a monument to one of the many failed attempts to build in this canyon.*

GETTING THERE
From Interstate 210 in Azusa, take exit 40 for Azusa Avenue (CA-39) and travel north for 11.8 miles, then turn right onto East Fork Road. In 3.3 miles, stay to the right to keep on East Fork Road and in 1.9 miles make a sharp left onto Camp Bonita Road. This road ends at the trailhead. Display your Adventure Pass.

ON THE TRAIL
Begin heading north from the oft-crowded trailhead as the trail drops down a wide fire road from the high ground above Coyote Flat to the lowlands of Heaton Flat, where there is a small hike-in campground, restroom, and a junction with the Heaton Flat Trail. Stay straight here as the trail hugs the bank of the East Fork, which—depending on water levels—will be a dry trail, a boulder hop, or your first experience fording the river. (I strongly recommend some quick-dry shoes or tough sandals for this hike.)

Sooner or later, all L.A. hikers make the pilgrimage to the Bridge to Nowhere.

The trail here is established but can change dramatically based on the level of water in the river and how many floods the canyon had in the previous season. Generally, if you just stay in the main canyon of the East Fork you'll be OK, but there are a few sections where the trail leaves the riverbed. The first section occurs at the 1-mile mark, where the trail rises on the west bank of the river and stays dry until 1.4 miles. Cross the river again here and climb to the east bank. Stay above the riverbed at 1.5 miles to follow the San Gabriel River as it turns northeast at

Shoemaker Canyon. Look to the northwest here to see one of the failed tunnels of Shoemaker Canyon Road from the 1950s, and look down to note chunks of asphalt from the failed attempt to build a road through this canyon in the 1930s. At 2.7 miles, the canyon makes a sharp turn north at Laurel Gulch. Just beyond this, note the odd ribbon of quartz on the western canyon wall known as Swan Rock and stay left (north) at Allison Gulch. The trail rises to the old road grade just north of Allison Gulch, but at 3.5 miles you should drop back into

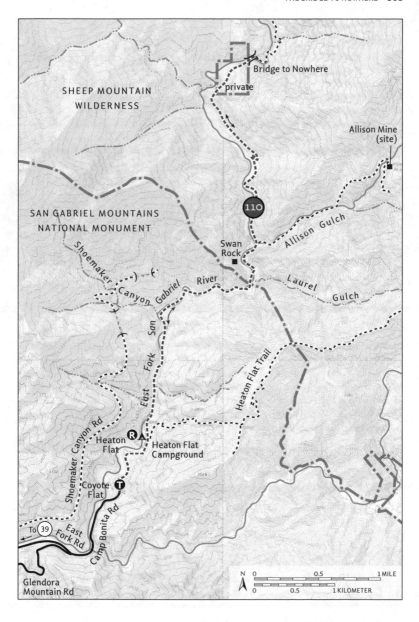

SHEEP MOUNTAIN
WILDERNESS

Bridge to Nowhere

private

Allison Mine
(site)

SAN GABRIEL MOUNTAINS
NATIONAL MONUMENT

110

Shoemaker

Canyon

Allison Gulch

Swan
Rock

San Gabriel River

Laurel Gulch

Fork

East

San

Heaton Flat Trail

Shoemaker Canyon Rd

R

Heaton
Flat

Heaton Flat
Campground

Coyote
Flat

T

To 39

East Fork Rd

Camp Bonita Rd

Glendora
Mountain Rd

N   0   0.5   1 MILE

0   0.5   1 KILOMETER

A LAND OF MANY USES

The East Fork San Gabriel River is often seen as ground zero in the sometimes prickly conflict between recreational use and wilderness preservation in the San Gabriel Mountains. In the lower reaches of the river, legal recreational activities like picnicking and bathing are causing excessive litter, graffiti, and other plagues of chronic overuse. Farther up the river, individual prospectors and miners are following in the historic footsteps of earlier gold seekers despite an official Forest Service ban on those activities on the East Fork (with the few private inholdings as notable exemptions from this ban). No one is getting rich from prospecting here, and although many in the prospecting community do haul out trash and truly care about the river, others alter the landscape with pickaxes and shovels, set prohibited campfires, stay in the area beyond the legal limit, and divert the river inside the federal wilderness area, which is also home to the endangered Santa Ana sucker fish. As the Forest Service develops a land-use plan for the newly designated San Gabriel Mountains National Monument and receives additional funding for patrols and law enforcement, expect additional changes and potential conflict inside this incredible canyon. Until then, please do your part and set a good example as a hiker. Be polite, adhere to the Leave No Trace ethics, and haul out any litter you can.

the riverbed to round a final curve in the canyon; staying up high here will put you on a narrow ridge of crumbling rock that is unnecessarily dangerous.

Stay in the riverbed until 3.8 miles, where a steep trail on the eastern bank returns you to the road grade. This rises above the river, entering a private inholding at 4.4 miles, and reaches the Bridge to Nowhere at 4.9 miles. It's a little underwhelming from this angle, but cross the bridge and look back to get a sense of just how weird it is to see something this huge this far back in the wilderness. A series of use-trails descends from the old road grade back down to the river, where there are dozens of incredible swimming holes—perfect places to watch weekend thrill seekers as they bungee jump from the edge of the bridge. Rest up and return the way you came in.

Opposite: Rugged, challenging, high-altitude hiking is the name of the game near Los Angeles County's tallest peak.

mount baldy area

The official name of the tallest peak in the San Gabriel Mountains is Mount San Antonio, in honor of the Franciscan priest Saint Anthony of Padua. It has been known as such since at least 1858.

The prospectors and pioneers who came later had no use for that fancy designation and just called the treeless summit "Old Baldy." "Mount Baldy" is the name that stuck with locals for the impressive gray mountain that stands guard over San Antonio Canyon, despite the USGS's dogged insistence on using the San Antonio label.

Hikers here can enjoy a high-elevation, conifer-covered wonderland on trails that don't seem like they have any business being in Southern California. Cascading mountain streams beckon hikers to backcountry camps in the Cucamonga Wilderness, shaded by towering Jeffrey pines and even taller peaks. Bighorn sheep roam the ridges here, putting the best mountain scramblers to shame, and the historic village of Mount Baldy is the perfect post-hike getaway for hungry hikers before returning to the world of freeways and deadlines.

111 Sunset Peak

RATING/ DIFFICULTY	ROUNDTRIP	ELEV GAIN/ HIGH POINT	SEASON
***/3	7.9 miles	1401 feet/ 5796 feet	Year-round

Map: USGS Mount Baldy; **Contact:** Angeles National Forest/San Gabriel Mountains National Monument, San Gabriel River Ranger District; **Notes:** Dogs allowed on leash. Roads may be closed during winter, or chains may be required; **GPS:** N 34.219058, W 117.712391

This moderate fire road hike takes you to a prominent peak in the Front Range of San Antonio Canyon and the remains of an old fire lookout. From here,

Sunset Peak may be the best place to enjoy the panorama near Mount Baldy.

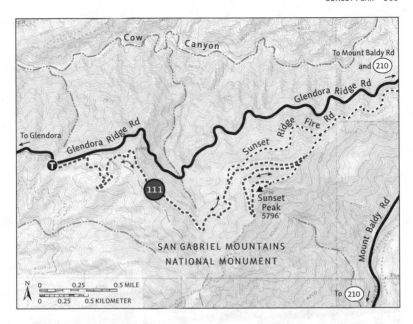

you'll have commanding views of the cities to the south and the impressive alpine summits of the Mount Baldy area.

GETTING THERE

From the Foothill Freeway (CA-210) in Claremont, take exit 52 at Base Line Road. Head west on Base Line Road at the exit and turn right onto Padua Avenue. In 1.8 miles, turn right onto Mount Baldy Road. Follow it for 7.1 miles and then make a sharp left onto Glendora Ridge Road. The fire road trailhead will be on the south side of the road in 4.2 miles.

ON THE TRAIL

Begin your hike heading east on a narrow fire road that closely parallels Glendora Ridge Road. You'll be on this road for almost the entirety of the trip, and while the trail

itself isn't necessarily the most interesting or exciting, the views are pretty top-notch. To the northeast, you'll see Lookout Mountain and the looming gray bulk of Mount San Antonio—visible for almost the entire hike. As the hike continues, you'll also make the transition from the upper limits of the south-facing chaparral into the pine forests of the higher elevations, making this hike one of the easiest ways to experience the transition between the two plant communities.

Most of this trail is on the north-facing side of the ridge, meaning it will be a bit cooler and shadier and more likely to hang onto snow in the winter months. Keep to the right at 2.1 miles and again at 2.7 miles, where a rugged ridgeline trail climbs to the peak from Cow Canyon Saddle below. Continue following the road as it makes a few broad switchbacks and reaches the summit just before 4 miles, unveiling a truly jaw-dropping panorama. Nearly all the major peaks of the Mount Baldy area are visible from here. Take it all in, decide which peaks you're going to visit next, and return the way you came.

112 Timber Mountain via Icehouse Canyon

RATING/ DIFFICULTY	ROUNDTRIP	ELEV GAIN/ HIGH POINT	SEASON
****/3	8.8 miles	3325 feet/ 8303 feet	May–Nov

Maps: USGS Mount Baldy, Cucamonga Peak; **Contact:** Angeles National Forest, San Gabriel River Ranger District; **Notes:**

Adventure Pass required at trailhead. Free wilderness pass required to enter the Cucamonga Wilderness, available at ranger stations and at the Mount Baldy Visitor Center (see Appendix I), open 9:00 AM–2:00 PM on weekdays, 7:00 AM–3:30 PM on weekends. Dogs allowed on leash; **GPS:** N 34.2500710, W 117.6361570

The first time you hike in Icehouse Canyon (named for an ice plant that supplied Los Angeles in the late 1850s), you can be forgiven for checking your map to make sure you're still in Los Angeles County. This cool, pine-lined alpine creek feels about a million miles away from city life—which is why it's one of the most popular day hikes in the region.

The old summit register on Timber Mountain still bears the family name of the owner of Icehouse Canyon Lodge.

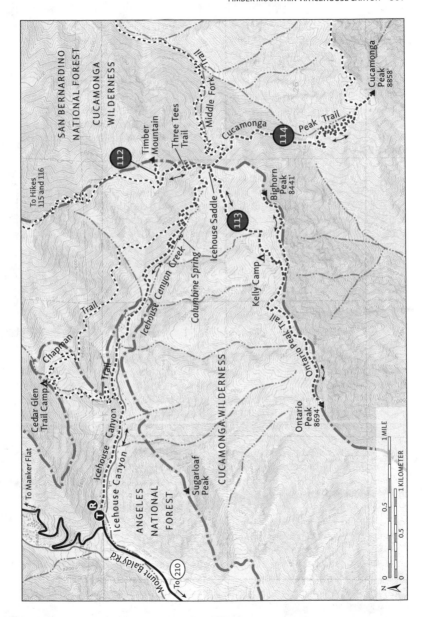

GETTING THERE

From the Foothill Freeway (CA-210) in Claremont, take exit 52 toward Base Line Road. Head west and turn right onto Padua Avenue. In 1.8 miles, turn right onto Mount Baldy Road. In 8.9 miles, take a slight right onto Icehouse Canyon Road and park at the trailhead.

ON THE TRAIL

Head east from the parking area and pass the ruins of the Icehouse Canyon Lodge, a beautiful two-story, wood-and-stone structure that provided warmth and hearty food to travelers from 1919 until it tragically burned down in 1988. The trail meanders alongside the year-round Icehouse Canyon Creek, slowly climbing through a magnificent forest of incense cedar and bigcone Douglas-fir. Stick to the trail or make the occasional side trip to the creek itself (just watch out for stinging nettle). At 1.1 miles ignore the Chapman Trail, which bends into Cedar Canyon and takes a higher route up Icehouse Canyon with an option to camp in Cedar Glen Trail Camp (overnight and camp stove permits required).

By 1.5 miles the creek tends to dry out, and you'll enter the Cucamonga Wilderness near some massive boulders at 1.7 miles. The canyon walls open up here and the forest cover thins, while the trail hops along the boulder-strewn floor before turning toward the northern wall at 2 miles. The trail hugs this area for the rest of the climb, passing the Chapman Trail again at 3 miles and reaching Icehouse Saddle at 3.5 miles. The saddle is a fine turnaround point but it's also a launching pad for adventures to nearby peaks. Head directly north on the Three Tees Trail toward Timber Mountain and keep right at 4.2 miles to head toward the peak, which

you'll reach at 4.4 miles. The iron summit register still bears the name of the founder of the Icehouse Canyon Lodge. Trek a bit to the north of the summit for some better views, then return the way you came.

EXTENDING YOUR TRIP

From Icehouse Saddle, ambitious hikers who want a little more elevation gain can head to Bighorn and Ontario peaks, passing (or staying at) Kelly Camp (Hike 113), or trek up to Cucamonga Peak (Hike 114). You can also continue on the Three Tees Trail to Telegraph Peak (Hike 116) and Thunder Mountain (Hike 115) and descend to Manker Flat, where, hopefully, you have a car shuttle back.

113 Bighorn and Ontario Peaks

RATING/ DIFFICULTY	ROUNDTRIP	ELEV GAIN/ HIGH POINT	SEASON
*****/4	13.9 miles	3698 feet/ 8696 feet	May–Nov

Maps: USGS Mount Baldy, Cucamonga Peak; **Contact:** Angeles National Forest, San Gabriel River Ranger District; **Notes:** Adventure Pass required at trailhead. Free wilderness pass required to enter the Cucamonga Wilderness, available at ranger stations and at the Mount Baldy Visitor Center (see Appendix I), open 9:00 AM–2:00 PM on weekdays, 7:00 AM–3:30 PM on weekends. Dogs allowed on leash. Overnight and camp stove permits required to stay at Kelly Camp; **GPS:** N 34.2500710, W 117.6361570

 *This fantastic trail takes you to the* site of Kelly Camp, one of the most remote former wilderness resorts. From this lofty backcountry base camp, the trail continues to

Clouds move in along the ridge to Bighorn Peak.

tackle nearby Bighorn Peak before traversing an epic ridgeline west to Ontario Peak. Along the way you'll have absolutely stunning views of Icehouse Canyon, the Baldy Bowl, and the foothill cities—and a better than decent chance of spotting some of the region's bighorn sheep, too.

GETTING THERE

From the Foothill Freeway (CA-210) in Claremont, take exit 52 toward Base Line Road. Head west and turn right onto Padua Avenue. In 1.8 miles, turn right onto Mount Baldy Road. In 8.9 miles, take a slight right onto Icehouse Canyon Road and park at the trailhead.

ON THE TRAIL

Follow the Timber Mountain route to Icehouse Saddle (Hike 112) at 3.5 miles. Take a hard right to join the Ontario Peak Trail and head west, back along the far southern rim of Icehouse Canyon. The trail blazes through fragrant pines and hearty manzanita and reaches Kelly Camp at 4.4 miles. The prospector John Kelly built a small gold mine and single log cabin here in 1905. The mine didn't make much, nor did the resort that followed. Today, only the stone foundations of guest cabins remain.

The Ontario Peak Trail climbs above Kelly Camp and at 4.8 miles meets the route that heads eastward to Bighorn Peak. Turn left here and follow the footpath through manzanita and loose talus, keeping a sharp eye out as the trail becomes slightly indistinct around 5.4 miles. Head to the northeast and continue dodging brush and boulders, topping out at the rocky summit of Bighorn at 5.6 miles. This region of the San Gabriels is not short on killer views, but in my opinion this is one of the best: the Baldy Bowl looms over the end of San Antonio Canyon, the deep gorge of Icehouse Canyon lies to your north, and straight ahead to the west is a sharp, steep ridgeline that divides the foothill cities from the mountain peaks. If you time it right, you can watch clouds from the basin whip up past the ridge and dissolve over the mountains—a sight you're not likely to forget.

Backtrack to the Ontario Peak Trail and continue west along that same ridgeline, passing through beautiful subalpine terrain and hiking quietly for a chance to spot some bighorn sheep. You'll reach the tiny summit of Ontario at 7.7 miles. Enjoy the views and solitude from your mountain perch and return the way you came.

114 Cucamonga Peak

RATING/ DIFFICULTY	ROUNDTRIP	ELEV GAIN/ HIGH POINT	SEASON
****/5	11.7 miles	3873 feet/ 8858 feet	May–Nov

Maps: USGS Mount Baldy, Cucamonga Peak; **Contact:** Angeles National Forest, San Gabriel River Ranger District and San Bernardino National Forest, Front Country Ranger District; **Notes:** Adventure Pass required to park at trailhead. Free wilderness pass required to enter the Cucamonga Wilderness, available at ranger stations and at the

Mount Baldy Visitor Center (see Appendix I), open 9:00 AM–2:00 PM on weekdays, 7:00 AM–3:30 PM on weekends. Dogs allowed on leash; **GPS:** N 34.2500710, W 117.6361570

  Cucamonga Peak rises in sharp relief above the foothill cities outside San Antonio Canyon, providing dramatic views of the valley below, deep quiet in the Cucamonga Wilderness, and an exhausting, leg-busting climb to its summit. In addition, the well-placed summit block can easily set you up with a photo that makes it look like you're on a much more precipitous drop than you actually are. Impress your social media friends and terrify your family back home!

GETTING THERE
From the Foothill Freeway (CA-210) in Claremont, take exit 52 toward Base Line Road. Head west and turn right onto Padua Avenue. In 1.8 miles, turn right on Mount Baldy Road. In 8.9 miles, take a slight right onto Icehouse Canyon Road and park at the trailhead.

ON THE TRAIL
Follow the route to Icehouse Saddle at 3.5 miles as described in Hike 112. From here, head southeast on the Cucamonga Peak Trail, keeping right at the junction with the Middle Fork Trail 0.1 mile later. The trail stays fairly level as it turns south on a long saddle between Cucamonga Peak to the east and Bighorn Peak to the west. Enjoy this brief respite, because by 4.6 miles you'll be staring up at a series of steep, tough switchbacks all the way to the summit.

Eventually the trail makes an eastward turn, and at 5.7 miles look for a spur trail on your right to the summit. On clear days, the views from here are shockingly vast,

The Icehouse Canyon Trail is a spectacular gateway to a number of peaks in the Mount Baldy area.

stretching to the distant San Jacintos and Santa Anas. Snag that summit photo and return the way you came in.

115 Thunder Mountain

RATING/ DIFFICULTY	ROUNDTRIP	ELEV GAIN/ HIGH POINT	SEASON
***/3	9.4 miles	2403 feet/ 8587 feet	May–Nov

Maps: USGS Mount San Antonio, Telegraph Peak; **Contact:** Angeles National Forest/ San Gabriel Mountains National Monument, San Gabriel River Ranger District; **Notes:** Adventure Pass required to park at trailhead. Route between Mount Baldy Notch and Thunder Mountain closed to hikers during ski season. Dogs allowed on leash. Check with Mount Baldy Ski Lifts (see Appendix I) for ski lift hours and prices; **GPS:** N 34.266125, W 117.626826

🦴 ⚫ 🌿 *I know what you're thinking: "A hike on fire roads and ski trails? Next." But this relatively mild route to the top of the ski lift at Thunder Mountain is a fantastic introduction to the grandeur of the Mount Baldy region, and the ability to take the Mount Baldy ski lift up or down (or both) means this peak is within reach for almost every hiker.*

GETTING THERE

From the Foothill Freeway (CA-210) in Claremont, take exit 52 toward Base Line Road. Head west and turn right onto Padua Avenue. In 1.8 miles, turn right onto Mount Baldy Road and follow it for 11.6 miles until you reach Manker Flat Campground. Park along the road (not in the sites). The trail begins on Falls Road. If you are planning on taking the ski lift, continue past the campground to the end of the road and use the ski lift's parking lot.

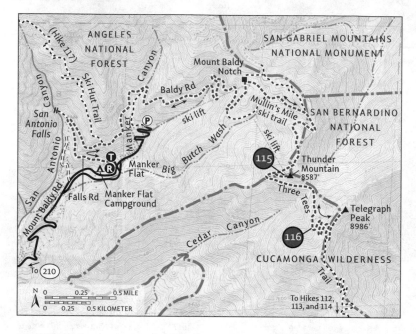

ON THE TRAIL

From the north end of Manker Flat, head west on Falls Road, which slowly rises above the Manker Flat area and the remnants of historic Camp Baldy. At 0.5 mile, there is a short spur trail to the base of San Antonio Falls, a beautiful, tiered cascade that is especially worth the side trip in the early spring. Head southeast on what is now on Baldy Road, keeping to the right at the junction with the Ski Hut Trail at 0.9 mile and ignoring the descending fire road at Manker Canyon at 1.6 miles. Keep to the left at 3 miles and you'll arrive at Mount Baldy Notch at 3.3 miles. This welcoming ski hut is open on the weekends during the summer months, offering casual food and cold drinks to weary hikers.

Head southeast from the notch on the Mullin's Mile ski trail, which scales the upper reach of Big Butch Wash before hitting a steep ridgeline drop-off at 3.9 miles. The trail stays on the west side of this ridge, ducking under the Thunder Mountain ski lift at 4.5 miles. Take a left just after this to hit Thunder's summit, then plot your next hiking trip or head back the way you came.

EXTENDING YOUR TRIP

Thunder Mountain is the northern terminus of the Three Tees Trail, and with a free wilderness permit (available at ranger stations and at the Mount Baldy Visitor Center, open 9:00 AM–2:00 PM on weekdays, 7:00 AM–3:30 PM on weekends; see Appendix I), you can continue south to Telegraph Peak (Hike 116) and Timber Mountain (Hike 112) before ending at Icehouse Saddle. From Icehouse Saddle there are many options, including an

Mount Baldy as seen from the Three Tees Trail

overnight stay at Kelly Camp or Cedar Glen Trail Camp (overnight and camp stove permits required), but the most popular route descends Icehouse Canyon and requires a car shuttle back to Manker Flat. It's an epic and challenging way to experience the beauty of the Cucamonga Wilderness.

116 Telegraph Peak

RATING/ DIFFICULTY	ROUNDTRIP	ELEV GAIN/ HIGH POINT	SEASON
*****/4	11.8 miles	2802 feet/ 8986 feet	May–Nov

Maps: USGS Mount San Antonio, Telegraph Peak; **Contact:** Angeles National Forest, San Gabriel River Ranger District; **Notes:** Adventure Pass required to park at trailhead. Route between Mount Baldy Notch and Thunder Mountain closed to hikers during ski season. Dogs allowed on leash. Check with Mount Baldy Ski Lifts (see Appendix I) for ski lift hours and prices; **GPS:** N 34.266125, W 117.626826

  Telegraph Peak, the highest point in the Cucamonga Wilderness, offers a bit more solitude and wild flavor than the shorter hike to nearby Thunder Mountain (Hike 115). From the narrow summit perch, you'll have tremendous views of the surrounding terrain, including some clear sight lines northeast to the San Bernardino Mountains across Cajon Pass.

GETTING THERE

From the Foothill Freeway (CA-210) in Claremont, take exit 52 toward Base Line Road. Head west and turn right onto Padua Avenue. In 1.8 miles, turn right onto Mount Baldy Road and follow it for 11.6 miles until

The weathered trunks and roots of old trees form alpine driftwood on the Three Tees Trail.

you reach Manker Flat Campground. Park along the road (not in the sites). The trail begins on Falls Road. If you are planning on taking the ski lift, continue past the campground to the end of the road and use the ski lift's parking lot.

ON THE TRAIL

Follow the route described in Thunder Mountain (Hike 115) to the 4.5-mile mark. Summit or bypass Thunder Mountain and continue on the wide path to the southwest, which wraps around Thunder Mountain and turns to the southeast at the Cucamonga

Wilderness boundary. Here it becomes a narrower single-track trail, making a slight dip into the upper reaches of Cedar Canyon. The trail makes its way through some gnarled pines and low manzanita and across a narrow talus ridge at 4.9 miles before heading south and rising up a series of switchbacks.

At 5.7 miles, keep left and follow the trail along a dramatic, narrow ledge to Telegraph Peak at 5.9 miles. The views are nothing short of epic from here and on clear days you can see all the way out to Catalina Island. The best part? You're likely to have this stretch of trail all to yourself, even while crowds are slogging their way up to the Mount Baldy summit within view. Return the way you came.

EXTENDING YOUR TRIP

The Three Tees Trail continues south to Timber Mountain (Hike 112) and down Icehouse Canyon, where a car shuttle can finish out a wonderful day spent in the wilderness. It is also possible to hike to Telegraph Peak from Icehouse Canyon, although you should be warned that the section from Timber to Telegraph has a lengthy series of steep switchbacks that will test the patience of even the most monkish hikers.

117 Mount Harwood and Mount San Antonio (Mount Baldy)

RATING/ DIFFICULTY	LOOP	ELEV GAIN/ HIGH POINT	SEASON
*****/5	10 miles	3911 feet/ 10,069 feet	May–Nov

Maps: USGS Mount San Antonio, Telegraph Peak; **Contact:** Angeles National Forest/San Gabriel Mountains National Monument, San Gabriel River Ranger District; **Notes:** Adventure Pass required at trailhead. While dogs are allowed on this route, we recommend taking your dogs only if they have experience on strenuous hikes. Check with Mount

Exhausted hikers rest on the summit of Mount Baldy after a taxing ascent.

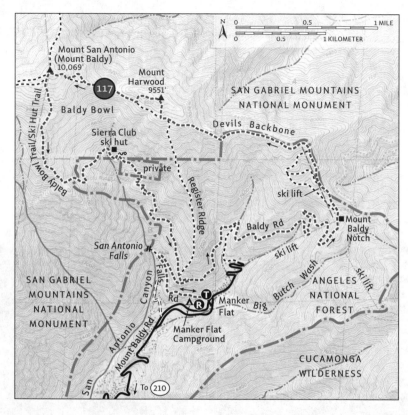

Baldy Ski Lifts (see Appendix I) for ski lift hours and prices and for hiking accessibility during winter months. Do not attempt this trail when ice or snow is present unless you have the proper training and equipment; **GPS: N 34.266125, W 117.626826**

This leg-busting ascent to the highest point in the San Gabriel Mountains (and Los Angeles County) is an absolute must-do for any serious hiker living in or visiting the region. This loop route traverses the infamous Devils Backbone and makes a short side trip to neighboring Mount Harwood before descending on the Ski Hut Trail. This route is challenging, rightfully popular, and stunning in every way.

GETTING THERE

From the Foothill Freeway (CA-210) in Claremont, take exit 52 toward Base Line Road. Head west and turn right onto Padua Avenue. In 1.8 miles, turn right onto Mount Baldy Road and follow it for 11.6 miles until

Hikers safely cross the Devils Backbone in calm summer weather.

you reach Manker Flat Campground. Park along the road (not in the sites). The trail begins on Falls Road.

ON THE TRAIL

Follow the route to Mount Baldy Notch described in Hike 115. From the notch, start hiking to the northwest. You'll be on ski routes here, and there aren't really a lot of signs to help hikers along the way. Keep to the right at junctions near another ski lift to take the most direct, though steepest, path. Heading left at either of the junctions offers a longer, more moderate climb, but all options meet at the northern end of the ski area at 3.9 miles. From here, the trail turns westward near the summit ridge, with

the broad expanse of Stockton Flat to the northeast.

Now you're about to leave the ski runs and hit the Devils Backbone—a narrow and precipitous stretch of trail that has given many Southern California hikers palpitations. With steep drop-offs to the north and south and the chance of gusty winds and lingering ice, this is definitely a place you want to watch your step; but in my opinion, the Backbone has a slightly more terrifying reputation than it probably deserves. Just take it easy and don't psych yourself out before you get here.

Past the Backbone, the trail narrows a bit and hugs a steep cliff face on the southern side of the ridge, then widens and heads directly toward the Baldy Bowl. At 5.1 miles, a use-trail extension of the unofficial (and unnecessarily steep) Register Ridge trail continues north to the top of barren Mount Harwood. This peak doesn't require a ton of extra effort or time from your Baldy target and is recommended. Unlike Baldy, on Harwood you'll likely have the summit entirely to yourself, and the views down the Baldy Bowl from its 9551-foot summit are no slouches, either. Descend back to the Devils Backbone Trail on a gentle use-trail along Harwood's western slope and steel yourself for the final climb to Baldy.

The steep switchbacks that follow often feel much longer than they actually are, but you'll reach the summit at 6.1 miles—a perfect place to celebrate your accomplishment with a lunch break and some panoramic summit selfies to take back to civilization with you.

From the summit, head due south and look for a sign marking the Baldy Bowl Trail (sometimes called the Ski Hut Trail by locals) to Manker Flat. This steep descent follows the western and southern edges of the Baldy Bowl—the wide, steep, treeless natural amphitheater just below the mountain's summit that's long been a favorite of wilderness skiers. The trail ducks inside the bowl itself and passes a spring and the Sierra Club ski hut at 7.7 miles. Follow this trail back to the fire road at 9.1 miles and return the way you came.

Opposite: Trails in the Puente and Chino hills are an invaluable resource for San Gabriel Valley hikers and cyclists.

puente-chino hills

Almost directly south from the San Gabriel Mountains lie the Puente and Chino hills, a series of low, rolling hills that separate the San Gabriel Valley from Orange County to the south.

Most of this area was agricultural in the past, but ranches and farms fell to factories and housing developments as the urbanized Los Angeles followed the freeways east. Large chunks of these hills have been preserved as wildlife corridors and state and local parks—a prized resource for locals who would otherwise have to travel great distances to find open spaces.

There isn't a ton of shade here, so hiking in the summer months can be a challenge for those who aren't willing to wake up extra early, but in the cooler months the hills turn a brilliant green and clear air provides some of the best views in all of Southern California.

Note that trails in the Puente Hills are closed for forty-eight hours following rainstorms and are open from sunrise to sunset. The Puente Hills Habitat Preservation Authority's website (see Appendix I) has updated trail closure information on its front page.

118 Hacienda Hills

RATING/ DIFFICULTY	LOOP	ELEV GAIN/ HIGH POINT	SEASON
****/3	4.7 miles	646 feet/ 1158 feet	Year-round (best in spring)

Maps: USGS Baldwin Park, El Monte;
Contact: Puente Hills Habitat Preservation

The Puma Trail provides excellent views of the San Gabriel Valley.

Authority; **Notes:** Park open sunrise–sunset. Trail open to horses and bicycles. Dogs allowed on leash; **GPS:** N 34.009594, W 117.993907

The Puente and Chino hills are covered in great hiking trails, but this loop in the Hacienda Hills is definitely one of the best. This developed trailhead has ample parking, water, restrooms, and a section of trail that's accessible for wheelchairs. On the trail, you'll enjoy beautiful views of the San Gabriel Mountains and some amazing riparian oak canyons.

GETTING THERE

From the Pomona Freeway (CA-60) eastbound in Hacienda Heights, take exit 14A for Seventh Avenue and head south for 0.7 mile. From CA 60 westbound, take exit 14 for Seventh Avenue, turn left onto Gale Avenue at the end of the ramp, then left onto Seventh. The trailhead is at the end of Seventh Avenue, at the intersection with Orange Grove Avenue. There is a very small parking area at the trailhead (including handicapped-accessible spots), but there is ample parking on Seventh Avenue just north of the trailhead, near the Orange Grove Middle School's outdoor space.

ON THE TRAIL

Head south past the trailhead gate along an easily graded path that meanders along the dirt and gravel extension of Seventh Avenue, lined with bioswales and recently planted California natives. In the spring, purple sage, California poppies, and goldfields put on quite a show here under the shade of young sycamores and native oaks. At 0.3 mile, turn left at a small, shaded bench to start hiking

on the hiker-only Coyote Trail, which wastes no time climbing up the north slope of the Hacienda Hills. Thankfully, this uphill stretch has decent shade and breaks in the foliage with excellent views of the San Gabriel Mountains. Be on the lookout for diminutive miner's lettuce, showy monkey flowers, and poison oak.

At 0.9 mile, the trail traverses a small ridge between the Hacienda Hills and a residential area along Oak Canyon Drive to the south. Ignore the spur trails near the impressive stands of prickly pear cactus and continue to the southwest. Join the Schabarum Trail heading west at 1.4 miles. At 1.5 miles, stay left at the junction with the Ahwinga Trail, then right at the junction with the Rattlesnake Ridge Trail, and continue on the Schabarum Trail as it turns north. On clear days you can get some excellent views of downtown Los Angeles and the Santa Monica Mountains to the west here—even though there are a lot of chain link fences around.

At 2 miles, leave the broad Schabarum Trail to join the more rugged Native Oak Trail, which makes a short, steep climb, then head right (east) onto the hiker-only Puma Trail at 2.1 miles. Unlike the Coyote Trail, the Puma Trail has almost no shade. While it may be a bit hotter here, you'll also have clear views in almost every direction as you switchback down to the Native Oak Trail again at 2.8 miles. Head south and at 3.1 miles the trail enters a shockingly lush and shaded riparian canyon—a welcome change indeed from the sunblasted Puma Trail. The trail climbs up again, meeting the Ahwinga Trail at 3.8 miles. Continue hiking east. You'll meet the remnants of a paved road at 4.1 miles and close the loop at 4.3 miles. Retrace your steps to the parking area.

119 Worsham Canyon

RATING/ DIFFICULTY	LOOP	ELEV GAIN/ HIGH POINT	SEASON
***/3	4.2 miles	615 feet/ 1358 feet	Year-round (best in spring)

Map: USGS Whittier; **Contact:** Puente Hills Habitat Preservation Authority; **Notes:** Park open sunrise–sunset. Trail open to horses and bicycles. Dogs allowed on leash; **GPS:** N 33.994090, W 118.012934

Less than a mile from the popular Turnbull Canyon (Hike 120) trail-head, this loop through Worsham Canyon provides many of the same experiences and views but with more-rugged trails, steeper inclines, and far fewer people. Although this trail is open year-round, it's best experienced in the spring when the winter rains have revitalized the native plants and grasses, and the sun isn't too brutal yet.

GETTING THERE

From Interstate 605 southbound in Whittier, take exit 16 for Beverly Boulevard and turn right (east). From the 605 northbound, at the bottom of the exit ramp, turn right on Pioneer Boulevard, then left onto Beverly Boulevard. Stay on Beverly and in 2.6 miles, it turns into Turnbull Canyon Road at Beverly Hills Drive. The trailhead is at a sharp curve approximately 1.2 miles past Beverly Hills Drive. The parking area at the trailhead is very, very small, so make sure you take as little room as possible when you park as street parking is prohibited here.

Worsham Canyon is a quiet hiking option in the Puente Hills.

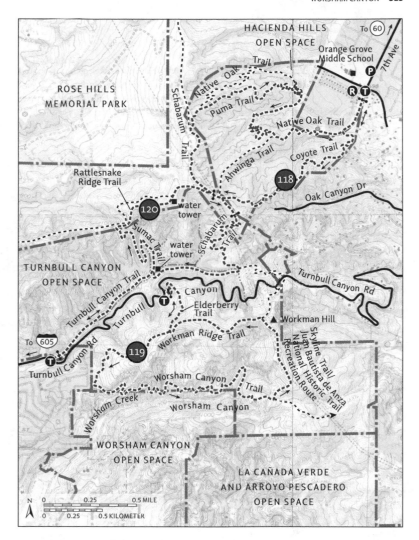

ON THE TRAIL

Begin on the Elderberry Trail, passing a gate and following an old dirt road that climbs through some extensive fields of nonnative (but still pretty in the spring) wild mustard before hitting the Workman Ridge Trail at 0.5 mile. Keep right here to make a southwesterly descent through the rolling Puente Hills.

The trail makes a sharp turn to the east at 1.1 miles, becoming the Worsham Canyon Trail. Ignore the spur trails—many of them head into the backyards of private homes. A very well-established use-trail at 1.3 miles heads south to an unofficial residential access point through private property. Continuing east, the trail meanders along the northern slope of Worsham Canyon. It's mostly grasses and sage scrub here, but just across the canyon you'll be able to see a healthy number of oak trees clinging to the side of the hill. As the canyon walls close in and you lose all sight of civilization, this stretch reveals itself to be an unbelievably secluded and quiet respite right in the thick of the SoCal sprawl.

At 2.3 miles, the trail crosses the bed of the mostly dry Worsham Creek and starts a moderately tough climb back up toward Workman Ridge. At 2.7 miles, turn left onto the Skyline Trail (also labeled the Juan Bautista de Anza National Historic Trail Recreation Route) and continue your climb to the north side of the ridge. Keep left at 3.2 miles to rejoin the Workman Ridge Trail and follow it west to close the loop at 3.8 miles, enjoying the inspiring views of the San Gabriel Mountains to the north on your way back to the trailhead.

120 Turnbull Canyon

RATING/ DIFFICULTY	LOOP	ELEV GAIN/ HIGH POINT	SEASON
**/2	4.3 miles	910 feet/ 1263 feet	Year-round (best in spring)

Maps: USGS Whittier, El Monte; **Contact:** Puente Hills Habitat Preservation Authority; **Notes:** Park open sunrise–sunset. Trail open to horses and bicycles. Dogs allowed on leash; **GPS:** N 33.995794, W 118.011378

This route takes you past a small but mature riparian canyon and up wildflower-covered hills to a ridge with some of the absolutely best views of Southern California you'll ever see (smog and haze permitting).

GETTING THERE
From Interstate 605 southbound in Whittier, take exit 16 for Beverly Boulevard and turn right (east). From the 605 northbound, at the bottom of the exit ramp, turn right on Pioneer Boulevard, then left onto Beverly Boulevard. Stay on Beverly and in 2.6 miles, it turns into Turnbull Canyon Road at Beverly Hills Drive. The trailhead is at a very small, dirt parking area 0.3 mile beyond this point. If you can't snag a spot, you'll have to turn around and park west of Greenleaf Avenue (about 0.8 mile from the trailhead) and walk back along the road; nearby residents keep restricting street parking for hikers.

ON THE TRAIL
Head into the canyon as its steep slope rises to your left. To the right of the broad fire road you're walking on is the narrow but mature strip of protected riparian woodland that hugs the canyon floor. Towering, tangled sycamores and live oaks give you a glimpse of the region's past as you hike alongside trail runners, equestrians, and mountain bikers.

At 0.7 mile, stay left to join the Sumac Trail as it starts to climb out of Turnbull Canyon. Here, you'll have even lovelier views of the hilly and green (in season) canyon sides as well as an unobstructed view into Whittier. On very clear days, you can see

California poppies put on a reliable springtime show in Turnbull Canyon.

down to Long Beach, Palos Verdes, and maybe even Catalina. At 1.4 miles, stay right to join the Rattlesnake Ridge Trail and in another 0.1 mile stay to the far right at a junction with another fire road and an old oil road to start the main ascent of the loop—a 200-foot gain over 0.3 mile to a prominent (and heavily graffitied) water tower.

From this ridge, you can lay your eyes on nearly every major mountain range in Southern California and see down the coast into Orange County . . . as well as admire the striking shape of the nearby Rose Hills Buddhist Columbarium to the west. Snap some photos before descending a short and steep fire road on the north side of the slope and continuing eastward. Just before the 1.9-mile mark, pass through an open gate and turn right onto the Schabarum Trail. Stay to the right at various junctions with use-trails and stay right to join the Turnbull Canyon Trail at 2.9 miles. Follow this trail to return to the three-way junction with the Turnbull Canyon and Sumac trails at 3.7 miles. Stay left to hike on the Turnbull Canyon Trail back to the trailhead.

121 Sycamore and Dark Canyons

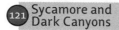

RATING/ DIFFICULTY	ROUNDTRIP	ELEV GAIN/ HIGH POINT	SEASON
****/3	4.6 miles	677 feet/ 977 feet	Year-round (best in spring)

Map: USGS Whittier; **Contact:** Puente Hills Habitat Preservation Authority; **Notes:** Park open sunrise–sunset. Trail open to hikers only. No dogs allowed; **GPS:** N 34.004040, W 118.055106

This pleasant out-and-back begins as a wide, sunny expanse and narrows into a shaded walkway framed with native oaks and its namesake sycamores. A steep switchback route gets your blood pumping before revealing the surrounding landscape on a high ridge above Whittier, and a quick trip into secluded Dark Canyon rounds out this trip.

GETTING THERE

From Interstate 605 southbound in Whittier, take exit 16 for Beverly Boulevard and turn right (east). From the 605 northbound, at the

A sprawling sycamore tree stands at the bottom of its namesake canyon.

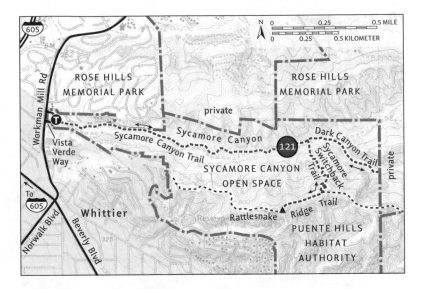

bottom of the exit ramp, turn right on Pioneer Boulevard, then left onto Beverly Boulevard. Head southeast on Beverly Boulevard for 0.7 mile, then turn left onto Workman Mill Road. In 0.4 mile, turn right onto Vista Verde Way. There is a small lot near the trailhead.

ON THE TRAIL

Head east on the dirt road called Sycamore Canyon Trail, following the signs for the trail as you pass the dirt access road for a controversial oil well. The road rises above the north side of the floor of Sycamore Canyon, passing a huge collection of prickly pear cacti near an open gate from the area's former life as a ranch. You'll pass more artifacts of the old days along the way, including old fences and water towers. About 0.7 mile in, the tree cover around the creek bed widens and the canyon takes on a more riparian flavor. At a particularly sprawling sycamore tree at 1.2

miles, turn right. The Sycamore Switchback Trail crosses the creek bed and makes a frontal assault on the ridge to the south, climbing upward in a series of tight switchbacks. Stay on the trail (no need to further erode the cuts) and enjoy the increasingly vast views that open up outside the canyon walls.

At 1.7 miles, head west on the Rattlesnake Ridge Trail to reach the trail's high point near a water tower at 1.9 miles. Soak in the views and backtrack to Sycamore Canyon Trail. At 2.6 miles, turn right to follow the trail into Dark Canyon for some more incredibly pleasant shaded canyon hiking. The trail turns south at 2.8 miles and dissolves into the oak forest at 3 miles. Any hiking that continues afterward is on unmaintained routes and is frowned upon, so just enjoy the shade and return to the trailhead the way you came in.

122 Powder Canyon

RATING/ DIFFICULTY	LOOP	ELEV GAIN/ HIGH POINT	SEASON
**/3	4.8 miles	721 feet/ 1311 feet	Year-round (best in spring)

Map: USGS La Habra; **Contact:** Puente Hills Habitat Preservation Authority and Peter F. Schabarum Regional Park; **Notes:** Park open sunrise–sunset. Schabarum Park open 7:00 AM–6:00 PM in the winter and 7:00 AM–8:00 PM in the summer. Dogs allowed on leash. A vehicle entry fee is required on weekends and holidays *only* if you begin in Schabarum Park; **GPS:** N 33.964243, W 117.921983

This trip forms a loop that takes you back up and over the Puente Hills, revealing dramatic views of the high San Gabriel Mountains before returning you to the shaded oak woodland charm of the canyon.

GETTING THERE
From the Pomona Freeway (CA-60) in Rowland Heights, take exit 19 for Fullerton Road and head south. Stay on Fullerton Road for about 2 miles, then take a slight right to stay on Fullerton Road. You'll pass the Rowland Water District buildings on your right and a dirt road. Take a right on the second dirt road you see (in about 0.2 mile). There's a small parking area near the Nogales trailhead. Continue past this to the larger parking area near the equestrian ring.

Share the broad fire roads of Powder Canyon with cyclists and equestrians.

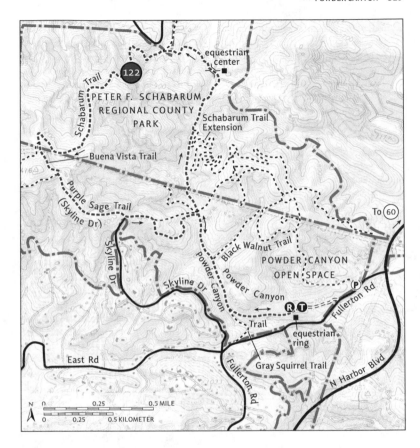

ON THE TRAIL

Head west from the small equestrian warm-up ring on a gravel road. Eventually the gravel gives way to dirt, and the trail dips out of the sun and into the welcome shade of a dense grove of native oaks. At 0.3 mile, keep right at the junction with the Gray Squirrel Trail to continue north. The oak forest falls behind you as you head toward the Puente Hills, keeping straight at 0.6 mile and reaching a major junction (and a crest)

at 0.8 mile. The sign here is a little confusing, but just continue heading north into Powder Canyon as the fire road begins a steady drop in elevation. (The other dirt road that heads to the northwest is a powerline access road that ends abruptly.)

Once inside the canyon proper, the fire road narrows a bit and its V-shaped walls provide an epic frame for the high San Gabriel Mountains in the distance. Pass the Schabarum Trail Extension at 1.2 miles and at

1.5 miles you'll reach the equestrian center at Peter F. Schabarum Regional County Park. Hug the edge of the parking area and look for a small footbridge across the creek bed to your west. Follow this trail as it skirts the southern edge of the park and keep to the left at 1.8 miles to continue on the Schabarum Trail.

The trail rises through rugged terrain covered in California sagebrush and prickly pear—a nice contrast to the nearby manicured lawns of homes and Schabarum Park. As the trail makes its way to the southwest, it also makes a noticeable gain in elevation with an equally noticeable lack of shade. Just before the 3-mile mark, the unmarked Buena Vista Trail branches off to the left and rises up the hill between the transmission towers. Take that steep trail to an access road and follow it to the Purple Sage Trail/ Skyline Drive at 3.2 miles. Turn left here and follow the dirt road east, closing the loop at 4 miles and returning to the trailhead the way you came in.

123 Telegraph Canyon

RATING/ DIFFICULTY	ROUNDTRIP	ELEV GAIN/ HIGH POINT	SEASON
****/4	12 miles	833 feet/ 1293 feet	Year-round (best in spring)

Maps: USGS Yorba Linda, Prado Dam; **Contact:** Chino Hills State Park; **Notes:** Park open 8:00 AM–5:00 PM Oct–Mar, 8:00 AM–7:00 PM Apr–Sep. Park may be closed after rain or during red flag warnings. No dogs allowed. $5 parking fee. Although this route is 12 miles roundtrip, there are several turnaround points that can make the trip shorter if desired; **GPS:** N 33.920358, W 117.827418

This route through the major east–west canyon in Chino Hills State Park takes hikers through some of the most beautiful oak woodland and riparian canyons in the Los Angeles region, offering a tremendous amount of natural solitude and birdsong all year round.

GETTING THERE

From CA-57 in Brea, take exit 10 for Lambert Road and head east. Lambert Road becomes Carbon Canyon Road (CA-142), and the Chino Hills State Park Discovery Center and parking lot will be on your right in 3.2 miles.

ON THE TRAIL

Head east from the Discovery Center past the overflow parking lot and native plant nursery. At 0.3 mile, keep right to stay on the Telegraph Canyon Trail, passing some old citrus orchards and the active facilities of the Robert B. Diemer Water Treatment Plant on your right. Ignore the locked and gated access roads and follow the trail as it heads east. Here, the canyon is fairly wide and shade is sporadic, but the trail is lined with fragrant sage scrub and the rare Southern California black walnut. In the late fall and early winter, the walnuts, sycamores, and poison oak all put on a little SoCal fall foliage display.

This route is easy to follow—just stay on the Telegraph Canyon Trail at every junction, ignoring side trails to your north and south. At 3.1 miles in, just past the Easy Street Trail, the canyon narrows considerably and the region's coast live oaks and sycamores (aliso in Spanish—also the name of the creek bed you're hiking along) take center stage. Keep your ears and eyes open for some of the park's wildlife, especially

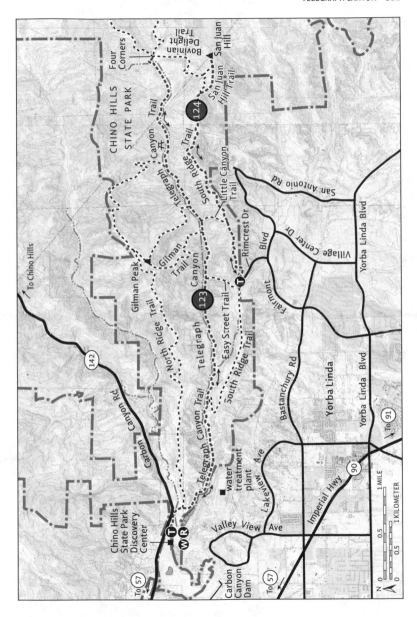

The native oaks and sycamores in Telegraph Canyon provide sporadic shade for hikers and plenty of habitat for birds.

its birds. You'll likely see woodpeckers storing their caches in the bark of oak trees and enormous red-tailed hawks circling high above. Attentive birders may catch a glimpse of rarer species such as the coastal cactus wren, least Bell's vireo, and California gnatcatcher.

There is a small but lovely shaded picnic area at 5 miles. Past this, the tree canopy diminishes and the landscape returns to rolling, grass-covered hills. The Four Corners trail junction is at mile 6—a good turnaround point for this canyon trek.

EXTENDING YOUR TRIP

From Four Corners, consider making the mile-long trip south to San Juan Hill, the highest point in Chino Hills State Park. Take the Bovinian Delight Trail south, passing a gas pipeline along the way. At 0.6 mile from Four Corners, keep right on a faded ranch road, which will take you to the South Ridge Trail. Turn left at this junction onto the San Juan Hill Trail for the steep climb to the top of San Juan Hill. Soak in the views and return the way you came or invert the directions for San Juan

Hill (Hike 124) and return to the Telegraph Canyon Trail on the Easy Street Trail. That route totals 13.7 miles.

124 San Juan Hill

RATING/ DIFFICULTY	ROUNDTRIP	ELEV GAIN/ HIGH POINT	SEASON
***/3	6 miles	794 feet/ 1781 feet	Year-round (best in spring)

Maps: USGS Yorba Linda, Prado Dam; **Contact:** Chino Hills State Park; **Notes:** Park open 8:00 AM–5:00 PM Oct–Mar, 8:00 AM–7:00 PM Apr–Sep. Park may be closed after rain or during red flag warnings. No dogs allowed; **GPS:** N 33.908912, W 117.780075

This no-nonsense fire road route is a popular fitness challenge for mountain bikers and trail runners, but hikers can also enjoy some spectacular views from the highest point in Chino Hills State Park. This is a great way to take in the scope of the Puente-Chino Hills biological corridor and get some absolutely jaw-dropping views of the Santa Ana and San Gabriel mountains.

San Juan Hill is a great vantage point for most of the mountain ranges in Southern California.

GETTING THERE

From CA-57 in Brea, take exit 9 for CA-90 and head east. After 3.3 miles turn left onto Bastanchury Road. In 2.7 miles, turn left onto Fairmont Boulevard and in 0.8 mile turn left onto Rimcrest Drive. Park near the end of Rimcrest Drive and pay attention to street parking regulations.

ON THE TRAIL

From the trailhead, it's a short walk north to a four-way junction in the shadow of the homes off Blue Gum Drive. Take a right onto the South Ridge Trail, which quickly climbs up above the residential neighborhood on a broad fire road heading east. After that first climb, though, the trail navigates a series of ups and downs as the towering Santa Ana Mountains loom to your southeast and the sprawl of Anaheim and Orange County lies behind you. Note that this route is entirely shadeless, so if you're hiking in the warmer months, be sure you get an early start to avoid the worst of the heat.

Stay on the South Ridge Trail, ignoring the side trails and utility spur roads along the way. At 2.9 miles, climb up the steep San Juan Hill Trail for a stunning visual on the area's landscape. Chino Hills State Park was founded in part to provide a biological corridor between the Santa Ana Mountains and the Puente Hills, and from this vantage point you can easily get an idea as to how these landscapes all interconnect. To your north, epic views of the tallest peaks in the San Gabriel Mountains lie ahead, while just a bit farther east you may be able to make out the San Bernardino and San Jacinto mountains as well. Retrace your steps to return to the trailhead.

125 Carbon Canyon Redwoods

RATING/ DIFFICULTY	LOOP	ELEV GAIN/ HIGH POINT	SEASON
***/1	2.6 miles	Negligible	Year-round (best in spring)

Map: USGS Yorba Linda; **Contact:** Carbon Canyon Regional Park; **Notes:** Park open 7:00 AM–6:00 PM in fall and winter, 7:00 AM–9:00 PM in spring and summer. Dogs allowed on leash. Parking fees vary: $3 on weekdays, $5 on weekends, higher on some holidays and during events; **GPS:** N 33.920984, W 117.829432

Who says you need to drive all the way up to Northern California to see the redwoods? This small, well-provisioned park has many amenities, including a pond stocked with fish for anglers, native plant and butterfly gardens, and the only successful nonnative coastal redwood grove in sunny Southern California.

GETTING THERE

From CA-57 in Brea, take exit 10 for Lambert Road and head east. Lambert Road becomes Carbon Canyon Road (CA-142), and the entrance to Carbon Canyon Regional Park is on the right at 3 miles. Follow the signs for the Redwood Trail to parking lot 5.

ON THE TRAIL

Head east from parking lot 5 and look for the signs for the Nature Trail. Over the next few years, these sages and buckwheats will become established and especially showy in the springtime. The trail passes a small

Yes, there are redwood trees right here in Southern California.

outdoor amphitheater, dips down into the bed of Carbon Canyon Creek, and hops to the south bank where it continues west past another section of a native plant garden. Here, a lone palo verde tree is the current highlight, but some woolly blue curls are sure to be showstoppers soon.

Benches provide rest stops along the way if you (or your smaller hiking companions) need them. The landscape transitions back to non-manicured sage scrub now, and at

0.8 mile stay to the left to continue toward the redwoods. Keep to the left again at 0.9 mile and soon you'll see some extremely out-of-place conifers rising above the horizon. There are 241 coastal redwoods here, all leftover promotional gifts for customers opening accounts at a local bank in 1970. While the redwoods farther north can reach heights of 370 feet, these specimens are a bit out of their element and the tallest is just above 90 feet in height. Although they're

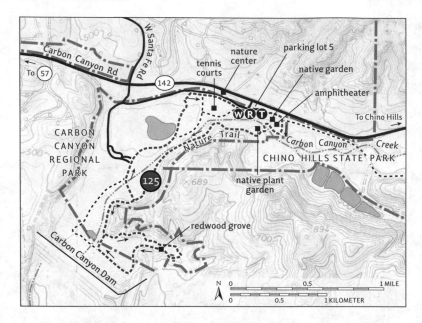

not quite as majestic as their natural brethren, walking beneath the canopy of these redwoods is a treat for hikers of all ages. It's a highly unusual experience to feel the natural air-conditioning of a redwood grove in Orange County.

Walk through the grove and turn right onto the cement flood control channel at 1.3 miles. Walk on this sidewalk-like structure until it returns to a dirt road before the enormous Carbon Canyon Dam comes into view before you. Surprise! This whole time, you've been walking inside a giant flood control feature! At 1.6 miles, turn right to return to the trail. You can either return to the trailhead the way you came or cross the flood channel at 1.9 miles to explore the park's picnic areas, pond, and playgrounds.

EXTENDING YOUR TRIP

There is a short connector trail that leads from the native plant garden to the Chino Hills State Park Discovery Center a short distance to the east. From here, you can explore Telegraph Canyon (Hike 123) or just enjoy the Discovery Center and a short interpretive trail without having to move your car and pay for parking again.

Appendix I:
Contact Information

Angeles National Forest/San Gabriel Mountains National Monument
www.fs.usda.gov/main/angeles/home

Headquarters
(626) 574-1613

Los Angeles River Ranger District
(818) 899-1900, ext. 221

San Gabriel River Ranger District
(626) 335-1251, ext. 221

Santa Clara/Mojave Rivers Ranger District
(661) 269-2808, ext. 221

Antelope Valley California Poppy Reserve State Natural Reserve
(661) 946-6092
(661) 724-1180 for wildflower info
www.parks.ca.gov/?page_id=627

Audubon Center at Debs Park
(323) 221-2255
www.debspark.audubon.org

Baldwin Hills Scenic Overlook
(310) 558-5547
www.parks.ca.gov/?page_id=22790

Bungee America
(310) 322-8892
www.bungeeamerica.com

California Department of Transportation (Caltrans) Road Condition Information
(800) 427-7623
www.dot.ca.gov/cgi-bin/roads.cgi

California State Parks
(800) 777-0369
www.parks.ca.gov

Camp Rotary/Corriganville Park
(805) 584-4400

Carbon Canyon Regional Park
(714) 973-3160
www.ocparks.com/parks/carbon

Charmlee Wilderness Park
(310) 457-7247

Chino Hills State Park
(951) 780-6222
www.parks.ca.gov/ChinoHillsSP

City of Burbank, Wildwood Canyon Park
(818) 238-5440

City of Duarte Parks and Recreation
(626) 359-4641, ext. 201
Transit (626) 359-1813
www.accessduarte.com

City of Glendale Community Services and Parks
(818) 548-2000

City of La Cañada Flintridge
(818) 790-8880

**City of Los Angeles Department
of Recreation and Parks**
(213) 738-2961
www.laparks.org

    Elysian Park
    (213) 485-5054
    www.laparks.org/dos/parks/facility
    /elysianPk.htm

    Ernest E. Debs Regional Park
    (213) 847-3989
    www.laparks.org/dos/parks/facility
    /debsEERegionalPk.htm

    Griffith Park
    (323) 644-2050
    www.laparks.org/dos/parks/griffithpk

    Runyon Canyon Park
    (323) 666-5046

    Wilacre Park
    (818) 766-8445

City of Sierra Madre
(626) 355-7135
www.cityofsierramadre.com/services
    /recreation/hiking

**Conejo Open Space Conservation
Agency**
(805) 381-2741
www.conejo-openspace.org

**County of Los Angeles Fire Department
Forestry Division**
(616) 794-0675 (Henninger Flats)
www.fire.lacounty.gov/forestry-division

**County of Los Angeles Parks
and Recreation**
(213) 738-2961
www.parks.lacounty.gov

    Kenneth Hahn State Recreation Area
    (323) 298-3660

Crystal Lake Campground
(626) 335-1251

Devils Punchbowl Natural Area
(661) 944-2743
www.devils-punchbowl.com

Eaton Canyon Nature Center
(626) 398-5420
www.ecnca.org

**Hill Canyon Wastewater
Treatment Plant**
(805) 491-8111

King Gillette Visitor Center
(805) 370-2301

Leo Carrillo State Park
(310) 457-8143
www.parks.ca.gov/?page_id=616

**Los Angeles Department of Water
and Power (LADWP)**
(323) 463-0830

Malibu Creek State Park
(818) 880-0367
www.parks.ca.gov/?page_id=614

    **Malibu Creek State Park
    Docent Association**
    www.malibucreekstatepark.org

Monrovia Canyon Park
(626) 256-8282
www.monroviacanyonpark.org

Mount Baldy Ski Lifts
(909) 982-0800
www.mtbaldyskilifts.com

Mount Baldy Visitor Center
(909) 982-2829

**Mountains Recreation and
Conservation Authority**
(323) 221-9944
www.mrca.ca.gov
www.lamountains.com

    Franklin Canyon Park
    (310) 858-7272

    Ranger Services
    (310) 456-7049

O'Melveny Park
(818) 363-3556

Peter F. Schabarum Regional Park
(626) 854-5560
www.parks.lacounty.gov/wps/portal/dpr
    /Parks/Peter_F_Schabarum
    _Regional_Park

Placerita Canyon State Park
(818) 880-0350
    Nature Center
    (661) 259-7721
    www.placerita.org

Point Mugu State Park
(310) 457-8143
www.parks.ca.gov/?page_id=630

**Puente Hills Habitat Preservation
Authority**
(562) 945-9003
www.habitatauthority.org
    Ranger Services
    (310) 858-7272, ext. 227

**Rancho Simi Recreation and
Park District**
(805) 584-4400
www.rsrpd.org

Saddleback Butte State Park
(661) 946-6092
www.parks.ca.gov/?page_id=618

San Bernardino National Forest
www.fs.usda.gov/sbnf

    Headquarters
    (909) 382-2600

    Front Country Ranger District
    (909) 382-2851

Santa Clarita Woodlands Park
(661) 255-3606

Santa Monica Mountains Conservancy
(310) 589-3200
www.smmc.ca.gov
www.lamountains.com

**Santa Monica Mountains National
Recreation Area**
(805) 370-2300
www.nps.gov/samo

Santa Susana Pass State Historic Park
(818) 784-4849
www.parks.ca.gov/?page_id=611

Topanga State Park
(310) 455-2465
www.parks.ca.gov/?page_id=629

Vasquez Rocks Natural Area Park
(661) 268-0840
www.parks.lacounty.gov/wps/portal/dpr
  /Parks/Vasquez_Rocks_Natural_Area

**Vulcan Materials Company Azusa
  Rock Quarry**
www.azusarock.com

Appendix II:
Outdoor Advocacy and Volunteer Groups

The following organizations are a mix of groups that inform and advocate for local outdoor issues as well as those who offer group hikes, training, and opportunities for volunteer and trail work.

American Hiking Society
www.americanhiking.org

Amigos de los Rios
www.amigosdelosrios.org

Angeles National Forest Fire Lookout Association
www.anffla.org

Angeles Volunteer Association
www.angelesvolunteers.org

Arroyo Seco Foundation
www.arroyoseco.org

Arroyos & Foothills Conservancy
www.arroyosfoothills.org

Audubon Center at Debs Park
www.ca.audubon.org/audubon center
-debs-park

Bike San Gabriel Valley
www.bikesgv.org

California Conservation Corps
www.ccc.ca.gov

California Native Plant Society

Los Angeles/Santa Monica Mountains Chapter
www.lasmmcnps.org

San Gabriel Mountains Chapter
www.cnps-sgm.org

Concerned Off-Road Bicyclists Association (CORBA)
www.corbamtb.com

Friends of Echo Mountain
www.facebook.com/Friendsofecho/

Friends of Griffith Park
www.friendsofgriffithpark.org

Friends of the Los Angeles River
www.folar.org

Los Angeles Conservation Corps
www.lacorps.org

Latino Outdoors
www.latinooutdoors.org

National Forest Foundation
www.nationalforests.org/ca

Pacific Crest Trail Association
www.pcta.org

San Gabriel Mountains Forever
www.sangabrielmountains.org

San Gabriel Mountains Trailbuilders
www.sgmtrailbuilders.org

Santa Monica Mountains Fund
www.samofund.org

Santa Monica Mountains Trail Council
www.smmtc.org

**Scenic Mount Lowe Railway
Historical Committee**
www.mtlowe.net

Sierra Club Angeles Chapter
www.angeles.sierraclub.org

Theodore Payne Foundation
www.theodorepayne.org

TreePeople
www.treepeople.org

The Trust for Public Land
www.tpl.org

**West Fork San Gabriel
River Conservancy**
www.westforksgrc.org

The Wilderness Society
www.wilderness.org

Appendix III:
Recommended Media

Andersen, Thom (director). *Los Angeles Plays Itself*. Thom Andersen Productions, 2003. Film.

Banham, Reyner. *Los Angeles: The Architecture of Four Ecologies*. Berkeley, CA: University of California Press, 2009.

Barbour, Michael G., Bruce M. Pavlik, and Susan Lindstrom. *California's Changing Landscapes: Diversity and Conservation of California Vegetation*. Sacramento, CA: California Native Plant Society, 1997.

Cunningham, Laura. *A State of Change: Forgotten Landscapes of California*. Berkeley, CA: Heyday, 2010.

Davis, Mike. *City of Quartz: Excavating the Future in Los Angeles*. New York City: Verso, 2006.

De Nevers, Greg, Deborah Stanger Edelman, and Adina Merenlender. *The California Naturalist Handbook*. Berkeley, CA: University of California Press, 2013.

Farmer, Jared. *Trees in Paradise: A California History*. New York: W. W. Norton & Company, 2013.

Lillard, Richard Gordon. *Eden in Jeopardy: Man's Prodigal Meddling with the Environment*. Santa Barbara, CA: Greenwood Press, 1971.

McPhee, John. *The Control of Nature*. New York: Farrar, Straus and Giroux, 1990.

Modern Hiker. Casey Schreiner. www.modernhiker.com.

Munz, Philip A. *Introduction to California Spring Wildflowers of the Foothills, Valleys, and Coast*. Berkeley, CA: University of California Press, 2004.

Quinn, Ronald D., and Sterling C. Keeley. *Introduction to California Chaparral*. Berkeley, CA: University of California Press, 2006.

Reisner, Marc. *Cadillac Desert: The American West and Its Disappearing Water*. New York: Penguin, 1993.

Robinson, John W. *Mines of the San Gabriels*. N.P.: La Siesta Press, 1990.

———. *The San Gabriels*. Monrovia, CA: Big Santa Anita Historical Society, 2001.

Rundel, Philip W., and Robert Gustafson. *Introduction to the Plant Life of Southern California*. Berkeley, CA: University of California Press, 2005.

Sheldon, Ian. *Animal Tracks of Southern California*. Auburn, WA: Lone Pine Publishing, 1998.

INDEX

1% for Parks
Outdoor Nonprofits in Partnership

Where would we be without parks and trails? Not very far into the wilderness.

That's why Mountaineers Books designates 1 percent of the sales of select guidebooks in our *Day Hiking* series toward park improvements and volunteer trail maintenance. Since launching this program, we've contributed more than $14,000 toward improving parks and trails.

For this book, our 1 percent of sales goes to **Western National Parks Association**. Western National Parks Association helps make the national park experience possible for everyone. As a nonprofit education partner of the National Park Service, WNPA supports 71 national park partners across the West, developing products, services, and programs that enrich the visitor experience. Their "Gateway to Nature" center in downtown Los Angeles connects diverse urban communities to our open public lands.

Mountaineers Books donates many books to nonprofit recreation and conservation organizations. Our 1% for Parks campaign is one more way we can help our fellow nonprofit organizations as we work together to get more people outside, to both enjoy and protect our wild public lands.

If you'd like to support Mountaineers Books and our nonprofit partnership programs, please visit our website to learn more or email mbooks@mountaineersbooks.org.

About the Author

Casey Schreiner is a seasoned television writer and producer who began his outdoor writing career in 2006 by founding the website *Modern Hiker* (www.modernhiker .com). The site is now the number-one hiking blog in California and is a source of in-depth trail info and outdoor journalism for the American West. Casey has been featured in regional and national media, including the *Los Angeles Times*, *New York Magazine*, *High Country News*, *National Public Radio*, and *Good Morning America*, and has broken multiple national news stories about vandalism in national parks. Casey was one of eight people chosen for the National Parks Foundation's Find Your Park Expedition and is dedicated to helping more people discover, enjoy, and protect their public lands. Casey lives near Griffith Park in Los Angeles with his partner, Daniel, and their pit bull, Emmy. When not hiking or writing, Casey is either tending to his small garden of California natives or trying to track down the best doughnuts in Southern California.

MOUNTAINEERS BOOKS is a leading publisher of mountaineering literature and guides—including our flagship title, *Mountaineering: The Freedom of the Hills*—as well as adventure narratives, natural history, and general outdoor recreation. Through our two imprints, Skipstone and Braided River, we also publish titles on sustainability and conservation. We are committed to supporting the environmental and educational goals of our organization by providing expert information on human-powered adventure, sustainable practices at home and on the trail, and preservation of wilderness.

The Mountaineers, founded in 1906, is a 501(c)(3) nonprofit outdoor activity and conservation organization whose mission is "to explore, study, preserve, and enjoy the natural beauty of the outdoors." One of the largest such organizations in the United States, it sponsors classes and year-round outdoor activities throughout the Pacific Northwest, including climbing, hiking, backcountry skiing, snowshoeing, bicycling, camping, paddling, and more. The Mountaineers also supports its mission through its publishing division, Mountaineers Books, and promotes environmental education and citizen engagement. For more information, visit The Mountaineers Program Center, 7700 Sand Point Way NE, Seattle, WA 98115-3996; phone 206-521-6001; www.mountaineers.org; or email info@mountaineers.org.

Our publications are made possible through the generosity of donors and through sales of more than 600 titles on outdoor recreation, sustainable lifestyle, and conservation. To donate, purchase books, or learn more, visit us online:

MOUNTAINEERS BOOKS
1001 SW Klickitat Way, Suite 201 • Seattle, WA 98134
800-553-4453 • mbooks@mountaineersbooks.org • www.mountaineersbooks.org

OTHER TITLES YOU MIGHT ENJOY FROM MOUNTAINEERS BOOKS

100 Classic Hikes in Southern California
Allen Riedel
Includes hikes in the San Bernardino National
Forest, Angeles National Forest, Santa Lucia
Mountains, Big Sur, and the Sierras

100 Classic Hikes in Northern California
John Soares and Marc Soares
Take some time to explore the Sierra Nevada,
Cascade Mountains, Klamath Mountains,
Coast Range and North Coast, and
the San Francisco Bay Area

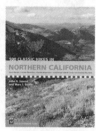

Best Hikes with Dogs Southern California
Allen Riedel
More than 60 dog-suitable trails, accessible
from Los Angeles, Palm Springs, San Diego,
and Santa Barbara

140 Great Hikes in and near Palm Springs
Philip Ferranti
Surreal lunar landscapes, high elevation
trails with spectacular views,
amazing wildflowers and more!

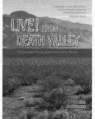

Live from Death Valley
John Soennichsen
"Eloquently written, Soennichsen's book
is a triumph of reportage reminiscent
of McPhee." —*Publishers Weekly*